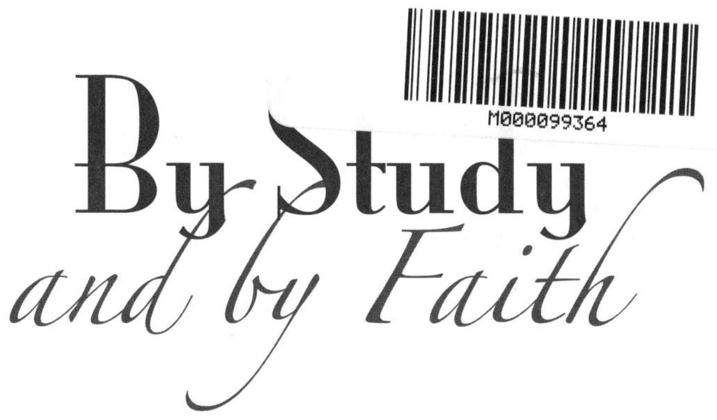

SELECTIONS FROM THE *RELIGIOUS EDUCATOR*

Edited by Richard Neitzel Holzapfel and Kent P. Jackson

RELIGIOUS STUDIES CENTER
BRIGHAM YOUNG UNIVERSITY

Published by the Religious Studies Center, Brigham Young University, Provo, Utah
http://religion.byu.edu/rsc_rec_pub.php

Printed in the United States of America by Sheridan Books, Inc.

ISBN 978-0-8425-2718-7
Retail U.S. $11.95

Cover photo by Glen Allison, Getty Images
Cover design by Kristin Call

Table of Contents

For ten years, the *Religious Educator* has provided a venue for scholars and students of the Restoration to explore Church history, ancient and modern scripture and doctrine, and approaches in understanding and teaching the principles of the gospel of Jesus Christ.

Photo by Richard B. Crookston

Introduction

Richard Neitzel Holzapfel and Kent P. Jackson

BYU Religious Education initiated the publication of the *Religious Educator* (*TRE*) in 2000 with the goal of providing another venue for scholars and students of the Restoration to explore our rich Church history, plumb the depths of ancient and modern scripture and doctrine, and highlight approaches in understanding and teaching the principles of the gospel of Jesus Christ.

Since the release of the first issue, hundreds of thoughtful, well-researched articles and essays have been published in *TRE* by dedicated scholars, teachers, and Church leaders, creating a remarkable library of historical, doctrinal, pedagogical, and devotional resources to inspire readers as they strive to understand, consider, apply, and teach the things that matter most.

As we prepared to publish the first issue of the tenth volume of *TRE* this past year, we decided to pull together a collection of articles and essays from past issues and publish them in a book that would provide us an occasion to introduce *TRE* to a new audience and to bring back in print some of the most significant essays from hard-to-find back issues that have long ago gone out of print. We enjoyed the opportunity to pore over the various issues and consider which essays have been well received and which articles might be considered some of the very best we have published in the past—the ones that we seem to go back to again and again because of their timeless message or the significant insights they provided.

The Religious Studies Center was established in 1975 by Jeffrey R. Holland, then dean of Religious Instruction at Brigham Young University, with the mission of encouraging and supporting the pursuit of truth through scholarship on gospel-related topics. This book, like all Religious Studies Center endeavors, is part of Religious Education's efforts to accomplish its overall mission of building the kingdom of God by teaching and preserving the sacred doctrine and history of the gospel of Jesus Christ.

We are thankful for the opportunity to provide our readers another opportunity to consider important matters related to the glorious gospel we have received. It is all "good news"!

Seek Learning by Faith

Elder David A. Bednar

***Elder David A. Bednar** is a member of the Quorum of the Twelve Apostles.*

This address was broadcast to Church Educational System religious educators on February 3, 2006.

I express my love to and for you—and the gratitude of the Brethren for the righteous influence you have upon the youth of the Church throughout the world. Thank you for blessing and strengthening the rising generation. I pray that the Holy Ghost will bless and edify us as we share this special time together.

Companion Principles: Preaching by the Spirit and Learning by Faith

We are admonished repeatedly in the scriptures to preach the truths of the gospel by the power of the Spirit (see D&C 50:14). I believe the vast majority of us as parents and teachers in the Church are aware of this principle and generally strive appropriately to apply it. As important as this principle is, however, it is only one element of a much larger spiritual pattern. We also frequently are taught to seek learning by faith (see D&C 88:118). *Preaching by the Spirit* and *learning by faith* are companion principles that we should strive to understand and apply concurrently and consistently.

I suspect we emphasize and know much more about a teacher teaching by the Spirit than we do about a learner learning by faith. Clearly, the principles and processes of both teaching and learning are spiritually essential.

However, as we look to the future and anticipate the ever more confused and turbulent world in which we will live, I believe it will be essential for all of us to increase our capacity to seek learning by faith. In our personal lives, in our families, and in the Church, we can and will receive the blessings of spiritual strength, direction, and protection as we seek by faith to obtain and apply spiritual knowledge.

Nephi teaches us, "When a man speaketh by the power of the Holy Ghost the power of the Holy Ghost carrieth [the message] unto the hearts of the children of men" (2 Nephi 33:1). Please notice how the power of the Spirit carries the message *unto* but not necessarily *into* the heart. A teacher can explain, demonstrate, persuade, and testify, and do so with great spiritual power and effectiveness. Ultimately, however, the content of a message and the witness of the Holy Ghost penetrate into the heart only if a receiver allows them to enter.

Brothers and sisters, learning by faith opens the pathway *into* the heart. We will focus upon the individual responsibility each of us has to seek learning by faith. We also will consider the implications of this principle for us as teachers.

The Principle of Action: Faith in the Lord Jesus Christ

The Apostle Paul defined faith as "the substance of things hoped for, [and] the evidence of things not seen" (Hebrews 11:1). Alma declared that faith is not a perfect knowledge; rather, if we have faith, we "hope for things which are not seen, [but] are true" (Alma 32:21). Additionally, we learn in the *Lectures on Faith* that faith is "the first principle in revealed religion, and the foundation of all righteousness" and that it is also "the principle of action in all intelligent beings."[1]

These teachings of Paul and of Alma and from the *Lectures on Faith* highlight three basic elements of faith: (1) faith as the *assurance* of things hoped for which are true, (2) faith as the *evidence* of things not seen, and (3) faith as the principle of *action* in all intelligent beings. I describe these three components of faith in the Savior as simultaneously facing the future, looking to the past, and initiating action in the present.

Faith as the assurance of things hoped for looks to the future. This assurance is founded upon a correct understanding about and trust in God and enables us to "press forward" (2 Nephi 31:20) into uncertain and often challenging situations in the service of the Savior. For example, Nephi relied upon precisely this type of future-facing spiritual assurance as he returned to Jerusalem to obtain the plates of brass—"not knowing beforehand the things which [he] should do. Nevertheless [he] went forth" (1 Nephi 4:6–7).

Faith in Christ is inextricably tied to and results in hope in Christ for our redemption and exaltation. And assurance and hope make it possible for us to walk to the edge of the light and take a few steps into the darkness—expecting and trusting the light to move and illuminate the way.[2] The combination of assurance and hope initiates action in the present.

Faith as the evidence of things not seen looks to the past and confirms our trust in God and our confidence in the truthfulness of things not seen. We stepped into the darkness with assurance and hope, and we received evidence and confirmation as the light in fact moved and provided the illumination we needed. The witness we obtained after the trial of our faith (see Ether 12:6) is evidence that enlarges and strengthens our assurance.

Assurance, action, and evidence influence each other in an ongoing process. This helix is like a coil, and as it spirals upward it expands and grows wider. These three elements of faith—assurance, action, and evidence—are not separate and discrete; rather, they are interrelated and continuous and cycle upward. And the faith that fuels this ongoing process develops and evolves and changes. As we again turn and face forward toward an uncertain future, assurance leads to action and produces evidence, which further increases assurance. Our confidence waxes stronger, line upon line, precept upon precept, here a little and there a little.

We find a powerful example of the interaction among assurance, action, and evidence as the children of Israel transported the ark of the covenant under the leadership of Joshua (see Joshua 3:7–17). Recall how the Israelites came to the river Jordan and were promised the waters would part, or "stand upon an heap" (Joshua 3:13), and they would be able to cross over on dry ground. Interestingly, the waters did not part as the children of Israel stood on the banks of the river waiting for something to happen; rather, the soles of their feet were wet before the water parted. The faith of the Israelites was manifested in the fact that they walked into the water *before* it parted. They walked into the river Jordan with a future-facing assurance of things hoped for. As the Israelites moved forward, the water parted, and as they crossed over on dry land, they looked back and beheld the evidence of things not seen. In this episode, faith as assurance led to action and produced the evidence of things not seen which were true.

True faith is focused in and on the Lord Jesus Christ and always leads to action. Faith as the principle of action is highlighted in many scriptures with which we are all familiar:

"For as the body without the spirit is dead, so *faith without works is dead* also" (James 2:26; emphasis added).

"But be ye *doers of the word*, and not hearers only" (James 1:22; emphasis added).

"But behold, if ye will awake and arouse your faculties, even to an *experiment upon my words*, and exercise a particle of faith" (Alma 32:27; emphasis added).

And it is faith as the principle of action that is so central to the process of learning and applying spiritual truth.

Learning by Faith: To Act and Not to Be Acted Upon

How is faith as the principle of action in all intelligent beings related to gospel learning? And what does it mean to seek learning by faith?

In the grand division of all of God's creations, there are things to act and things to be acted upon (see 2 Nephi 2:13–14). As sons and daughters of our Heavenly Father, we have been blessed with the gift of agency—the capacity and power of independent action. Endowed with agency, we are agents, and we primarily are to act and not only to be acted upon—especially as we seek to obtain and apply spiritual knowledge.

Learning by faith and from experience are two of the central features of the Father's plan of happiness. The Savior preserved moral agency through the Atonement and made it possible for us to act and to learn by faith. Lucifer's rebellion against the plan sought to destroy the agency of man, and his intent was that we as learners would only be acted upon.

Consider the question posed by Heavenly Father to Adam in the Garden of Eden, "Where art thou?" (Genesis 3:9). Obviously the Father knew where Adam was hiding, but He, nonetheless, asked the question. Why? A wise and loving Father enabled His child to act in the learning process and not merely be acted upon. There was no one-way lecture to a disobedient child, as perhaps many of us might be inclined to deliver. Rather, the Father helped Adam as a learner to act as an agent and appropriately exercise his agency.

Recall how Nephi desired to know about the things his father, Lehi, had seen in the vision of the tree of life. Interestingly, the Spirit of the Lord begins the tutorial with Nephi by asking the following question, "Behold, what desirest thou?" (1 Nephi 11:2). Clearly the Spirit knew what Nephi desired. So why ask the question? The Holy Ghost was helping Nephi to act in the learning process and not simply be acted upon. (I encourage you at a later time to study chapters 11–14 in 1 Nephi and notice how the Spirit both asked questions and encouraged Nephi to "look" as active elements in the learning process.)

From these examples we recognize that as learners, you and I are to act and be doers of the word and not simply hearers who are only acted upon. Are you and I agents who act and seek learning by faith, or are we waiting to be taught and acted upon? Are the students we serve acting and seeking to learn by faith, or are they waiting to be taught and acted upon? Are you and I encouraging and helping those whom we serve to seek learning by faith? You and I and our students are to be anxiously engaged in asking, seeking, and knocking (see 3 Nephi 14:7).

A learner exercising agency by acting in accordance with correct principles opens his or her heart to the Holy Ghost—and invites His teaching, testifying power, and confirming witness. Learning by faith requires spiritual, mental, and physical exertion and not just passive reception. It is in the sincerity and consistency of our faith-inspired action that we indicate to our Heavenly Father and His Son, Jesus Christ, our willingness to learn and receive instruction from the Holy Ghost. Thus, learning by faith involves the exercise of moral agency to act upon the assurance of things hoped for and invites the evidence of things not seen from the only true teacher, the Spirit of the Lord.

Consider how missionaries help investigators to learn by faith. Making and keeping spiritual commitments, such as studying and praying about the Book of Mormon, attending Church meetings, and keeping the commandments, require an investigator to exercise faith and to act. One of the fundamental roles of a missionary is to help an investigator make and honor commitments—to act and learn by faith. Teaching, exhorting, and explaining, as important as they are, can never convey to an investigator a witness of the truthfulness of the restored gospel. Only as an investigator's faith initiates action and opens the pathway to the heart can the Holy Ghost deliver a confirming witness. Missionaries obviously must learn to teach by the power of the Spirit. Of equal importance, however, is the responsibility missionaries have to help investigators learn by faith.

The learning I am describing reaches far beyond mere cognitive comprehension and the retaining and recalling of information. The type of learning about which I am speaking causes us to put off the natural man (see Mosiah 3:19), to change our hearts (see Mosiah 5:2), and to be converted unto the Lord and to never fall away (see Alma 23:6). Learning by faith requires both "the heart and a willing mind" (D&C 64:34). Learning by faith is the result of the Holy Ghost carrying the power of the word of God both unto and into the heart. Learning by faith cannot be transferred from an instructor to a student through a lecture, a demonstration, or an experiential exercise; rather, a student must exercise faith and act in order to obtain the knowledge for himself or herself.

The young boy Joseph Smith instinctively understood what it meant to seek learning by faith. One of the most well-known episodes in the life of Joseph Smith was his reading of verses about prayer and faith in the book of James in the New Testament (see James 1:5–6). This text inspired Joseph to retire to a grove of trees near his home to pray and to seek for spiritual knowledge. Please note the questions Joseph had formulated in his mind and felt in his heart—and which he took into the grove. He clearly had prepared himself to "ask in faith" (James 1:6) and to act.

> In the midst of this war of words and tumult of opinions, I often said to myself: What is to be done? Who of all these parties are right; or, are they all wrong together? If any one of them be right, which is it, and how shall I know it? . . .
>
> My object in going to inquire of the Lord was to know which of all the sects was right, that I might know which to join. No sooner, therefore, did I get possession of myself, so as to be able to speak, than I asked the Personages who stood above me in the light, which of all the sects was right . . . and which I should join (Joseph Smith—History 1:10, 18).

Notice that Joseph's questions focused not just on what he needed to know but also on what he needed to do. And his very first question centered on action and what was to be done! His prayer was not simply which church is right. His question was which church should he join. Joseph went to the grove to learn by faith. He was determined to act.

Ultimately, the responsibility to learn by faith and apply spiritual truth rests upon each of us individually. This is an increasingly serious and important

The Lord invites us to seek learning by study and also by faith
(see D&C 88:118).

responsibility in the world in which we do now and will yet live. What, how, and when we learn is supported by—but is not dependent upon—an instructor, a method of presentation, or a specific topic or lesson format.

Truly, one of the great challenges of mortality is to seek learning by faith. The Prophet Joseph Smith best summarizes the learning process and outcomes I am attempting to describe. In response to a request by the Twelve Apostles for instruction, Joseph taught, "The best way to obtain truth and wisdom is not to ask it from books, but to go to God in prayer, and obtain divine teaching."[3]

And on another occasion, the Prophet Joseph explained that "reading the experience of others, or the revelation given to them, can never give us a comprehensive view of our condition and true relation to God."[4]

Implications for Us as Teachers

The truths about learning by faith we have discussed thus far have profound implications for us as teachers. Let us now consider together three of these implications.

Implication 1. The Holy Ghost is the only true teacher. The Holy Ghost is the third member of the Godhead, and He is the teacher and witness of all truth. Elder James E. Talmage explained: "The office of the Holy Ghost in His ministrations among men is described in scripture. He is a teacher sent from the Father; and unto those who are entitled to His tuition He will reveal all things necessary for the soul's advancement."[5]

We should always remember that the Holy Ghost is the teacher who, through proper invitation, can enter into a learner's heart. Indeed, you and I have the responsibility to preach the gospel by the Spirit, even the Comforter, as a prerequisite for the learning by faith that can be achieved only by and through the Holy Ghost (see D&C 50:14). In this regard, you and I are much like the long, thin strands of glass used to create the fiber-optic cables through which light signals are transmitted over very long distances. Just as the glass in these cables must be pure to conduct the light efficiently and effectively, so we should become and remain worthy conduits through whom the Spirit of the Lord can operate.

But brothers and sisters, we must be careful to remember in our service that we are conduits and channels; we are not the light. "For it is not ye that speak, but the Spirit of your Father which speaketh in you" (Matthew 10:20). It is never about me and it is never about you. In fact, anything you or I do as an instructor that knowingly and intentionally draws attention to self—in the messages we present, in the methods we use, or in our personal demeanor—is a form of priestcraft that inhibits the teaching effectiveness of the Holy Ghost. "Doth he preach it by the Spirit of truth or some other way? And if it be by some other way it is not of God" (D&C 50:17–18).

Implication 2. We are most effective as instructors when we encourage and facilitate learning by faith. We are all familiar with the adage that giving a man a fish feeds him for one meal. Teaching the man to fish, on the other hand, feeds him for a lifetime. As gospel instructors, you and I are not in the business of distributing fish; rather, our work is to help individuals learn to "fish" and to become spiritually self-reliant. This important objective is best accomplished as we encourage and facilitate learners acting in accordance with correct principles—as we help them to learn by doing. "If any man will do his will, he shall know of the doctrine, whether it be of God" (John 7:17).

Please notice this implication in practice in the counsel given to Junius F. Wells by Brigham Young as Brother Wells was called in 1875 to organize the young men of the Church:

> At your meetings you should begin at the top of the roll and call upon as many members as there is time for to bear their testimonies and at the next meeting begin where you left off and call upon others, so that all shall take part and get into the practice of standing up and saying something. Many may think they haven't any testimony to bear, but get them to stand up and they will find the Lord will give them utterance to many truths they had not thought of before. More people have obtained a testimony while standing up trying to bear it than down on their knees praying for it.[6]

President Boyd K. Packer has given similar counsel in our day:

> Oh, if I could teach you this one principle. A testimony is to be found in the bearing of it! Somewhere in your quest for spiritual knowledge, there is that "leap of faith," as the philosophers call it. It is the moment when you have gone to the edge of the light and stepped into the darkness to discover that the way is lighted ahead for just a footstep or two. "The spirit of man," as the scripture says, indeed "is the candle of the Lord." (Prov. 20:27.)
>
> It is one thing to receive a witness from what you have read or what another has said; and that is a necessary beginning. It is quite another to have the Spirit confirm to you in your bosom that what you have testified is true. Can you not

> see that it will be supplied as you share it? As you give that which you have, there is a replacement, with increase![7]

I have observed a common characteristic among the instructors who have had the greatest influence in my life. They have helped me to seek learning by faith. They refused to give me easy answers to hard questions. In fact, they did not give me any answers at all. Rather, they pointed the way and helped me take the steps to find my own answers. I certainly did not always appreciate this approach, but experience has enabled me to understand that an answer given by another person usually is not remembered for very long, if remembered at all. But an answer we discover or obtain through the exercise of faith, typically, is retained for a lifetime. The most important learnings of life are caught—not taught.

The spiritual understanding you and I have been blessed to receive, and which has been confirmed as true in our hearts, simply cannot be given to another person. The tuition of diligence and learning by faith must be paid to obtain and personally "own" such knowledge. Only in this way can what is known in the mind be transformed into what is felt in the heart. Only in this way can a person move beyond relying upon the spiritual knowledge and experience of others and claim those blessings for himself or herself. Only in this way can we be spiritually prepared for what is coming. We are to "seek learning, even by study and also by faith" (D&C 88:118).

Implication 3. An instructor's faith is strengthened as he or she helps others seek learning by faith. The Holy Ghost, who can "teach [us] all things, and bring all things to [our] remembrance" (John 14:26), is eager to help us learn as we act and exercise faith in Jesus Christ. Interestingly, this divine learning assistance is perhaps never more apparent than when we are teaching, either at home or in Church assignments. As Paul made clear to the Romans, "Thou therefore which teachest another, teachest thou not thyself?" (Romans 2:21).

Please notice in the following verses from the Doctrine and Covenants how teaching diligently invites heavenly grace and instruction: "And I give unto *you* a commandment that *you* shall teach one another the doctrine of the kingdom. Teach ye diligently and my grace shall attend *you*, that *you* may be instructed more perfectly in theory, in principle, in doctrine, in the law of the gospel, in all things that pertain unto the kingdom of God, that are expedient for *you* to understand" (D&C 88:77–78; emphasis added).

Consider that the blessings described in these scriptures are intended specifically for the teacher: "Teach . . . diligently and my grace shall attend you"—that you, the teacher, may be instructed! The same principle is evident in verse 122 from the same section of the Doctrine and Covenants: "Appoint among yourselves a teacher, and let not *all* be spokesmen at once; but let one speak at a time and let *all* listen unto his sayings, that when *all* have spoken that *all* may be edified of *all*, and that every man may have an equal privilege" (D&C 88:122; emphasis added).

As all speak and as all listen in a dignified and orderly way, all are edified. The individual and collective exercise of faith in the Savior invites instruction and strength from the Spirit of the Lord.

Seek Learning by Faith: A Recent Example

All of us were blessed by the challenge from the First Presidency last August to read the Book of Mormon by the end of 2005. In extending the challenge, President Gordon B. Hinckley promised that faithfully observing this simple reading program would bring into our lives and into our homes "an added measure of the Spirit of the Lord, a strengthened resolution to walk in obedience to His commandments, and a stronger testimony of the living reality of the Son of God."[8]

Please note how this inspired challenge is a classic example of learning by faith. First, you and I were not commanded, coerced, or required to read. Rather, we were invited to exercise our agency as agents and act in accordance with correct principles. President Hinckley, as an inspired teacher, encouraged us to act and not just be acted upon. Each of us, ultimately, had to decide if and how we would respond to the challenge—and if we would endure to the end of the task.

Second, in proffering the invitation to read and to act, President Hinckley was encouraging each of us to seek learning by faith. No new study materials were distributed to members of the Church, and no additional lessons, classes, or programs were created by the Church. Each of us had our copy of the Book of Mormon—and a pathway into our heart opened wider through the exercise of our faith in the Savior as we responded to the First Presidency challenge. Thus, we were prepared to receive instruction from the only true teacher, the Holy Ghost.

In recent weeks I have been greatly impressed by the testimonies of so many members concerning their recent experiences reading the Book of

Mormon. Important and timely spiritual lessons have been learned, lives have been changed for the better, and the promised blessings have been received. The Book of Mormon, a willing heart, and the Holy Ghost—it really is that simple. My faith and the faith of the other Brethren have been strengthened as we have responded to President Hinckley's invitation and as we have observed so many of you acting and learning by faith.

As I stated earlier, the responsibility to seek learning by faith rests upon each of us individually, and this obligation will become increasingly important as the world in which we live grows more confused and troubled. Learning by faith is essential to our personal spiritual development and for the growth of the Church in these latter days. May each of us truly hunger and thirst after righteousness and be filled with the Holy Ghost (see 3 Nephi 12:6)—that we might seek learning by faith.

I witness that Jesus is the Christ, the Only Begotten Son of the Eternal Father. He is our Savior and Redeemer. I testify that as we learn of Him, listen to His words, and walk in the meekness of His Spirit (see D&C 19:23), we will be blessed with spiritual strength, protection, and peace.

As a servant of the Lord, I invoke this blessing upon each of you: even that your desire and capacity to seek learning by faith—and to appropriately help others to seek learning by faith—will increase and improve. This blessing will be a source of great treasures of spiritual knowledge in your personal life, for your family, and to those whom you instruct and serve. In the sacred name of Jesus Christ, amen.

Notes

1. Joseph Smith, comp., *Lectures on Faith* (Salt Lake City: Deseret Book, 1985), 1.
2. See Boyd K. Packer, "The Candle of the Lord," *Ensign*, January 1983, 54.
3. Joseph Smith, *History of the Church of Jesus Christ of Latter-day Saints*, ed. B. H. Roberts, 2nd ed. rev. (Salt Lake City: Deseret Book, 1957), 4:425.
4. Smith, *History of the Church*, 6:50.
5. James E. Talmage, *The Articles of Faith*, 12th ed. (Salt Lake City: Deseret Book, 1924), 162.
6. Brigham Young, in Junius F. Wells, "Historic Sketch of the YMMIA," *Improvement Era*, June 1925, 715.
7. Boyd K. Packer, "The Candle of the Lord," *Ensign*, January 1983, 54–55.
8. Gordon B. Hinckley, "A Testimony Vibrant and True," *Ensign*, August 2005, 6.

The Atonement and the Resurrection

Elder D. Todd Christofferson

Elder D. Todd Christofferson *is a member of the Quorum of the Twelve Apostles.*

This article is adapted from an address given at BYU on March 26, 2005.

I am honored to share a few thoughts on the Atonement and Resurrection of Jesus Christ. I have struggled, as many of you have, with a finite mind to comprehend that infinite sacrifice of the Savior. I do not pretend to be able to plumb the depths of the subject, but I hope that I can offer an insight or two that would be helpful and encouraging to us as we think again on the great events of those few days that mean all the difference in our existence.

In your mind, try to place yourselves back in time at that first Easter weekend. Today is Saturday, the Jewish Sabbath. Here we are—the events of yesterday and the day before have made a tremendous impact upon us. It was Thursday evening when the Last Supper took place. Afterward Jesus passed over the brook and into the Garden of Gethsemane and suffered there in a way that none of us have fully witnessed and certainly none comprehend. It was perhaps into the wee hours of yesterday morning that that continued. Yesterday He was assaulted and abused by those in authority, both Jewish and Roman. He was condemned finally by Pilate and scourged. It has been less than twenty-four hours since we witnessed the awful scene of His Crucifixion, as He hung there on the cross and suffered intensely again. It was a very, very dark time, and it has not been many hours ago. We hurriedly placed His body in the tomb before sunset yesterday. Now here we are on this Sabbath.

It is midday, and we are wondering, in doubt, and confused. We had thought it had been He who would rescue Israel. We had thought it had been He who was the Messiah, and yet He is gone; He is dead.

Just before He died yesterday, He uttered those words: "It is finished" (John 19:30). What did He mean? Did He mean He had failed? He would never return? He is gone and it is over? Is there something more? Unbeknownst to you and me in this setting, in this Sabbath of doubt, He, His spirit, has been occupied elsewhere. This morning He entered the world of spirits. Future records will confirm that He was expected there.

> [There were assembled a multitude of the righteous] awaiting the advent of the Son of God into the spirit world [just this morning], to declare their redemption from the bands of death.
>
> Their sleeping dust was to be restored unto its perfect frame, bone to his bone, and the sinews and the flesh upon them, the spirit and the body to be united never again to be divided, that they might receive a fulness of joy.
>
> While this vast multitude waited and conversed, rejoicing in the hour of their deliverance . . . , the Son of God appeared, declaring liberty to the captives who had been faithful;
>
> And there he preached to them the everlasting gospel, the doctrine of the resurrection and the redemption of mankind from the fall, and from individual sins on conditions of repentance. (D&C 138:16–19)

That is what He has been doing this morning. And in the language of President Joseph F. Smith, "He [has] organized his forces and appointed messengers, clothed with power and authority, and commissioned them to go forth and carry the light of the gospel to them that were in darkness, even to all the spirits of men" (D&C 138:30). And thus will the gospel be preached to them that are dead. Now, what awaits tomorrow we do not know. But in good time joy incomprehensible will come to us. Tomorrow morning Mary and other women will be at the tomb. They will find it empty. Angels will declare that the Savior, not there, has risen. Peter and John will enter that tomb and find it empty. Later that morning, with the sun perhaps barely up, Jesus Himself will appear to Mary and speak to her, the first mortal ever to see the resurrected Lord. He will show Himself to other women and to Peter individually. He will be with two of you on the road to Emmaus, and then toward evening, show

Himself to His Apostles and perhaps some of us, gathered together, wondering and pondering over the marvelous witness of those who saw Him earlier. That is what awaits us tomorrow, and it is glorious to contemplate.

I wonder if we appreciate the expectations that devolve upon us because of what He has done and what He now offers to us. In perhaps the earliest reference to Him and His role in our lives, this is the comment from God to Moses: "But, behold, my Beloved Son, which was my Beloved and Chosen from the beginning, said unto me—Father, thy will be done, and the glory be thine forever" (Moses 4:2).

In one simple sentence, I believe the Savior revealed what was and always has been His overriding purpose and His motivation. His purpose is to do the will of the Father, and His motivation is to glorify the Father. I believe it required all of that devotion, the full measure of His devotion to doing the will of the Father and the motive of glorifying the Father, for Him to be able to endure what He had to endure and see the Atonement through to its conclusion.

The accounts of His suffering found in Matthew, Mark, and Luke, speaking of Gethsemane, emphasize how much He endured. (It has interested me that there is no account of Gethsemane in John, at least in what we have of John. I wonder if it was something he felt too sacred to touch or just too tender to recount.) At least three times, it appears, He pled with the Father that He might not have to drink the bitter cup. In Matthew the account is:

> He went a little further, and fell on his face, and prayed, saying, O my Father, if it be possible, let this cup pass from me: nevertheless not as I will, but as thou wilt.
>
> And he cometh unto the disciples, and findeth them asleep, and saith unto Peter, What, could ye not watch with me one hour?
>
> Watch and pray, that ye enter not into temptation: the spirit indeed is willing, but the flesh is weak.
>
> He went away again the second time, and prayed, saying, O my Father, if this cup may not pass away from me, except I drink it, thy will be done.
>
> And he came and found them asleep again: for their eyes were heavy.
>
> And he left them, and went away again, and prayed the third time, saying the same words. (Matthew 26:39–44)

This really is all we have (repeated in a varied form in Mark and Luke) of what was in that prayer. I am sure there was much more. But that was the most compelling, saying essentially: "Father, if it be possible, take this cup from me. If there is any way that this can be accomplished short of my having to drink it, that is what I plead with thee to do. Nevertheless, not my will, but thine be done."

Luke records that because of His agony, "His sweat was as it were great drops of blood falling down to the ground" (Luke 22:44). The Savior Himself, when He described it to the Prophet Joseph Smith, said it was not sweat but, in fact, blood that He bled from every pore. Luke records that an angel came to strengthen Him in that ordeal (see Luke 22:43). And later as that suffering resumed on the cross, it seemed compounded as the Father withdrew His Spirit in order that the Son might tread the winepress alone. "And at the ninth hour Jesus cried with a loud voice, saying, Eloi, Eloi, lama sabachthani? which is, being interpreted, My God, my God, why hast thou forsaken me?" (Mark 15:34).

Always, however, in all of this agony and all of this pleading for relief was His submission to the Father's will—"Nevertheless not as I will, but as thou wilt" (Matthew 26:39). "Father, if this cup may not pass away from me, except I drink it, thy will be done" (Matthew 26:42). As He described the Atonement and the concern that He not shrink and fail fully to drain that bitter cup, He expressed once again the overriding motivation that saw Him through that incomprehensible suffering: "Nevertheless, *glory be to the Father*, and I partook and finished my preparations unto the children of men" (D&C 19:19; emphasis added).

Had Jesus not devoted Himself to the Father and to the Father's will, throughout His life and throughout His existence prior to this life, He might not have been able to see the Atonement through to its conclusion. As He expressed it in John: "When ye have lifted up the Son of man, then shall ye know that I am he, and that I do nothing of myself; but as my Father hath taught me, I speak these things. And He that sent me is with me: the Father hath not left me alone; for I do always those things that please him" (John 8:28–29).

In the Book of Mormon, He stated: "Behold, I am Jesus Christ, whom the prophets testified shall come into the world. And behold, I am the light and the life of the world; and I have drunk out of that bitter cup which the Father hath given me, and have glorified the Father in taking upon me the sins of the world, in the which I have suffered the will of the Father in all things from the beginning" (3 Nephi 11:10–11).

Later, in that same book of 3 Nephi: "Behold I have given unto you my gospel, and this is the gospel which I have given unto you—that I came into the world to do the will of my Father, because my Father sent me" (3 Nephi 27:13). And Abinadi's unforgettable words: "Yea, even so he shall be led, crucified, and slain, the flesh becoming subject even unto death, the will of the Son being swallowed up in the will of the Father" (Mosiah 15:7).

I wonder if we, in order to hold on our way, to persevere and endure to the end, to reap the full benefits of His Atonement, must similarly devote ourselves to the will and glory of the Father and the Son. Is it not logical that you and I, to be able to receive what He offers, would have to do as He did and make our greatest ambition to do the will of God and our greatest desire to glorify Him?

I read earlier some verses from section 138 of the Doctrine and Covenants, referring to the Savior's advent in the spirit world before the Resurrection. There is an interesting description given there of the body of righteous people who were awaiting that advent. Here is how they were described: "There were gathered together in one place an innumerable company of the spirits of the just, who had been faithful in the testimony of Jesus while they lived in mortality; and who had offered sacrifice in the similitude of the great sacrifice of the Son of God, and had suffered tribulation in their Redeemer's name. All these had departed the mortal life, firm in the hope of a glorious resurrection, through the grace of God the Father and his Only Begotten Son, Jesus Christ" (D&C 138:12–14).

What interests me particularly there is that phrase "who had offered sacrifice in the similitude of the great sacrifice of the Son of God." They had not offered an equivalent sacrifice but something in the similitude, of the same nature. And because of that they were firm in the hope of a glorious or celestial resurrection. What would be an offering in the similitude of the great offering of the Son of God?

We have the familiar statement given to Adam: "And after many days an angel of the Lord appeared unto Adam, saying: Why dost thou offer sacrifices unto the Lord? And Adam said unto him: I know not, save the Lord commanded me. And then the angel spake, saying: *This thing is a similitude of the sacrifice of the Only Begotten of the Father, which is full of grace and truth.* Wherefore, thou shalt do all that thou doest in the name of the Son, and thou shalt repent and call upon God in the name of the Son forevermore" (Moses 5:6–8; emphasis added).

We know that when He appeared in this hemisphere, following His resurrection and ascension, He ended that kind of sacrifice in the similitude of the Only Begotten; that is, the animal sacrifice. But He reemphasized one aspect of the commandment to Adam—"Thou shalt repent and call upon God in the name of the Son forevermore"—when He later said, "Ye shall offer for a sacrifice unto me a broken heart and a contrite spirit. And whoso cometh unto me with a broken heart and a contrite spirit, him will I baptize with fire and with the Holy Ghost" (3 Nephi 9:20). It is, then, our sacrifice in the similitude of His that we would submit ourselves entirely to God.

As it says in section 20 of the Doctrine and Covenants: "Wherefore, the Almighty God gave his Only Begotten Son, as it is written in those scriptures which have been given of him. He suffered temptations but gave no heed unto them. He was crucified, died, and rose again the third day; and ascended into heaven, to sit down on the right hand of the Father, to reign with almighty power according to the will of the Father. [For what purpose?] That as many as would believe and be baptized in his holy name, and endure . . . to the end, should be saved" (D&C 20:21–25).

That is our sacrifice in the similitude of His, being baptized in His holy name and enduring to the end. May I remind you of two familiar verses from a sacramental hymn, "God Loved Us, So He Sent His Son."

> God loved us, so he sent his Son,
> Christ Jesus, the atoning One,
> To show us by the path he trod
> The one and only way to God.

And then the fourth verse that we rarely sing:

> In word and deed he doth require
> My will to his, like son to sire,
> Be made to bend, and I, as son,
> Learn conduct from the Holy One.[1]

That learning, that submission to Him and to His will that would permit us to reap the benefit of the Atonement, may involve a number of things. The one revelation recorded in the canon of scripture that was given to Brigham Young includes this verse: "My people must be tried in all things, that they may be prepared to receive the glory that I have for them, even the glory of Zion; and he that will not bear chastisement is not worthy of my kingdom" (D&C 136:31).

Early in my tenure as a Seventy, I was companion to Elder Russell M. Nelson in a stake conference. We had a wonderful experience together, and as we finished and were driving home, I said to him, "Elder Nelson, I hope if you ever see an error in me or some mistake or shortcoming, you would tell me about it." He replied, "I will." I was a little unnerved by his seeming anxiousness to comply with my request, but then He said, "That is one of the ways we show our love for one another." And I believe that is indeed a true principle.

The Savior said: "I am the true vine, and my Father is the husbandman. Every branch in me that beareth not fruit he taketh away: and every branch that beareth fruit, he purgeth it, that it may bring forth more fruit" (John 15:1–2). What form the purging might take, what sacrifices it might entail for any of us, we probably will not know in advance. But if with the rich young ruler, we asked, "What lack I yet?" (Matthew 19:20), the Savior's answer would probably be the same, "Follow me" (Matthew 19:21)—or, in the language of King Benjamin, "[Become] as a child, submissive, meek, humble, patient, full of love, willing to submit to all things which the Lord seeth fit to inflict upon him, even as a child doth submit to his father" (Mosiah 3:19). Here is another way of stating it: "Then said Jesus unto his disciples, If any man will come after me, let him deny himself, and take up his cross, and follow me [and this addition from the Joseph Smith Translation]. And now for a man to take up his cross, is to deny himself all ungodliness, and every worldly lust, and keep my commandments" (Matthew 16:24; Joseph Smith Translation, Matthew 16:26).

We must be able to say, with Job, that our submission to Him, to His will, is so complete that "though he slay me, yet will I trust in him" (Job 13:15). I think this is perfectly described in poetic form in the hymn "When I Survey the Wondrous Cross" by Isaac Watts.

> When I survey the wondrous cross
> On which the Prince of Glory died,
> My richest gain I count but loss
> And pour contempt on all my pride.

Forbid it, Lord, that I should boast
Save in the death of Christ, my God.
All the vain things that charm me most,
I sacrifice them to His blood.

See, from His head, His hands, His feet,
Sorrow and love flow mingled down;
Did e'er such love and sorrow meet,
Or thorns compose so rich a crown.

Were the whole world of nature mine,
That were a present far too small;
Love so amazing, so divine,
Demands my soul, my life, my all.[2]

Indeed, it does deserve our all.

While we may not immediately attain to the Savior's perfect example of always doing those things that please the Father and always living our lives in a way to glorify Him, we can progress as the Savior Himself did, from grace to grace, until we obtain a fulness. "I, John, bear record that I beheld his glory, as the glory of the Only Begotten of the Father, full of grace and truth, . . . which came and dwelt in the flesh, and dwelt among us. And I, John, saw that he received not of the fulness at first, but received grace for grace; and he received not of the fulness at first, but continued from grace to grace, until he received a fulness; and thus he was called the Son of God, because he received not of the fulness at the first" (D&C 93:11–14).

A few years back in general conference, I quoted this reassuring statement from President Brigham Young, who seemed to understand the challenge we face:

> After all that has been said and done, after he has led this people so long, do you not perceive that there is a lack of confidence in our God? Can you perceive it in yourselves? You may ask, "[Brother] Brigham, do you perceive it in yourself?" I do, I can see that I yet lack confidence, to some extent, in him whom I trust.—Why? Because I have not the power, in consequence of that which the fall has brought upon me. . . .

> Something rises up within me, at times[,] that . . . draws a dividing line between my interest and the interest of my Father in heaven; something that makes my interest and the interest of my Father in heaven not precisely one. . . .
>
> We should feel and understand, as far as possible, as far as fallen nature will let us, as far as we can get faith and knowledge to understand ourselves, that the interest of that God whom we serve is our interest, and that we have no other, neither in time nor in eternity.[3]

With you, I bear witness of the fruits of that great Atonement. To me, they come under three headings.

Forgiveness. The first is forgiveness, or as we sometimes say, justification. "It shall come to pass, that whoso repenteth and is baptized in my name shall be filled; and if he endureth to the end, behold, him will I hold guiltless before my Father at that day when I shall stand to judge the world" (3 Nephi 27:16).

"Behold I say unto you, that whosoever has heard the words of the prophets, yea, all the holy prophets who have prophesied concerning the coming of the Lord—I say unto you, that all those who have hearkened unto their words, and believed that the Lord would redeem his people, and have looked forward to that day for a remission of their sins, I say unto you, that these are his seed, . . . the heirs of the kingdom of God" (Mosiah 15:11).

And this witness from section 20: "We know that justification through the grace of our Lord and Savior Jesus Christ is just and true" (D&C 20:30).

Sanctification. A second fruit is the cleansing or, as we sometimes say, sanctification that comes through His grace. "No unclean thing can enter into his kingdom; therefore nothing entereth into his rest save it be those who have washed their garments in my blood, because of their faith, and the repentance of all their sins, and their faithfulness unto the end. Now this is the commandment: Repent, all ye ends of the earth, and come unto me and be baptized in my name, that ye may be sanctified by the reception of the Holy Ghost, that ye may stand spotless before me at the last day" (3 Nephi 27:19–20).

In Moroni, we read: "Again, if ye by the grace of God are perfect in Christ, and deny not his power, then are ye sanctified in Christ by the grace of God, through the shedding of the blood of Christ, which is in the covenant of the Father unto the remission of your sins, that ye become holy, without spot" (Moroni 10:33).

And again, from section 20, a testimony: "We know also, that sanctification through the grace of our Lord and Savior Jesus Christ is just and true, to all those who love and serve God with all their mights, minds, and strength" (D&C 20:31).

Resurrection. The third glorious fruit of the Atonement is the Resurrection itself, which comes because He atoned for Adam's transgression. "The Lord said unto Adam: Behold I have forgiven thee thy transgression in the Garden of Eden. Hence came the saying abroad among the people, that the Son of God hath atoned for original guilt, wherein the sins of the parents cannot be answered upon the heads of the children, for they are whole from the foundation of the world" (Moses 6:53).

In section 88, we learn: "Now, verily I say unto you, that through the redemption which is made for you is brought to pass the resurrection from the dead. And the spirit and the body are the soul of man. And the resurrection from the dead is the redemption of the soul" (D&C 88:14–16).

Regarding the Resurrection, we read: "They who are of a celestial spirit shall receive the same body which was a natural body; even ye shall receive your bodies, and your glory shall be that glory by which your bodies are quickened. Ye who are quickened by a portion of the celestial glory shall then receive of the same, even a fulness" (D&C 88:28–29).

The power of the Atonement to pardon, to sanctify, to give new life, even eternal and immortal life, came to me in a simple but powerful experience some years ago. Again, it is one of many witnesses. On this occasion I had been assigned by the First Presidency to interview a woman for the possible restoration of her temple blessings. She had committed some grievous transgressions, had been excommunicated, then baptized again, and now had applied for the privilege of returning to the temple. That required this interview and the ordinance of laying on of hands to restore those blessings and rights to her. As I prepared for that interview and read the summary of what had happened in her life, I was astonished. I could not believe that there could be so much of the sordid and evil in one life. As I read, I asked myself, *How could the First Presidency ever suppose that this person would again qualify to enter the house of the Lord?* When she came into the room to be interviewed, she seemed to have a glow about her, a light within. As we spoke, there came upon me a sense that she was pure—perhaps one of the purest souls I had ever met. I looked at her, and I looked at the paper describing the past, and I could not believe it was the same woman. And in a real sense, she was a different person. The Atonement had transformed her. It gave me to understand, powerfully, the depth and breadth and scope of the atoning grace of Jesus Christ. He is real, and His grace is very real.

Conclusion

It is appropriate to consider the testimony of the Prophet Joseph Smith as we conclude this reflection on the Atonement and Resurrection. Martyrdom endows a prophet's testimony with a special validity. The Greek root *martireo*, from which the English word *martyr* is derived, means "witness," or "to bear witness." The prophet Abinadi is described as having sealed the words, or the truth of his words, by his death (see Mosiah 17:20). Jesus's own death was a testament of His divinity and His mission. He is declared in Hebrews to be "the mediator of the new testament" (Hebrews 9:15), validated by His death, "for where a testament is, there must also of necessity be the death of the testator. For a testament is of force after men are dead" (Hebrews 9:16).

Like most of the Lord's anointed in ancient time, Joseph Smith sealed his mission and his works with his own blood. In a hail of bullets on the afternoon of June 27, 1844, in Carthage, Joseph and his brother Hyrum were cut down for the religion and the testimony they professed. And as the latter-day Apostles then announced: "The testators are now dead, and their testament is in force. . . . Their *innocent blood* on the banner of liberty, and on the *magna charta* of the United States, is an ambassador for the religion of Jesus Christ, that will touch the hearts of honest men among all nations" (D&C 135:5, 7; emphasis in original).

The Savior has not had among mortals a more faithful witness, a more obedient disciple, a more loyal advocate than Joseph Smith.

I close with his great witness of the Savior, making it my own, joining it with yours:

> We beheld the glory of the Son, on the right hand of the Father, and received of his fulness;
>
> And [we] saw the holy angels, and them who are sanctified before his throne, worshiping God, and the Lamb, who worship him forever and ever.

> And now, after the many testimonies which have been given of him, this is the testimony, last of all, which we give of him: That he lives!
>
> For we saw him, even on the right hand of God; and we heard the voice bearing record that he is the Only Begotten of the Father—
>
> That by him, and through him, and of him, the worlds are and were created, and the inhabitants thereof are begotten sons and daughters unto God. (D&C 76:20–24)

This is the most significant aspect of our entire existence. It is real. He is real. "He is not here, but is risen" (Luke 24:6). He lives. In the name of Jesus Christ, amen.

Notes

1. "God Loved Us, So He Sent His Son," *Hymns* (Salt Lake City: The Church of Jesus Christ of Latter-day Saints, 1985), no. 187.
2. "When I Survey the Wondrous Cross," *Westminster Choir College Library* (Bryn Mawr, PA: Theodore Presser, 1970).
3. Brigham Young, *Deseret News*, September 10, 1856, 212.

The Precise Purposes of the Book of Mormon

Elder Jay E. Jensen

Elder Jay E. Jensen *is a member of the First Quorum of the Seventy.*

As a young student in grade school and high school, I developed a love for reading good books. I am certain that much of my motivation came from my mother. Good books were always available at home. We also had the local public library. Saturdays were shopping days, and Mother drove the short distance from Mapleton to Springville, Utah, to do the weekly grocery shopping. The city library was one block from the market, and I often spent my time reading in the library rather than following her through the aisles of the store—a boring task.

Somehow, through all those early years of reading, I failed to learn the significance of reading the prefaces or introductions to books, and I am confident the fault was mine, not the fault of my teachers. Later on in college, I learned that reading the preface is one of the most important things to do, for in them I learned the authors' stated purposes or intents and important background information concerning the text.

Moroni's Purpose Statement on the Title Page

Reading and understanding the introductions to the four standard works and their stated purposes is no exception; this practice is particularly true for the Book of Mormon. Unique to this volume of scripture are two significant introductions: (1) the title page, written by Moroni, and (2) the introduction, written under the direction of the First Presidency and the Quorum of the

Twelve. The three other introductory sections to the Book of Mormon—The Testimony of the Three and Eight Witnesses, Testimony of the Prophet Joseph Smith, and A Brief Explanation about the Book of Mormon—are also important because of the useful background and contextual information they provide, but not because they are statements of intent.

Moroni states the precise purposes of the Book of Mormon on the title page—"Which is to show unto the remnant of the House of Israel

1. "what great things the Lord hath done for their fathers; and
2. "that they may know the covenants of the Lord, that they are not cast off forever—And also
3. "to the convincing of the Jew and Gentile that JESUS is the CHRIST, the ETERNAL GOD, manifesting himself unto all nations."

To this list we might add Moroni's last words on the title page, "That ye may be found spotless at the judgment-seat of Christ," a vital part of the Book of Mormon's purpose.

A worthwhile scripture study exercise is to take three separate pieces of paper and write one of the statements at the top of each and then begin a careful study of the Book of Mormon, writing scripture references supporting each purpose. My own efforts showed that the longest list of references is under the third purpose, substantiating the truth that the Book of Mormon is the most Christ-centered book ever written and truly "Another Testament of Jesus Christ."

In the first two purpose statements, "what great things the Lord hath done for their fathers," and "that they may know the covenants of the Lord," Moroni clearly established that people in the Book of Mormon are Israelites and inheritors of the promises made to the fathers. Specifically, the term *fathers* referred to in the first statement may refer to specific ancestral lines and to all the great prophets and patriarchs in the Old Testament, but quite often the fathers are the three great patriarchs, Abraham, Isaac, and Jacob, with whom the Lord made covenants. Thus, the first statement leads to the second: "that they may know the covenants of the Lord."[1]

Nephi is the principal writer and author of the small plates, and Mormon and Moroni are the principal compilers and writers of the large plates. These three writers were clear in their purposes for writing, all of which generally tie into the title page of the Book of Mormon; but, as will be shown below, it was probably Nephi who started the basic themes that helped all other writers and compilers with their focus, resulting in the title page as we know it today.

Nephi's Purposes in Writing

So significant are the small plates, and especially the writings of Nephi, that the Lord declared, "Behold, there are many things engraven upon the plates of Nephi *which do throw greater views upon my gospel*" (D&C 10:45; emphasis added). This greater view appears early on in 1 Nephi. In fact, the more I read, study, ponder, and pray over the Book of Mormon, the more I am convinced that Lehi and Nephi set the major doctrinal themes for all other writers. If this is so, then the small plates of Nephi (1 and 2 Nephi, Jacob, Enos, Jarom, and Omni) are a preface to the entire 531 pages (English edition). Perhaps it is even safe to say that those themes are established by the dream and vision of Lehi (see 1 Nephi 8; 10) and Nephi's subsequent vision of the same (see 1 Nephi 11–14). Also, it is important to include Nephi's commentary on Lehi's vision or dream as found in chapter 15. In summary, 1 Nephi chapters 8 through 15 (inclusive) are the most complete preface to the entire Book of Mormon, and all else that follows in this magnificent book grows out of and is in harmony with these eight chapters.[2]

Lehi and Nephi focus on covenants, the Messiah, the gathering of Israel, the Gentiles, and the Restoration in these early chapters, but it is Nephi's commentary on them that establishes the centrality of the themes Moroni outlined in the title page. For me, 1 Nephi 15 is one of the most important chapters in the entire Book of Mormon. The setting for it is that Laman and Lemuel had not understood Lehi's words "concerning the natural branches of the olive-tree, and also concerning the Gentiles" (1 Nephi 15:7). Nephi answered them by teaching them about Israel and its scattering and subsequent gathering in the latter days, beginning with the coming forth of the Book of Mormon, which he said contains the fulness of the gospel and would "come unto the Gentiles, and from the Gentiles unto the remnant of our seed" (1 Nephi 15:13). As a result of the Book of Mormon, the remnant of their seed and all the house of Israel would know

1. "that they are of the house of Israel, and
2. "that they are the covenant people of the Lord; and
3. "then shall they know and come to the knowledge of their forefathers, and also

4. "to the knowledge of the gospel of their Redeemer which was ministered unto their fathers by him; wherefore,
5. "they shall come to the knowledge of their Redeemer and the very points of his doctrine, that they may know how to come unto him and be saved" (1 Nephi 15:14).

Those who come to this knowledge will rejoice and come into the true fold of God and be grafted into the true olive tree (see 1 Nephi 15:15–16). To be grafted in, by scriptural definition, is to "come to the knowledge of the true Messiah, their Lord and their Redeemer" (1 Nephi 10:14). As people come to this knowledge and are grafted in, we see the grand fulfillment of the promises made to Abraham, "pointing to the covenant which should be fulfilled in the latter days; which covenant the Lord made to our father Abraham, saying: In thy seed shall all the kindreds of the earth be blessed" (1 Nephi 15:18).

The kindreds or families spoken of will be converted through the power of the Spirit as they read, ponder, and pray about the Book of Mormon and will be led to the holy temple, where families are sealed together in fulfillment of the promises made to Abraham.

All other Book of Mormon writers and prophets received revelation from the Holy Ghost, from heavenly messengers, and from the Savior Himself that build upon and expand the simple, profound truths that Lehi and Nephi received by revelation. This revelation shows that Jesus Christ "is the same yesterday, to-day, and forever; and the way is prepared for all men from the foundation of the world, if it so be that they repent and come unto him" (1 Nephi 10:18).

Nephi concluded his portion of the plates by teaching us what he hoped his writings would do—and, for emphasis, I identify them in outline form with this introductory statement by Nephi: "And the words which I have written in weakness will be made strong unto them; for

1. "it persuadeth them to do good;
2. "it maketh known unto them of their fathers;
3. "and it speaketh of Jesus, and persuadeth them to believe in him, and to endure to the end, which is life eternal.
4. "And it speaketh harshly against sin" (2 Nephi 33:4–5).

Other Purposes of the Book of Mormon as Described by Nephi

In addition to the declared purposes discussed thus far, Nephi shared poignant thoughts and feelings about what he had written and what he hoped his writings would do. For example, Nephi included the writings of Isaiah with the hope that we would liken them and that they would "persuade them [us in these latter days] that they would remember the Lord their Redeemer . . . and believe in [Him]" (1 Nephi 19:18, 23). Furthermore, speaking about the plates of brass, Nephi testified that by likening them to ourselves, we will know they "are true; and they testify that a man must be obedient to the commandments of God" (1 Nephi 22:30).

Nephi's understanding about these things, the writings on the small plates, is clearly stated with his interpretation of his father's dream, and we can read between the lines to discern his deep feelings: "I said unto them that it [the iron rod] was the word of God; and whoso would hearken unto the word of God, and would hold fast unto it, they would never perish; neither could the temptations and the fiery darts of the adversary overpower them unto blindness, to lead them away to destruction" (1 Nephi 15:24).

In the so-called Psalm of Nephi, we glimpse his feelings about the plates: "And upon these I write the things of my soul. . . . For my soul delighteth in the scriptures, and my heart pondereth them, and writeth them for the learning and the profit of my children. Behold, my soul delighteth in the things of the Lord; and my heart pondereth continually upon the things which I have seen and heard" (2 Nephi 4:15–16).

After Nephi had included the writings of Isaiah and his commentaries and prophecies of the same, he said he was satisfied except for "a few words which I must speak concerning the doctrine of Christ" (2 Nephi 31:2). Following that statement he wrote about what the Lord had showed to him, perhaps as part of the vision described in 1 Nephi 11–14, about the Savior, His baptism, and why we must follow Him and stay on the path He marked (see 2 Nephi 31; compare to 1 Nephi 8, Lehi's dream). Then Nephi gave first what I call an if-then proposition concerning the words of Christ: "*If* ye shall press forward, feasting upon the word of Christ, and endure to the end, behold [then], thus saith the Father: Ye shall have eternal life" (2 Nephi 31:20; emphasis added). This strong invitation was followed by this command: "Feast upon the words of Christ; for behold, the words of Christ will tell you all things what ye should do" (2 Nephi 32:3).

Finally, he brought his portion of the small plates to a close by stating that "I, Nephi, have written what I have written, and I esteem it as of great worth" (2 Nephi 33:3). He was commanded to write these things, knowing that they are the words of Christ and that we and Nephi "shall stand face to face" and be judged according to what we have done with the words he wrote, for they will either condemn us or bless us with life eternal (see 2 Nephi 33:11–15).

Jacob's Purpose Statement

Jacob adhered to the intent established by Nephi and the important focus on the themes of what the Lord had done for their fathers, that Israel may know the covenants of the Lord, and to the convincing of Jew and Gentile that Jesus is the Christ. These are found in 2 Nephi 6 through 10, especially chapters 9 and 10, and Jacob 1 through 6. In the following meaningful purpose statement, Jacob expressed his hopes for what he had written: "And we labor diligently to engraven these words upon plates, hoping that our beloved brethren and our children will receive them with thankful hearts, and look upon them that they may learn with joy and not with sorrow, neither with contempt, concerning their first parents. For, for this intent have we written these things, that they may know that we knew of Christ, and we had a hope of his glory many hundred years before his coming; and not only we ourselves had a hope of his glory, but also all the holy prophets which were before us" (Jacob 4:3–4).

This precise statement of intent is then illustrated by the magnificent allegory in Jacob chapter 5 and his summary of that allegory in chapter 6, specifically that God will remember the house of Israel and His covenant with them, exhorting them to "repent, and come with full purpose of heart, and cleave unto God" and not "reject all the words which have been spoken concerning Christ" (Jacob 6:5, 8), which he and Nephi had been so careful in writing and preserving.

Fulfillment of the Writers' Intents in the Book of Alma

In Mormon's abridgment of Alma's teachings and experiences, the following summary of what the plates had accomplished thus far illustrates the fulfillment of intent. If we change the verb tense from the past to the present or future, these truths also may be considered as statements of purpose.

"And now, it has hitherto been wisdom in God that these things should be preserved; for behold they [the writings on the plates] have

1. "enlarged the memory of this people, yea, and
2. "convinced many of the error of their ways, and
3. "brought them to the knowledge of their God unto the salvation of their souls.
4. "Yea, I say unto you, were it not for these things that these records do contain, which are on these plates, Ammon and his brother could not have convinced so many thousands of the Lamanites of the incorrect tradition of their fathers; yea, these records and their words brought them unto repentance; that is, they brought them to the knowledge of the Lord their God, and to rejoice in Jesus Christ their Redeemer" (Alma 37:8–9).

This work of supernal significance offers a convincing testimony that Jesus is the Christ, the Eternal God, who manifests Himself to all who repent and come unto Him, especially Lehi's posterity, whom the Lord loves—His covenant people, the children of Israel.

A Purpose Statement from the Doctrine and Covenants

In a revelation to the Prophet Joseph Smith in 1828, the following declaration appears. Note how it parallels the title page and Lehi's and Nephi's visions. Again, I emphasize the introductory words *purpose* and *that*, which establish intent:

"And for this very *purpose* are these plates preserved, which contain these records—

1. "*that* the promises of the Lord might be fulfilled, which he made to this people; And
2. "*that* the Lamanites might come to the knowledge of their fathers, and
3. "*that* they might know the promises of the Lord, and
4. "*that* they may believe the gospel and rely upon the merits of Jesus Christ, and be glorified through faith in his name, and
5. "*that* through their repentance they might be saved" (D&C 3:19–20; emphasis added).

A Purpose Statement from the Book of Ether

When Moroni included his abridgment of the plates of Ether, he inserted this short purpose statement:

"Wherefore, I, Moroni, am commanded to write these things

1. "*that* evil may be done away, and
2. "*that* the time may come that Satan may have no power upon the hearts of the children of men, but
3. "*that* they may be persuaded to do good continually,
4. "*that* they may come unto the fountain of all righteousness and be saved" (Ether 8:26; emphasis added).

Notice how the fourth purpose above parallels the words established by Lehi and Nephi in the tree-of-life dream as illustrated by the metaphor of coming unto the fountain of all righteousness and being saved (see 1 Nephi 8:15–16, 30; 11:25).

Comparison of Mormon's and Moroni's Purpose Statements

Sons learn from their fathers in both word and deed. Moroni surely learned much from his father Mormon, as illustrated by comparing three purpose statements, two of Mormon's and the title page written by Moroni.

Note the emphasis on the judgment-seat in Mormon 3 and in the title page and, as was stated earlier, the role of the Book of Mormon in helping us to prepare for the judgment.

Mormon's Purpose Statement No.1	**Mormon's Purpose Statement No. 2**	**Title Page (Moroni's Purpose Statement)**
Therefore I write unto you, Gentiles and also unto you, house of Israel. . . . Yea, behold, I write unto all the ends of the earth. . . .	Now these things are written unto the remnant of the house of Jacob. . . . And behold, they shall go unto the unbelieving of the Jews;	Written to the Lamanites, who are a remnant of the house of Israel; and also to Jew and Gentile. . . .
And I write also unto the remnant of this people. . . . Therefore, I write unto you all. And for this cause I write unto you, that ye may know that ye must all stand before the judgment-seat of Christ; . . . and ye must stand to be judged of your works, whether they be good or evil;		Which is to show unto the remnant of the House of Israel what great things the Lord hath done for their fathers; and that they may know the covenants of the Lord, that they are not cast off forever—
And also that ye may believe the gospel of Jesus Christ, which ye shall have among you; And also that the Jews, the covenant people of the Lord, shall have other witnesses besides him whom they saw and heard, that Jesus, whom they slew, was the very Christ and the very God. And I would that I could persuade all ye ends of the earth to repent and prepare to stand before the judgment-seat of Christ. (Mormon 3:17–22)	And for this intent shall they go—that they may be persuaded that Jesus is the Christ, the Son of the living God; that the Father may bring about, through his most Beloved, his great and eternal purpose, in restoring the Jews, or all the house of Israel, to the land of their inheritance, which the Lord their God hath given them, unto the fulfilling of his covenant; and also that the seed of this people may more fully believe his gospel. (Mormon 5:12, 14–15)	And also to the convincing of the Jew and Gentile that JESUS is the CHRIST, the ETERNAL GOD, manifesting himself unto all nations. . . . Wherefore, condemn not the things of God, that ye may be found spotless at the judgment-seat of Christ. (title page)

Mormon's Final Purpose Statement

As seen in the parallels above (Mormon 3:17–22; Mormon 5:12, 14–15; and the title page), Mormon clearly understood the intended purpose of the Book of Mormon. If we look at the chronology of Mormon's writings, it appears that Mormon chapter 7 is his final message. (Moroni concluded the plates and inserted two epistles from his father, Moroni 8 and 9, that were probably written earlier in his ministry, making Mormon chapter 7 his final written message on the plates.) Mormon's final hope and counsel are that the remnant of this people in the Book of Mormon will know the following:

1. The things of their fathers (v. 1);
2. That they are the house of Israel (v. 2);
3. What they must do to be saved (vv. 3–4);
4. That they must come to the knowledge of their fathers (v. 5);
5. That they must believe in Jesus Christ and in His mission, Atonement, and Resurrection and that there will be a final judgment (vv. 5–6);
6. That those who believe in the Book of Mormon will believe the Bible and vice versa (v. 9);
7. That they are the seed of Jacob (Israel) and that if they believe in Jesus Christ, repent, are baptized, and receive the Holy Ghost, it will be well with them in the day of judgment (v. 10).

Moroni's Final Purpose Statements

Moroni received the records from his father, Mormon, and then added his words (see Mormon 8–9, Moroni 1–10, and portions of Ether). Moroni said that "my father hath made this record, and he hath written the intent thereof" (Mormon 8:5; see also 3:20–22; 5:14–15; and 7). Moroni summarized his father's intent by saying that he hoped the record would help its writers to "rid our garments of the blood of our brethren" (Mormon 9:37) and that these brethren would be restored to the knowledge of Jesus Christ and that God, the Father, would "remember the covenant which he hath made with the house of Israel" (Mormon 9:37).

I continue to marvel at the precise parallels found in all these purpose statements, all of them so beautifully summarized in the title page to the Book of Mormon.

In addition to the title page, the concluding chapter of the Book of Mormon, Moroni 10, contains eight truths relating to all these purpose statements. Each truth begins with an exhortation.

1. "I would exhort you . . . that ye would remember how merciful the Lord hath been . . . and ponder it in your hearts" (v. 3).
2. "I would exhort you that ye would ask God, the Eternal Father, in the name of Christ, if these things are not true" (v. 4).

3. "I would exhort you that ye deny not the power of God" (v. 7).
4. "I exhort you, my brethren, that ye deny not the gifts of God" (v. 8).
5. "I would exhort you . . . that ye remember that every good gift cometh of Christ" (v. 18).
6. "I would exhort you . . . that ye remember that he is the same yesterday, today, and forever" (v. 19).
7. "I exhort you to remember these things" (v. 27).
8. "I would exhort you that ye would come unto Christ" (v. 30).

The last two exhortations focus on "these things" and on Jesus Christ. "These things" refers to the written records, and Moroni's exhortation parallels Nephi's: there will be a final judgment, and we will see Nephi and Moroni, to ensure an accountability concerning what we have done with the records (see 2 Nephi 33:10–15). Finally, Moroni invites us to come unto Christ and be perfected in Him (see Moroni 10:30, 32). Thus end the large plates, with this stirring Christ-centered invitation.

But what about the end of the small plates? It is no surprise that the small plates, those magnificent writings that Nephi started and that Amaleki concluded, parallel Moroni's exhortations:

> I shall deliver up these plates unto him, *exhorting* all men to come unto God, the Holy One of Israel, and believe in prophesying, and in revelations, and in the ministering of angels, and in the gift of speaking with tongues, and in the gift of interpreting languages, and in all things which are good; for there is nothing which is good save it comes from the Lord: and that which is evil cometh from the devil.
>
> And now my beloved brethren, I would that ye should come unto Christ, who is the Holy One of Israel, and partake of his salvation, and the power of his redemption. Yea, come unto him, and offer your whole souls as an offering unto him, and continue in fasting and praying, and endure to the end; and as the Lord liveth ye will be saved. (Omni 1:25–26; emphasis added)

The Prophet Joseph Smith translated the small and large plates by the gift and power of God and declared to the world that "the Book of Mormon was the most correct of any book on earth, and the keystone of our religion, and a man would get nearer to God by abiding by its precepts, than by any other book."[3]

This bold declaration takes on greater meaning when it is harmonized with the declared purposes of the Book of Mormon.

Notes

1. A summary of those covenants that God made with Abraham is that Jesus Christ would be born in Abraham's lineage, that Abraham's posterity would be more numerous than the stars or sand on the seashores, that his posterity would bless all nations, and, finally, that they were promised a land of inheritance (see Genesis 17; 22; Abraham 2:6–11; Bible Dictionary, "Abraham" and "Abraham, Covenant of," 601–2).
2. See also the excellent article by Andrew C. Skinner, "The Foundational Doctrine of 1 Nephi 11–14," *Religious Educator* 2, no. 2 (2001): 139–55.
3. Joseph Smith, *History of the Church of Jesus Christ of Latter-day Saints*, ed. B. H. Roberts, 2nd ed. rev. (Salt Lake City: Deseret Book, 1957), 4:461.

Our Creator's Cosmos

Elder Neal A. Maxwell

Elder Neal A. Maxwell *(1926–2004) was a member of the Quorum of the Twelve Apostles.*

This address was delivered at the Twenty-sixth Annual Church Educational System Religious Educators Conference on August 13, 2002, at Brigham Young University.

The religious education of our youth and young adults in our seminaries and institutes of religion, our Church schools, and colleges and universities is one of the most effective and high-yield programs of the Church!

While it is your duty to serve the "rising generations," I am confident that your duty has long since become your delight. Thank you from the bottom of my heart! And thanks to Brother Randy McMurdie, who has helped so much with arranging the special visuals.

My special appreciation goes to Professor Eric G. Hintz of Brigham Young University, an observational astronomer, for his very helpful, substantive suggestions concerning these remarks. Through him I have been pleased to learn of the increasing numbers of Latter-day Saint students pursuing advanced astronomy and astrophysics. For them and all of us, these words of Anselm constitute good counsel: "Believe in order to understand," rather than "understand in order to believe."[1] I, and I alone, am responsible for what I say. My theme is "Our Creator's Cosmos."

I plead for the vital help of the Spirit as I speak to you as an Apostle, not an astrophysicist. As a special witness, I will speak about the witnessing universe: "The scriptures are laid before thee, yea, and all things denote there is a God; yea, even the earth, and *all things* that are upon the face of it, yea, and its motion, yea, and also all the planets which move in their regular form *do witness that there is a Supreme Creator* " (Alma 30:44; emphasis added).

May what follows—not my words, but the stunning words of scripture along with some breathtaking visuals—bring additional awe and reverence concerning the wonders the Father and Son have wrought to bless us.

Under the Father's direction, Christ was and is the Lord of the universe, "the same which *looked upon the wide expanse of eternity* " (D&C 38:1; emphasis added).

The late Carl Sagan, who communicated effectively about science and the universe, perceptively observed that

> in some respects, science has far surpassed religion in delivering awe. How is it that hardly any major religion has looked at science and concluded, "This is better than we thought! The Universe is much bigger than our prophets said—grander, more subtle, more elegant. God must be even greater than we dreamed"? Instead, they say, "No, no, no! My god is a little god, and I want him to stay that way." A religion, old or new, that stressed the magnificence of the Universe as revealed by modern science might be able to draw forth reserves of reverence and awe hardly tapped by the conventional faiths. Sooner or later, such a religion will emerge.[2]

Latter-day Saints certainly should not lack reverence and awe—especially when we contemplate the universe in the context of divinely revealed truths. Yes, the cosmos "as revealed by modern science" is "elegant," as Sagan wrote. But the universe is also pulsating with divine purpose, so our awe is "added upon," providing even greater reasons for reverential awe regarding "the magnificence of the Universe"!

Of course, the Church does not align itself with the astrophysics of 2002, nor does it endorse any particular scientific theory about the creation of the universe.

As astrophysicists pursue their important work, they use the scientific method and are not in pursuit of spiritual answers. A few scientists share our belief in religious explanations concerning these vast creations, but some view ours as an unsponsored universe. Bereft of belief in cosmic meaning, some, as portrayed by one writer, view humans as being "wrenched whimpering into an alien universe."[3]

Resoundingly, the restored scriptures tell us otherwise!

But do the sweeping, scriptural words with which we have been blessed stir us enough? Are we steadily becoming the "manner of people" who reflect such soaring doctrines by our increased spiritual sanctification? Brothers and sisters, God is giving away the spiritual secrets of the universe, but are we listening?

In daily discipleship, we are rightly instructed to "lift up the hands which hang down" (Hebrews 12:12). Why not also strive to "lift up" the sometimes passive and provincial *minds* that also "hang down," unnoticing of the stunning scope of it all?

Given all that God has done to prepare a place for us in the stretching universe, might we not develop and display greater faith? In the perplexities and crunches of life, will we have faith in the Creator's having made "ample provision" to bring all His purposes to pass? [4]

Years ago, President J. Reuben Clark Jr. made this comforting comment: "Our Lord is not a novice, he is not an amateur; he has been over this course time and time and time again."[5]

Brothers and sisters, has not the Lord described His course as "one eternal round"? (D&C 35:1; see also 1 Nephi 10:19; Alma 7:20; D&C 3:2).

Greater appreciation for the greater universe will also help us to live more righteously in our own tiny universes of daily life. Likewise, a better understanding of God's governance of the vast galaxies can lead to our better self-governance.

Now for a mixture of scriptures, illustrations, and scientific commentary.

Consider first this photo of our beautiful earth as viewed with our moon in the foreground:

Reflect upon how long it took man to reach the moon, and yet it is located in our own backyard!

The resources so necessary to sustain human life are so generously provided on this particular planet; unless they are mismanaged, we are told that there is "enough and to spare" (D&C 104:17). Yet as big as this earth is—and all of us jet-laggers can so attest—Stephen W. Hawking provided for us some sobering perspective: "[Our] earth is a *medium-sized* planet orbiting around an average star in the outer suburbs of an *ordinary* spiral galaxy, which is itself only one of about a million million galaxies in the observable universe."[6]

One scientist who does not believe in divine design nevertheless noted that "as we look out into the universe and identify the many accidents . . . that have worked together to our benefit, it almost seems as if the universe must in some sense have known that we were coming."[7]

Arrangements on this earth are apparently more favorable than any in our stretching solar system.

If, for example, the planet earth were closer to the sun, we would fry, and if it were more distant, we would freeze.

Now note the arrow, which points to about where our solar system is situated amid the incredible vastness of our own Milky Way Galaxy.

In this visual, though our solar system is stretched out over millions of millions of miles, it is too tiny to see! Oh, the sweeping scope of it all!

On a clear night, you and I can see some portions of the Milky Way, but what if a view of sparkling stars occurred only once every thousand years? Ralph Waldo Emerson wrote of how then "men [would] believe and adore; and preserve for many generations the remembrance of the city of God which had been shown!"[8]

No wonder the scriptures tell how wide and varied God's witnessing to us is: "Behold, . . . all things are created and made to bear record of [God], . . . things which are in the heavens above, and things which are on the earth . . . : *all things bear record of [God]* " (Moses 6:63; emphasis added).

Next, contemplate what constitutes but one section within our vast Milky Way Galaxy:

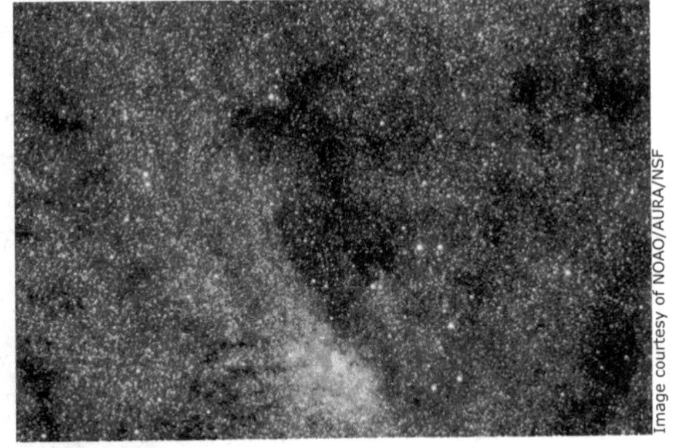

Image courtesy of NOAO/AURA/NSF

Isn't it breathtaking? Especially when we realize that the distances between those bright dots are so great!

Whatever the *how* of God's creative process, spiritually reassuring things are set forth about the beginning—"back of the beyond," so very long ago.

"And there stood one among them that was like unto God, and he said unto those who were with him: We will go down, *for there is space there,* and we will take of these materials, and we will make an earth whereon these may dwell; . . . And they went down *at the beginning*, and they . . . *organized and formed the heavens and the earth*" (Abraham 3:24; 4:1; emphasis added).

Strikingly, according to some scientists, "Our galaxy, the Milky Way, is located in *one of the relatively empty spaces* between the Great Walls."[9]

There is space there.

As able scientists continue to probe beyond our galaxy with the Hubble space telescope, they discover stunning things like the Keyhole Nebula with its own stars.

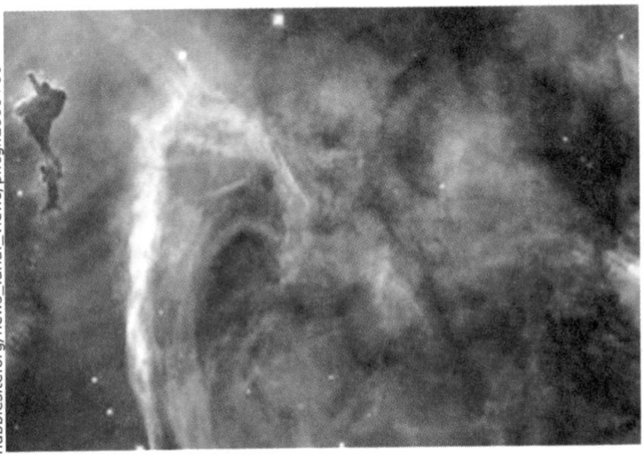

hubblesite.org/news_.and._views/pr.cgi.2000+06

The Hubble telescope has shown us so much more; and, to use one of your students' favorite words, it is awesome!

This next view is of a star-forming region involving *unorganized material.*

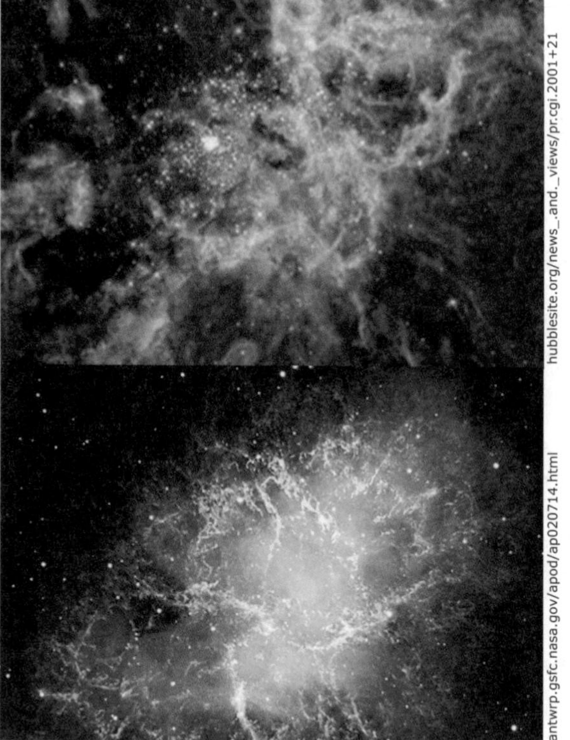

"And as one earth shall pass away, and the heavens thereof even so shall another come" (Moses 1:38).

Next, we see a visual of what is "left over" after a star dies.

"For behold, there are many worlds that have passed away by the word of my power" (Moses 1:35).

In the words of the hymn "How Great Thou Art," of the universe and the Atonement, we sing that we "scarce can take it in."[10]

Whatever God's initial process, there apparently was some divine overseeing: "And the Gods watched those things which they had ordered *until* they obeyed" (Abraham 4:18; emphasis added).

Very significantly, we here on this earth are not alone in the universe. In the Doctrine and Covenants, which will be the focus of your study this year, we read that "by [Christ], and through him, and of him, the *worlds* are and were created, *and the inhabitants thereof* are begotten sons and daughters unto God" (D&C 76:24; emphasis added; see also Moses 1:35).

We do not know *where* or *how many* other inhabited planets there are, even though we appear to be alone in our own solar system.

As to the Lord's continuing role amid His vast creations, so little has been revealed. There are inklings, however, about kingdoms and inhabitants.

"Therefore, unto this parable I will liken all these kingdoms, and the inhabitants thereof—every kingdom in its hour, and in its time, and in its season, even according to the decree which God hath made" (D&C 88:61).

The Lord even invites us to "ponder in [our] hearts" that particular parable (v. 62). Such pondering does not mean idle speculation, but rather, patient and meek anticipation of further revelations. Besides, God gave only *partial* disclosure—"not all"—to Moses, with "only an account of this earth" (Moses 1:4, 35), but Moses still learned things he "never had supposed" (v. 10). Nevertheless, we do not worship a one-planet God!

Now, cast your eyes on this view of what is called "deep space":

Almost every dot you see in this frame, courtesy of the Hubble telescope, is a galaxy! Think of our own Milky Way Galaxy. I am told that each galaxy represented here has on the order of 100 *billion* stars. Just this little wedge of the universe has almost innumerable worlds.

Earlier believers in divine design included the articulate Alexander Pope. He reacted thusly to the marvels of this universe:

> A mighty maze! but not without a plan. . . .
> Thro' worlds unnumber'd tho' the God be known,
> 'Tis ours to trace him only in our own. . . .
> [Though] other planets circle other suns.[11]

Happily for us, brothers and sisters, the *vastness* of the Lord's creations is matched by the *personalness* of His purposes!

"For thus saith the Lord that created the heavens; God himself that formed the earth and made it; he hath established it, he created it not in vain, he formed it to be inhabited" (Isaiah 45:18; see also Ephesians 3:9; Hebrews 1:2).

"And worlds without number have I created; and I also created them for mine own purpose; . . .

". . . For behold, there are many worlds that have passed away by the word of my power. And there are many that now stand, and innumerable are they unto man; but all things are numbered unto me, for they are mine and I know them" (Moses 1:33, 35).

One may ask what is God's purpose for the inhabitants? It is best expressed in that terse verse with which you are all so familiar: "For behold, this is my work and my glory—to bring to pass the immortality and eternal life of man" (Moses 1:39).

Therefore, in the expansiveness of space, there is stunning *personalness*, for God knows and loves each of us! (see 1 Nephi 11:17). We are not ciphers in unexplained space! While the Psalmist's query was, "What is man, that thou art mindful of him?" (Psalm 8:4), mankind is at the very center of God's work. We are the sheep of His hand and the people of His pasture (see Psalms 79:13; 95:7; 100:3). His work includes our immortalization—accomplished by Christ's glorious Atonement! Think of it, brothers and sisters, even with their extensive longevity, stars are not immortal, but you are.

The revelations give us very little information about *how* the Lord created it all. Scientists meanwhile focus on *how* and *what* and *when.* Nevertheless, some of them acknowledge the puzzlement over *why.* Hawking said: "Although science may solve the problem of *how* the universe began, it cannot answer the question: *Why* does the universe bother to exist? I don't know the answer to that."[12]

Albert Einstein said of his desires: "I want to know *how* God created this world. I am not interested in this or that phenomenon, in the spectrum of this or that element. I want to know His thoughts; the rest are details."[13]

Dr. Allen Sandage, a believer in divine design, was an assistant to Edwin Hubble. Sandage wrote: "Science . . . is concerned with the *what, when,* and *how.* It does not, and indeed cannot, answer within its method (powerful as that method is), *why.*"[14]

Mercifully, we are given vital and pivotal answers to the *why* questions in revelations that contain the answers that matter most to us anyway! Having seen vast and spectacular things, Enoch rejoiced—but over what? He rejoiced over his personal assurance about God: "Yet thou art there" (Moses 7:30). Enoch even saw God weep over needless human suffering, which tells us so much about divine character (see vv. 28–29). But that is a topic for another time.

Alas, even given the remarkable revelations about the cosmos and God's purposes, people can still drift away. These people did: "And it came to pass that . . . the people began to forget those signs and wonders which they had heard, and began to be less and less astonished at a sign or a wonder from heaven, insomuch that they began to be hard in their hearts, and blind in

Image courtesy of White Flower Farm

their minds, and began to disbelieve all which they had heard and seen" (3 Nephi 2:1).

So, as you and I ponder God's creative grandeur, we are also told to consider the beauty of the lilies of the field. Remember, "all things" bear witness of Him! (see Alma 30:44).

In this visual we see lilies, and then, in close-up, divine design. The same divine design in the universe is miniatured in the lilies of the field (see Matthew 6:28–29; 3 Nephi 13:28–29; D&C 84:82).

The miracle of this planet has so many ongoing, marvelous subtleties. Wendell Berry writes:

"Whoever really has considered the lilies of the field or the birds of the air and pondered the improbability of their existence *in this warm world within the cold and empty stellar distances* will hardly balk at the turning of water into wine—which was, after all, a very small miracle. We forget the greater and still continuing miracle by which water (with soil and sunlight) is turned into grapes."[15]

As we reverence what the Lord has created, we are to reverence Him and His character enough to strive to become ever more like Him, as He has directed (see Matthew 5:48; 3 Nephi 12:48; 27:27). Unsurprisingly, therefore, the power of godliness revealed in lilies is likewise revealed in the ordinances of His gospel (see D&C 84:20). Thematically, these ordinances concern our cleansing, covenanting, obeying, and preparing—all behaviorally necessary in order for us to be empowered to make the homeward journey.

These personalized expressions of divine love and power matter much more to us anyway than trying to number the wondrous galaxies or comparing the number of planets to stars. We lay people could not comprehend it anyway. Achieving spiritual sanctification matters so much more than cosmic quantifications.

Thus, as we enlarge our views both of the universe and of God's stretching purposes, we, too, can reverently exclaim, "O how great the plan of our God!" (2 Nephi 9:13).

Therefore, as we probe, ponder, and learn, we certainly should be filled with awe, and we should also be intellectually meek. King Benjamin counseled us with these simple but profound words:

"Believe in God; believe that he is, and that he created all things, both in heaven and in earth; believe that he has all wisdom, and all power, both in heaven and in earth; *believe that man doth not comprehend all the things which the Lord can comprehend*" (Mosiah 4:9; emphasis added).

Alas, in our age, brothers and sisters, we have some who believe that if they cannot comprehend something, then God cannot comprehend it either. Ironically, some do actually prefer a "little god." Better for all of us—scientists and nonscientists alike—instead of trying to downsize divinity, to upsize our personal humility!

As spectacular as what science has learned about the witnessing universe so far, it is still such a small sample. Of the 1995 Hubble picture of a "deep field," it was said that "the sampled segment—the deepest image ever taken of the heavens—covered . . . 'a speck of the sky only about the width of a dime located 75 feet away.'"[16]

The soul trembles, brothers and sisters!

Whatever Moses' own sample, no wonder he was overwhelmed and "fell unto the earth" say-that "man is nothing" (Moses 1:9–10).

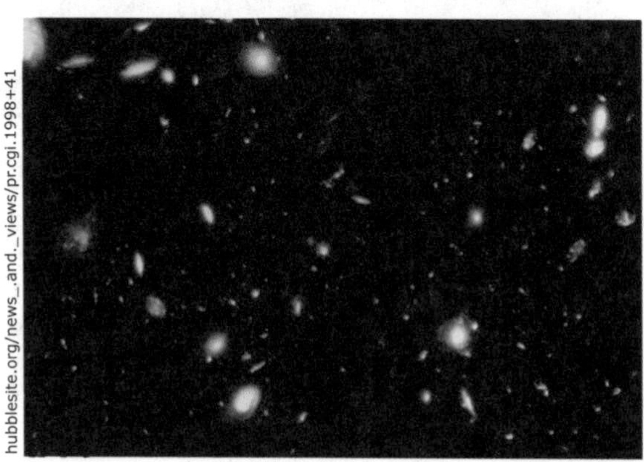
hubblesite.org/news_.and._views/pr.cgi.1998+41

Mercifully, though struck, the revelations as-us of God's love: "Now brethren, we see that God mindful of every people, whatsoever land they be in; yea, he numbereth people, and his bowels of mercy are over all the earth. Now this is my joy, and my great thanksgiving; yea, and I will give thanks unto my God forever" (Alma 26:37).

So, brothers and sisters, the Lord is mindful of each of His vast creations. Look once more at the many "dots" in just one portion of our ordinary-sized Milky Way Galaxy:

He knows them all. Think of it. Just as the Lord knows each owf these creations, so also He knows and loves each of those seen in this or any crowd—indeed, each and all of mankind! (see 1 Nephi 11:17).

Divine determination is so reassuring, as these words in Abraham set forth: "There is nothing that the Lord thy God shall take in his heart to do but what he will do it" (Abraham 3:17). His capacity is so remarkable that two times in two verses in the Book of Mormon He courteously but pointedly reminds us that He really is "able" to do His own work (see 2 Nephi 27:20–21). Is He ever!

Furthermore, order is reflected in God's creations!

"And I saw the stars, that they were very great, and that one of them was nearest unto the throne of God; and there were many great ones which were near unto it; . . .

"And thus there shall be the reckoning of the time of one planet above another, until thou come nigh unto Kolob, which Kolob is after the reckoning of the Lord's time; which Kolob is set nigh unto the throne of God, to govern all those planets *which belong to the same order as that upon which thou standest*" (Abraham 3:2, 9; emphasis added).

One scientist is reported as saying of cosmic configuration, "We may be living among huge honeycomb structures or cells."[17] Some scientists say of certain nonrandom galaxies that they "appear to be arranged in a network of strings, or filaments, surrounding large, relatively empty regions of space known as voids."[18] Other astronomers say they have discovered an "enormous . . . wall of galaxies, . . . the largest structure yet observed in the universe."[19] Commendably, such able scientists continue to press forward.

For us, however, clearly the earth never was the center of the universe, as many once provincially believed! Nor has it been many decades since many likewise believed our Milky Way Galaxy was the only galaxy in the universe.

But the more we know, the more vital the *why* questions and the answers thereto become. Yet the answers to the *why* questions are obtainable only by revelations given by God the Creator, and more is yet to come:

> All thrones and dominions, principalities and powers, shall be revealed and set forth upon all who have endured valiantly for the gospel of Jesus Christ.
>
> And also, if there be bounds set to the heavens or to the seas, or to the dry land, or to the sun, moon, or stars—
>
> All the times of their revolutions, all the appointed days, months, and years, and all the days of their days, months, and years, and all their glories, laws, and set times, shall be revealed in the days of the dispensation of the fulness of times (D&C 121:29–31).

Therefore, brothers and sisters, as we look at the universe, we do not see unexplained chaos or cosmic churn. Instead, the faithful see God "moving in His majesty and power" (D&C 88:47). It is like viewing a divinely choreographed, cosmic ballet—spectacular, subduing, and reassuring!

Even so, in the midst of our feeling overcome by the wonder and awe, the "cares of the world" can overcome us (see D&C 39:9). Humdrum routineness and repetition can cause us to look indifferently downward instead of reverently upward and outward. We can become estranged from the Creator, who then seems like a far, distant star: "For how knoweth a man the master whom he has not served, and who is a stranger unto him, and is far from the thoughts and intents of his heart?" (Mosiah 5:13).

We know the Creator of the universe is also the Author of the plan of happiness. We can trust Him. He knows perfectly what brings happiness to His children (see Mosiah 2:41; Alma 41:10).

Meanwhile, as some experience daily life situations in which they are or feel unloved and unappreciated, they can nevertheless know that God loves them! His creations so witness.

Therefore, we can confess His hand in our individual lives just as we can confess His hand in the astonishing universe (see D&C 59:21). If we will so confess His hand now, one day we who are "cradled" amidst His creations can even know what it is like to be "clasped in the arms of Jesus" (Mormon 5:11).

The reverent rejoicing being now encouraged by these remarks was there a long, long time ago. As the Creator's plan was presented premortally, some even "shouted for joy" (Job 38:7). Why not? For "men are, that they might have joy" (2 Nephi 2:25). May you be blessed to convey to your students the contagion of your reverence and awe concerning the Lord's creations and His plans for us.

In conclusion, I testify that the astonishing work of God is greater than the known universe. Further, I testify that God's plans for His children predate His provision of this beautiful planet for us! In the holy name of Jesus Christ, amen.

Notes

1. Saint Anselm: *Basic Writings*, trans. Sidney Norton Deane, 2nd ed. (La Salle, IL: Open Court Publishing, 1962), 7.
2. Carl Sagan, *Pale Blue Dot: A Vision of the Human Future in Space* (New York: Ballantine Books, 1994), 50.
3. Morris L. West, *The Tower of Babel* (New York: William Morrow, 1968), 183.
4. Joseph Smith, *Teachings of the Prophet Joseph Smith*, comp. Joseph Fielding Smith (Salt Lake City: Deseret Book, 1976), 220.
5. J. Reuben Clark Jr., *Behold the Lamb of God* (Salt Lake City: Deseret Book, 1962), 17.
6. Stephen W. Hawking, *A Brief History of Time: From the Big Bang to Black Holes* (New York: Bantam Books, 1988), 126.
7. Freeman J. Dyson, "Energy in the Universe," *Scientific American* 224, no. 3 (September 1971): 59.
8. Ralph Waldo Emerson, "Nature," in *The Complete Works of Ralph Waldo Emerson*, centenary edition, 12 vols. (Boston: Houghton Mifflin, 1903), 1:7.

9. Stephen Strauss, "Universe May Have Regular Pattern of Galaxies, New Findings Suggest," *Deseret News*, March 4, 1990, 2S.
10. Stuart K. Hine, "How Great Thou Art," *Hymns* (Salt Lake City: The Church of Jesus Christ of Latter-day Saints, 1985), no. 86.
11. Alexander Pope, "Essay on Man," in *The Poems of Alexander Pope*, ed. John Butt (New Haven, CT: Yale University Press, 1963), 504–505.
12. Stephen Hawking, *Black Holes and Baby Universes and Other Essays* (New York: Bantam Books, 1993), 99.
13. Albert Einstein, in Ronald W. Clark, *Einstein: The Life and Times* (New York: World Publishing Company, 1971), 19.
14. Allen Sandage, "A Scientist Reflects on Religious Belief," *Truth Journal*, Internet edition, vol. 1 (1985), *leaderu.com/truth/1truth15.html.*
15. Wendell Berry, "Christianity and the Survival of Creation," in *Sex, Economy, Freedom, and Community: Eight Essays* (New York and San Francisco: Pantheon Books, 1993), 103.
16. Michael Benson, "A Space in Time," *Atlantic Monthly* 290, no. 1 (July–August 2002): 105.
17. David Koo, in Strauss, "Universe May Have Regular Pattern," 2S.
18. Chaisson and Steve McMillan, *Astronomy Today* (Englewood Cliffs, NJ: Prentice Hall, 1993), 559.
19. Corey S. Powell, "Up against the Wall," *Scientific American* 262, no. 2 (February 1990): 19.

The "How" of Scriptural Study

Joseph Fielding McConkie

Joseph Fielding McConkie *is a professor emeritus of ancient scripture at BYU.*

This address was given at Campus Education Week, August 2006.

If the heavens were to open today and God were to speak, would you not want to listen to what He had to say? In like manner, were a messenger to come in His stead, would your interest be any the less? If the message were written, would you not want to read it?

A great many faithful people gave their lives so that the word of the Lord as given to His people anciently would be preserved for us. Careful study of this record can only be a source of great blessing to us, while failure to become acquainted with it would be a great loss.

Let Correct Principles, Not Techniques, Direct Our Study

Over the years many of my students and others have come to my office inquiring as to how they might become better students of the scriptures. I have also frequently been asked how men like my father, Elder Bruce R. McConkie, and my grandfather President Joseph Fielding Smith, both of whom had the reputation of being gospel scholars, studied the scriptures. Implicit in such questions is the idea that there is some methodology or secret known to but a few, and that secret gives those who know it a marked advantage in scriptural understanding. Indeed, I will reveal the great and grand secret. It is that there is no secret.

As to my father and my grandfather, their method consisted in not having a method. Methods are not the answer! Effective scriptural study has nothing to do with the marking system you use. It has nothing to do with the choice of a blue marking pencil over a red one. It has nothing to do with whether you study a particular subject chronologically or topically. It has nothing to do with your using a quad instead of a triple combination. It has nothing to do with the size of the type unless you are getting older.

It has everything to do with the *intensity* and *consistency* with which you study. There are no shortcuts; there are no secrets.

There are, however, basic principles that are fundamental to a correct understanding of scripture. I will present seven such principles. Each brings with it additional light. Together they can increase your scriptural understanding sevenfold and more.

It Takes the Spirit of Revelation to Understand Revelation

The first and most basic principle of scriptural understanding is that revelation given by the Spirit can only be understood with the Spirit.

An acceptance of scripture as such requires a belief in the principle of revelation. It requires a belief that God can and does convey His mind and will to us. Most scripture is written only in the hearts and minds of people. This form of scripture is known as the Light of Christ. It is universal to the children of men and always has the purpose of preparing them to receive greater light. Scripture also embraces all that is spoken under the influence of the Holy Ghost. The Holy Ghost is a revelator. As the third member of the Godhead, His purpose is to teach and testify of the truths of salvation. Thus, the voice of the Holy Ghost is reserved for a higher order of truths than those dispensed through the Light of Christ.

While right to the Light of Christ is universal, revelation from the Holy Ghost requires faith in Christ and compliance with principles of righteousness. Nephi teaches the principle in this language:

> I, Nephi, having heard all the words of my father, concerning the things which he saw in a vision, and also the things which he spake by the power of the Holy Ghost, which power he received by faith on the Son of God—and the Son of God was the Messiah who should come—[Note that it was faith in Christ that granted Nephi the right to the companionship of the Holy Ghost.] I, Nephi, was desirous also that I might see,

> and hear, and know of these things, by the power of the Holy Ghost, which is the gift of God unto all those who diligently seek him, as well in times of old as in the time that he should manifest himself unto the children of men.
>
> For he is the same yesterday, to-day, and forever; and the way is prepared for all men from the foundation of the world, if it so be that they repent and come unto him.
>
> For he that diligently seeketh shall find; and the mysteries of God shall be unfolded unto them, by the power of the Holy Ghost, as well in these times as in times of old, and as well in times of old as in times to come; wherefore, the course of the Lord is one eternal round. (1 Nephi 10:17–19)

Among the countless revelations that have come from the God of heaven some few have found their way into writing. Among their number fewer still have found their way into a collection of such writings that have been preserved for us in book form. One such collection of inspired writings is known to us as the Holy Bible. The word *bible* comes from the Greek *biblia*, which means "the books." Thus, the Bible is a library of books believed to be sacred or holy.

It is important to note that Catholics, Protestants, and Jews disagree as to which books ought be included in this collection. The Latter-day Saint library of sacred books contains appreciably more scriptural records than is found in the libraries of other faiths. While others cannot agree among themselves as to which books ought be in the Library of Faith—or the Bible, as we call it—they regard our adding to that library as an act of heresy.

We, on the other hand, believe that if we have the same faith the ancients had, we will receive revelation that is immediate to our situation just as they did. The ancients were edified by the revelation given to people who had preceded them, but they were not limited to old revelation. As it was with them, so it is with us. Indeed, this principle is fundamental to our understanding and interpretation of all we read in the canon of scripture. By breaking communication with the heavens—that is, by saying that the library of revelation is closed—we lose not only the opportunity to receive additional revelation but also the key to understand all we possess. Nephi explained the principle in these words:

> Yea, wo be unto him that saith: We have received, and we need no more!
>
> And in fine, wo unto all those who tremble, and are angry because of the truth of God! For behold, he that is built upon the rock receiveth it with gladness; and he that is built upon a sandy foundation trembleth lest he shall fall.
>
> Wo be unto him that shall say: We have received the word of God, and we need no more of the word of God, for we have enough!
>
> For behold, thus saith the Lord God: I will give unto the children of men line upon line, precept upon precept, here a little and there a little; and blessed are those who hearken unto my precepts, and lend an ear unto my counsel, for they shall learn wisdom; for unto him that receiveth I will give more; and *from them that shall say, We have enough, from them shall be taken away even that which they have.* (2 Nephi 28:27–30; emphasis added)

Never in all the eternities has the Lord revealed that there would be no more revelation. To do so would rob us of the ability to understand the revelation He has already given us. He would hide the evidence of His existence and camouflage gospel truths.

The Bible is a very different book in the hands of someone who rejects the spirit of revelation and in the hands of someone who is open to that spirit. The words are the same, but the vision is entirely different. A book that came by revelation is only revelation to people who have the spirit of revelation.

The spirit you bring to the reading of a book predetermines what you are going to get out of it. The Gospel of Matthew read by one man may be scripture but, when read by another, may not be scripture. They may be in the same room together sharing the same book, and it may be scripture to one and not to the other. The difference is not in what has been written but in the spirit in which it is read. Holy writ read in the spirit of contention is not scripture; it is not the voice of the Lord, and it does not represent His Spirit. It is simply black ink on white paper. If the spirit in which something is read is not right, then the interpretation of what was written cannot be right either.

Let me share two classic scriptural texts that teach this principle. The first comes from a revelation given to teach us how to discern truth and error, good spirits from bad spirits, correct doctrine from false doctrine. As we begin our reading, the Lord, the master teacher, provokes thinking on this matter of discerning spirits with a question:

> Wherefore, I the Lord ask you this question—unto what were ye ordained? [Then in response to His own question, the Lord says,]
>
> To preach my gospel by the Spirit, even the Comforter which was sent forth to teach the truth.
>
> And then received ye spirits which ye could not understand, and received them to be of God; and in this are ye justified? . . .
>
> Verily I say unto you, he that is ordained of me and sent forth to preach the word of truth by the Comforter, in the Spirit of truth, doth he preach it by the Spirit of truth or some other way? [Note that the text assumes that what we are teaching is true—that is not the issue—the issue is the Spirit in which it is being taught.]
>
> And if it be by some other way it is not of God.
>
> And again, he that receiveth the word of truth, doth he receive it by the Spirit of truth or some other way?
>
> If it be some other way it is not of God.
>
> Therefore, why is it that ye cannot understand and know, that he that receiveth the word by the Spirit of truth receiveth it as it is preached by the Spirit of truth? (D&C 50:13–21)

Did you see it? The truths of heaven are not the truths of heaven if we attempt to justify them in any manner other than by the spirit of revelation. If we are to be "edified and rejoice together" we must both teach and learn by the spirit of revelation.

As a second illustration of this principle, consider the words of an earlier revelation, a revelation given to the Quorum of the Twelve six years before they were called. Speaking of the Book of Mormon, the Lord says, "These words are not of men nor of man, but of me; wherefore, you shall testify they are of me and not of man; for it is my voice which speaketh them unto you; for they are given by my Spirit unto you, and by my power you can read them one to another; and save it were by my power you could not have them; wherefore, you can testify that you have heard my voice, and know my words" (D&C 18:34–36).

The principle does not confine itself to the Quorum of the Twelve. No gospel principle does. We only have one gospel, and it must apply to all who are honest in heart in like manner. When you or I read or study scripture under the direction of the Lord's Spirit, we are hearing the voice of the Lord and can so testify. To read scripture without that Spirit is an entirely different matter.

Thus, the first principle of scriptural understanding is that scripture must be understood by the same spirit by which it was written. Without the spirit of revelation, there is no scripture. Some would say this is circular reasoning, and so it is. It takes life to give life. You cannot read in the dark. You cannot see and hear the things of the Spirit without the Spirit. As light cleaves to light, so darkness is the parent of the deeds of darkness.

There Is But One Gospel

Our second principle centers on the eternal nature of the gospel. All gospel principles are absolute; from eternity to eternity they are the same. They were the same in our pre-earth life as they are in this our second estate. They do not change in the world to which our spirits go at death, nor will their weight and measurement be any more or less in the Resurrection. There are no principles of salvation that were not decreed before the foundations of the earth. The Lord declared His house to be a house of order, not a house of confusion. In a revelation given to the Prophet Joseph Smith, the Lord dramatizes this principle by asking three rhetorical questions. First, "Will I accept of an offering . . . that is not made in my name?" Second, "Will I receive at your hands that which I have not appointed?" And third, "Will I appoint unto you, . . . except it be by law, even as I and my Father ordained unto you, before the world was?" (D&C 132:9–11).

The answer to each of these questions is a resounding no. Their purpose is to dramatize that there is but one gospel, one plan of salvation, one system of authority, and one organization in which legal and lawful administrators can be found. If God's house is a house of order, it will not be governed by laws of someone else's making, and it will not honor offerings made to other gods, nor will ordinances performed without its permission or authority be accepted.

Without proper legal authority, I cannot become your heir by reading your journal and learning of the promises your father made to you. In like manner, without the proper spirit of revelation you cannot be God's heir by reading the promises He made to people in an earlier day. Your salvation and mine require revelation that is immediate and personal.

It would be equally true that if people could legitimately claim the right to teach the gospel and act in the name of the Lord by reading the Bible, they could also become the president of the United States simply by reading our nation's Constitution.

"Seek Learning, Even by Study and Also by Faith"

I take our third principle from the curriculum given by the Lord to the school of the prophets: "Seek learning, even by study and also by faith" (D&C 88:118). The statement first affirms the importance of study and then suggests the necessity of reaching beyond our study to embrace the principle of faith.

Let me illustrate what is involved here. The Prophet Joseph Smith was studying the book of James when he came to a passage that directed him to ask of God and to do so in faith with nothing wavering (see James 1:5–6). When he set the book down and went in search of a quiet place to pray, his faith supplanted his study, and by that faith he was able to do what his biblical mentors had done: open the heavens.

My faith that the Book of Mormon has a proper place in the library of sacred books grants me a great host of knowledge that I would not otherwise enjoy. It restores to me the knowledge of the plain and precious things that were taken from the Bible. From it I learn that the peoples of the Old Testament had what is known to us as the Melchizedek Priesthood. They also had baptism, the gift of the Holy Ghost, and all other saving principles and ordinances of the gospel. From the Book of Mormon I can gain more knowledge and understanding of what was taught in Old and New Testament times than I can from reading all the scholarly commentaries ever written on the matter.

From the book of Abraham, I learn that the peoples of the Old Testament had the Abrahamic covenant with the promise of the continuation of seed and the eternal family unit. By faith in Joseph Smith's translation of the book of Moses, I learn that Jesus, the Messiah, was known to Adam, Enoch,

Noah, and Abraham and that the plan of salvation they knew is the same as the plan of salvation we know today.

This is not a retreat to the anti-intellectual stance common to much of the historical Christian world. It is the bold declaration that bringing faith to the act of study is like a loving couple bringing a child into the world. The child is a living thing who brings to his or her parents a depth of love and understanding that they never could have known before. Similarly, my faith in Jesus of Nazareth as the long-sought Messiah, Savior, and Redeemer of mankind gives me an entirely different understanding of the Old Testament than I could otherwise have.

All things produce after their own kind, and so it is that faith begets faith. Faith in one gospel principle will infuse faith in another. My faith in the Resurrection—that is, the inseparable union of body and spirit (an idea that is not scientifically defensible)—infuses faith in the story of the Creation (a matter over which there are endless scientific arguments).

It is only by adding faith to our scripture study that we capture the essence of what we read. True religion is a living thing. It demands that signs follow believers. It speaks of miracles so that we will know that we can work miracles. It describes the voice of God so that we will know His voice when we hear it. It reports the ministering of angels so that we will know that we may entertain the same; if we have planted the same seeds as did those of whom we read in holy writ, then we may harvest as they harvested.

Keep Things in Context

The fourth principle I would call to your attention is the need to keep things in their proper context. Context gives color to or changes the color of everything we or anyone else says. When my wife tells me that I ought to say "I love you" more often, she does mean that I should say it to other women. Every scriptural text has two contexts: the immediate moment or circumstance that evoked the statement and the larger context in relation to all other correct principles or utterances. An obscure or isolated statement will not be called on to bear the weight of the gospel or to assume the responsibility to establish any principle essential to salvation.

When Christ said, "In the resurrection they neither marry, nor are given in marriage" (Matthew 22:23–30), we need to know whether He was speaking of every soul that ever lived or of the Sadducees (who had rejected Him as their Messiah), who had asked the question that sparked Jesus's response.

When He said, "Take therefore no thought for the morrow" (Matthew 6:34), was He speaking to you and me, or was He speaking to the Twelve who had been called to the full-time ministry?

When He said, "Father, forgive them; for they know not what they do" (Luke 23:34), did He have in mind the Roman soldiers who drove the nails in His hands and feet, or did He mean everyone throughout all history who seeks to crucify Him afresh?

When Christ said, "Go ye into all the world, and preach the gospel" (Mark 16:15), was He giving a commission to everyone who feels so inclined, or was He speaking to the Twelve whom He had commissioned and trained?

When the Apostle Paul said, "If they cannot contain, let them marry: for it is better to marry than to burn" (1 Corinthians 7:9), was he suggesting that marriage is for people who are innately weak and lack moral character, or was he suggesting that those then laboring as missionaries ought to wait until they had completed their missions before they married?

When John warned that none were to add to or take from what he had written, was he forbidding others from tampering with the words of his epistle, or was he announcing that all other inspired writing had ceased? (see Revelation 22:18–19).

The immediate context answers each of the questions just raised, but if we are still confused, we must defer to the greater context of all that has been revealed on the matter in question.

As a young man, I served as a chaplain in the military. Whenever our unit received orders to go into combat, some of the soldiers discovered that they were conscientious objectors and could not take up arms. Their claims were always treated with respect, and among other things they were sent to see the chaplain to seek his aid in establishing their case, if indeed they had one. In such cases I would ask if there was any religious basis against their new military profession. The only answer to this question I can remember being given was that God commanded Moses, saying, "Thou shalt not kill" (Exodus 20:13).

Without describing all of the discussions I had with these young men, I note that without exception they were surprised to learn that the word translated *kill* in this text comes from a Hebrew word meaning *murder*. They were further surprised to learn that the penalty for murdering in the days of Moses was death. They were equally surprised to learn that Moses himself was a great general who repeatedly led the army of Israel to battle against their enemies whom they killed in rather staggering numbers.

The point here is that this is the greater context for the sixth commandment. It places it in an entirely different context than the young men I worked with had previously understood.

Balance Correct Principles

Our fifth principle concerns the balance necessary among gospel principles. Correct principles often conflict with each other—a difficulty we can trace all the way back to Eden. God deliberately placed Adam and Eve in a position in which they had to make a choice between conflicting commandments. They had been commanded to multiply and replenish the earth, something they could not do without partaking of the tree of the knowledge of good and evil, which they had been commanded not to do. Their situation required them to make a choice and then live with its consequences. Wisely and properly they chose to keep the greater of the two commandments, that being to have children, which, of course, required their partaking of the tree of the knowledge of good and evil. We refer to this event as Adam's *transgression*, not Adam's *sin*. Transgression involves the breaking of a law. Sin, on the other hand, is willful disobedience. In this matter there was no sin, but there was a broken law. The consequences of this broken law, known to us as the Fall, created the need for Christ and His Atonement.

What I desire to call your attention to in the context of our discussion is that on occasion—appreciably more often than we would like—correct principles conflict with each other. We, like Adam and Eve, are often faced with conflicting commandments. Like them, we too must make a choice as to which is the greater and which is lesser, and, like our first parents, we too must live with the consequences of those choices.

Consider these illustrations. On the one hand we want to be honest; on the other we do not want to be hurtful or insensitive. Both are virtues, but any virtue overdone becomes a vice. We are taught to be forgiving and merciful, and yet, as any good bishop knows, mercy cannot deny justice. Were it to do so, it would destroy personal responsibility, the doctrine of repentance, and ultimately the entire plan of salvation.

There is a letter of the law and a spirit, and a time and place for each to take center stage. So it is that there is a balance to maintain between gospel principles. The doctrine of grace, as marvelous as it is, cannot be allowed to become a bully and chase all other gospel principles out of the chapel. We cannot get so infatuated with one principle that it overshadows the others. The world is full of examples of this kind of gospel mutiny, wherein the ship of faith has been taken over by one principle, and the others are either enslaved or forced overboard.

What must be remembered here is that no principle remains a correct principle when used incorrectly. Any principle that is isolated from the body of principles becomes corrupted in its isolation. What frequently happens is that we are invited to give a lesson on a particular principle. So we isolate it from its companion principles for study. We then do such a good job of explaining its importance that when we are through, it has been inflated to the point that it no longer fits in with the other principles, so they have to be evicted to make room for it. The recipe of gospel principles does not permit the omission of one ingredient to be made up with a double dose of another. All principles, properly understood, must remain in their proper relationship with all other gospel principles.

Thus life is full of choices, and even the best of choices comes with consequences. Indeed, the best of choices generally comes at a high cost. We did not come to this earth to see how many difficulties we could avoid or how long we could rest in the shade, but rather to see if we would choose to stand in the light and labor energetically in the cause of truth.

Use Commentaries and Common Sense

The sixth principle of scriptural study is to freely seek help from sources that may exceed your knowledge on any particular matter. We have a number of excellent helps provided for us in the Church's latest edition of the scriptures. Chapter headings not only give a concise summary of chapter content but also often contain explanation and commentary. The footnotes can be helpful, but do not suppose that they themselves are scripture. In the Church's English edition of the Bible, the Topical Guide, Bible Dictionary, lengthy extracts from the Joseph Smith Translation, and the maps are also very helpful. Secular commentaries can be helpful in matters of history and geography. In doctrinal matters the help they give is very limited. As for Latter-day Saint commentaries, no one is going to be right about everything, but that does not mean they cannot help in some things.

It has frequently been said that the best commentary on scripture is scripture. Certainly this is the case, but it is not just a matter of using one verse to interpret another; it is seeing that the Old Testament is a marvelous commentary on the New Testament and that the New Testament is equally important in unlocking or understanding the Old Testament. Additionally it is not sufficient for us as Latter-day Saints to see the Book of Mormon as "Another Testament of Jesus Christ"; we must also recognize that it is a key with which we unlock the true meaning of the Old and New Testaments. It is the stick of Joseph spoken of by Ezekiel that was to become one with the stick of Judah for the purpose of gathering scattered Israel (see Ezekiel 37:19).

Thus Joseph of Egypt said: "Wherefore, the fruit of thy loins shall write [speaking to those of his own seed]; and the fruit of the loins of Judah shall write; and that which shall be written by the fruit of thy loins, and also that which shall be written by the fruit of the loins of Judah, shall grow together, unto the confounding of false doctrines and laying down of contentions, and establishing peace among the fruit of thy loins, and bringing them to the knowledge of their fathers in the latter days, and also to the knowledge of my covenants, saith the Lord" (2 Nephi 3:12; Joseph Smith Translation, Genesis 50:31).

The point is that the message of the two books is the same. Properly understood, they are teaching the same principles, testifying of the same God, and leading us to the same end. The Book of Mormon restores to our understanding many of the "plain and precious things" that were lost or taken from Bible manuscripts before they were printed in book form. No book of scripture is threatened by another book of scripture. Though they differ in detail, the Gospels sustain each other. So it is with what we call the standard works. They are not competitors; they are companions.

I have heard many disparaging remarks about commentaries. Remember that much of scripture, if not most, is commentary on other scripture. Anything written or said about the gospel is commentary on the gospel; even the statement that we should not use commentaries is a commentary.

It might also be noted that few things are more important in understanding scripture than common sense. No scriptural passage cannot be misunderstood, and perhaps no scriptural text has not been misused. Bad causes and bad politics are often sustained with scriptural quotations. It was with scriptural arguments that those of Jesus's day rejected Him. To those who sought His death, Christ said,

> Search the scriptures; for in them ye think ye have eternal life: and they [that is, the scriptures] are they which testify of me.
>
> And ye will not come to me, that ye might have life.
>
> I receive not honour from men.
>
> But I know you, that ye have not the love of God in you.
>
> I am come in my Father's name, and ye receive me not: if another shall come in his own name, him ye will receive.
>
> How can ye believe, which receive honour one of another, and seek not the honour that cometh from God only?
>
> Do not think that I will accuse you to the Father: there is one that accuseth you, even Moses, in whom ye trust.
>
> For had ye believed Moses, ye would have believed me: for he wrote of me.
>
> But if ye believe not his writings, how shall ye believe my words? (John 5:39–47)

As for scriptural mischief, the grand key is to declare the figurative literal and the literal figurative. In so doing, you can profess a love for scripture while turning its meaning upside down.

In the book of Moses we read that Adam was created from the "dust" of the earth (see Moses 3:7). Some would argue that the first man was made from clay. However, the same text states that you and I "were born into the world by water, and blood, and the spirit," which God had made "and so became of dust a living soul" (Moses 6:59). The same author who used "dust" to describe Adam's birth uses it to describe yours and mine also.

In this same context, we read that Eve was created from Adam's rib (see Moses 3:21–22). The text does not bother to tell us that this is figurative, that it is a metaphor to teach that the place of the woman is at the side of man. Scripture does not tell us this. We must deduce it. Our understanding comes from the "doctrine of common sense." Little girls are not made from sugar and spice, nor are they made from their husband's rib. Some things we are just left to figure out on our own.

When we studied algebra, we learned we could take the known and use it to solve for the unknown. We can do the same with gospel principles. If, for instance, we know that a people had the Melchizedek Priesthood, then we know they also had the gift of the Holy Ghost because it is the Melchizedek Priesthood that bestows this gift.

I have had students ask for evidence that the principle of eternal marriage was practiced in Old Testament times. Would it not stand to reason that if we got the authority to perform eternal marriage from Abraham or someone from his dispensation that the authority must have existed in that dispensation? In like manner, we would reason that if baptism is an ordinance of the Aaronic Priesthood, then a people having the Aaronic Priesthood would also have the ordinance of baptism.

Knowing that God is eternal and that the saving principles that come from Him are absolute repeatedly opens the scriptures to our understanding. It defies, for instance, the idea that there was one plan of salvation for people in Old Testament times and a different plan of salvation for people in New Testament times and still another for people living in the present era. It surely sets aside the idea that there was no Church of Christ before New Testament times.

"Liken Them unto Yourselves" (1 Nephi 19:24)

The seventh and final principle that I would suggest to enhance your scriptural study is that of applying, or likening, the scriptures unto yourselves (see 1 Nephi 19:23–24). In a number of Doctrine and Covenants revelations the Lord says, "What I say unto one I say unto all" (D&C 93:49). For instance, Doctrine and Covenants 25 records a revelation to Emma Smith in which He calls her "an elect lady" (v. 3). She is given the specific assignment to compile a hymnbook for the use of the young Church and then is given some general counsel. At the conclusion of this revelation, the Lord says, "And verily, verily, I say unto you, that this is my voice unto all" (D&C 25:16). Thus, every member of the Church has equal claim to this revelation. It is as much ours as it is Emma's.

Understanding this principle requires a little of the common sense of which we have spoken. The Lord did not intend that every member of the Church should compile a hymnbook but rather that we should all avoid the temptation to "murmur" about our lot, we should seek the Holy Ghost to aid in our learning, and we should lay aside the things of this world and seek for the things of a better one, as Emma was instructed to do. In so doing, we have the same promise that Emma did—we will receive a "crown of righteousness" with all the blessings that go with it.

In like manner, the Lord gave a revelation to Joseph Smith Sr. It is a revelation on service, and it is found in the fourth section of the Doctrine and Covenants. Missionaries quote it frequently when they meet together, but the revelation really belongs to all of us. It is ours because the principles in it apply to us in exactly the same manner they applied to Joseph Smith Sr.

So it is that we take the cloth of scripture and tailor it to fit our own circumstances. We do so with integrity, laying hold to eternal principles and leaving to the primary subject of each revelation the promises that were his or hers alone.

Conclusion

This brings us full circle. It welds our seven principles together. We began with the idea that scripture, meaning revelation, is only revelation when it is attended by the spirit of revelation.

Joseph Smith and Oliver Cowdery provide us with a remarkable illustration of this principle. After John the Baptist had restored the Aaronic Priesthood to them and after they had been baptized and the Holy Ghost had fallen upon them, Joseph Smith said, "Our minds being now enlightened, we began to have the scriptures laid open to our understanding, and the true meaning and intention of their more mysterious passages *revealed unto us in a manner which we never could attain to previously, nor ever before had thought of*" (Joseph Smith—History 1:74; emphasis added).

We add to that a second principle, the idea that gospel principles are everlastingly the same. All scripture comes from the same source, has the same purpose, and teaches the same doctrine. The gospel of Jesus Christ did not and does not evolve. It is not subject to change; it is absolute and eternal. The doctrine by which Adam and Eve found salvation is one and the same with the doctrine by which each of their children through all generations of time will find salvation. It will center on the same Savior, the same Atonement, obedience to the same laws and ordinances, and require the same priesthood.

As there is but one Savior, so there is but one gospel. When the resurrected Christ visited the people in the New World, He did as He had done in the Old World. He went to His temple, He called and ordained twelve men to be special witnesses of His name, and He taught the same gospel He had taught to those of His own nation. The gospel and its covenants and promises remain everlastingly the same. There was not one gospel for the pioneers and another for us, or one for apostles and prophets and another for the rest of the Church. We only have one gospel just as we only have one Savior. Each of us makes the same covenants, and each of us receives the same promise of blessings. In this context the promises in the revelations are ours, they were given to us, we can read our names into them.

Our third principle was that of seeking learning by both study and faith. It must be obvious that the only way we can truly learn faith is to exercise it. The idea that we are to seek learning by both study and faith suggests that faith does not require us to leave our minds at the door when we go to Sunday School class or when we seek to learn about the gospel. It does suggest, however, that it would be a puny gospel that did not reach beyond the bounds of our understanding and the knowledge we have accumulated. The same revelation that tells us to seek learning by faith also tells us that God, not nature, is the author of all laws. This revelation declares that all law, light, and life come from God and that He is above them all. He is their maker, not their copartner.

Our fourth principle noted that everything has it proper context. All gospel principles have an immediate context and a more general context which is the fulness of the gospel. No gospel principle was intended to stand alone. Isolating any principle from the congregation of principles that constitute the gospel is perverting that principle. The gospel does not consist of grace alone, love alone, faith alone, or any principle alone. Gospel principles sustain each other.

Thus we noted as our fifth principle the balance necessary among gospel principles. Ignorance cannot nurture faith, nor can the intellect substitute for it. The Bible remains a sealed book to those who worship at the shrine of their own intellect. Its meaning and purpose are also lost upon those who reduce its message to a few phrases that they endlessly quote to justify the shallowness of their understanding and the quickness with which they embrace that which has no place in the household of faith.

Our sixth principle encouraged seeking the wisdom and help of any and all sources that lead us to a greater understanding. No source would exceed the voice of a living prophet; indeed, the united voice of all past prophets tells us to listen to the living prophet.

We observe in our seventh and final principle that we seek the same destination as did the faithful of ages past, and thus the path they marked in their writings is of great value to us. To be of help to us, we must align the map they have given us with the same principles known to them and read it by the light of the same Spirit known to them.

Anytime anyone interprets a passage of scripture, we get a measure of their common sense and their spiritual integrity. What you do with scripture, including the neglect thereof, is a wonderful way for the Lord to get a measure of your soul. That each of us might give Him a good measure is my prayer.

When we teach diligently using the tools the Lord has provided, His grace will attend us.

What Is Our Doctrine?

Robert L. Millet

Robert L. Millet *is a professor of Church history and doctrine and former dean of Religious Education at BYU.*

We have been charged to "teach one another the doctrine of the kingdom. Teach ye diligently," the Lord implores, "and my grace shall attend you, that you may be instructed more perfectly in theory, in principle, in doctrine, in the law of the gospel, in all things that pertain unto the kingdom of God, that are expedient for you to understand" (D&C 88:77–78). But what exactly are we to teach? What is doctrine?

Before beginning this discussion, let me affirm that I understand implicitly that the authority to declare, interpret, and clarify doctrine rests with living apostles and prophets. This article will thus speak only *about* doctrine and in no way attempt to reach beyond my own stewardship.

Doctrine: Its Purpose, Power, and Purity

Doctrine is "the basic body of Christian teaching or understanding (2 Timothy 3:16). Christian doctrine is composed of teachings which are to be handed on through instruction and proclamation. . . . Religious doctrine deals with the ultimate and most comprehensive questions."[1]

Further, "gospel doctrine is synonymous with the truths of salvation. It comprises the tenets, teachings, and true theories found in the scriptures; it includes the principles, precepts, and revealed philosophies of pure religion; prophetic dogmas, maxims, and views are embraced within its folds; the

Articles of Faith are part and portion of it, as is every inspired utterance of the Lord's agents."[2]

The central, saving doctrine is that Jesus is the Christ, the Son of God, the Savior and Redeemer of humankind; that He lived, taught, healed, suffered, and died for our sins; and that He rose from the dead the third day with a glorious, immortal, resurrected body (see 1 Corinthians 15:1–3; D&C 76:40–42). It was the Prophet Joseph Smith who spoke of these central truths as the "fundamental principles" of our religion to which all other doctrines are but appendages.[3]

President Boyd K. Packer observed: "Truth, glorious truth, proclaims there is . . . a Mediator. . . . Through Him mercy can be fully extended to each of us without offending the eternal law of justice. This truth is the very root of Christian doctrine. You may know much about the gospel as it branches out from there, but if you only know the branches and those branches do not touch that root, if they have been cut free from that truth, there will be no life nor substance nor redemption in them."[4]

Such counsel really does point us toward that which is of most worth in sermons and in the classroom, that which should receive our greatest emphasis. There is power in doctrine, power in the word (see Alma 31:5), power to heal the wounded soul (see Jacob 2:8), power to transform human behavior. "True doctrine, understood, changes attitudes and behavior," President Packer taught. "The study of the doctrines of the gospel will improve behavior quicker than a study of behavior will improve behavior. That is why we stress so forcefully the study of the doctrines of the gospel."[5]

Elder Neal A. Maxwell also pointed out that "doctrines believed and practiced do change and improve us, while ensuring our vital access to the Spirit. Both outcomes are crucial."[6]

Those of us who are teachers associated with the Church of Jesus Christ are under obligation to learn the doctrines, teach them properly, and bind ourselves to speak and act in harmony with them. Only in this way can we perpetuate truth in a world filled with error, avoid deception, focus on what matters most, and find joy and happiness in the process. "I have spoken before," President Gordon B. Hinckley stated, "about the importance of keeping the doctrine of the Church pure, and seeing that it is taught in all of our meetings. I worry about this. Small aberrations in doctrinal teaching can lead to large and evil falsehoods."[7]

How Do We "Keep the Doctrine Pure"? What Might We Do?

1. *We can teach directly from the scriptures, the standard works.* The scriptures contain the mind and will and voice and word of the Lord (see D&C 68:3–4) to men and women in earlier days and thus contain doctrine and applications that are both timely and timeless. "And all scripture given by inspiration of God, is profitable for doctrine, for reproof, for correction, for instruction in righteousness: that the man [or woman] of God may be perfect, thoroughly furnished unto all good works" (Joseph Smith Translation, 2 Timothy 3:16–17).

2. *We can present the doctrine the same way the prophets in our own day present it (see D&C 52:9, 36)—in terms of both content and emphasis.* Mormon wrote: "And it came to pass that Alma, having authority from God, ordained priests; . . . and he commanded them that *they should teach nothing save it were the things which he had taught* " (Mosiah 18:18–19; emphasis added). "Therefore they did assemble themselves together in different bodies, being called churches; every church having their priests and their teachers, and *every priest preaching the word according as it was delivered to him by the mouth of Alma.* And thus, notwithstanding there being many churches they were all one church, yea, even the church of God" (Mosiah 25:21–22; emphasis added).

3. *We can pay special attention to the scriptural commentary offered by living apostles and prophets in general conference addresses, cross-reference the same in our scriptures, and teach this commentary in conjunction with the scriptures.* For example, we can study what

- Elder Jeffrey R. Holland taught concerning the parable of the prodigal son in the April 2002 general conference;
- Elder Robert D. Hales taught concerning the covenant of baptism in October 2000;
- Elder Joseph B. Wirthlin taught concerning the principles of fasting as found in Isaiah 58 in April 2001;
- Elder Dallin H. Oaks taught concerning conversion and "becoming" as well as his thoughtful commentary on the parable of the workers in the vineyard in October 2000;
- Elder M. Russell Ballard taught concerning "Who is my neighbor?" and what may be called the doctrine of inclusion in October 2001.

4. *We can teach the gospel with plainness and simplicity, focus on fundamentals, and emphasize what matters most.* We do not tell all we know, nor do we teach on the edge of our knowledge. The Prophet Joseph Smith explained that "it is not always wise to relate all the truth. Even Jesus, the Son of God, had to refrain from doing so, and had to restrain His feelings many times for the safety of Himself and His followers, and had to conceal the righteous purposes of His heart in relation to many things pertaining to His Father's kingdom."[8]

5. *We can acknowledge that there are some things we simply do not know.* President Joseph F. Smith declared: "It is no discredit to our intelligence or to our integrity to say frankly in the face of a hundred speculative questions, 'I do not know.' One thing is certain, and that is, God has revealed enough to our understanding for our exaltation and for our happiness. Let the Saints, then, utilize what they already have; be simple and unaffected in their religion, both in thought and word, and they will not easily lose their bearings and be subjected to the vain philosophies of man."[9]

Doctrinal Parameters

In recent years, I have tried to look beneath the surface and discern the nature of the objections that so many in the religious world have toward the Latter-day Saints. To be sure, the growth of the Church poses a real threat to many—more specifically, the Christian groups resent the way we "steal their sheep." We are not in the line of historic Christianity and thus are neither Catholic nor Protestant. We believe in scripture beyond the Bible and in continuing revelation through apostles and prophets. We do not accept the concepts concerning God, Christ, and the Godhead that grew out of the post–New Testament church councils. All these things constitute reasons why many Protestants and Catholics label us as non-Christian. We have tried, with some success I think, to speak of ourselves as "Christian but different." But there is another reason we are suspect, one that underlies and buttresses large amounts of anti-Mormon propaganda—namely, what they perceive to be some of our "unusual doctrines," much of which was presented by a few Church leaders of the past.

Let me illustrate with an experience I had just a few months ago. A Baptist minister was in my office one day. We were chatting about a number of things, including doctrine. He said to me, "Bob, you people believe in such strange things!" "Like what?" I asked. "Oh, for example," he said, "you believe in blood atonement. And that affects Utah's insistence on retaining death by a firing squad." I responded, "No, we don't." "Yes, you do," he came right back. "I know of several statements by Brigham Young, Heber C. Kimball, and Jedediah Grant that teach such things." "I'm aware of those statements," I said. I then found myself saying something that I had never voiced before: "Yes, they were taught, but *they do not represent the doctrine of our Church.* We believe in the blood atonement of Jesus Christ, and that alone." My friend didn't skip a beat: "What do you mean they don't represent the doctrine of your Church? They were spoken by major Church leaders."

I explained that such statements were made, for the most part, during the time of the Mormon Reformation and that they were examples of a kind of "revival rhetoric" in which the leaders of the Church were striving to "raise the bar" in terms of obedience and faithfulness. I assured him that the Church, by its own canonical standards, does not have the right or the power to take a person's life because of disobedience or even apostasy (see D&C 134:10). I read to him a passage from the Book of Mormon in which the Nephite prophets had resorted to "exceeding harshness, . . . continually reminding [the people] of death, and the duration of eternity, and the judgments and the power of God, . . . and exceedingly great plainness of speech" in order to "keep them from going down speedily to destruction" (Enos 1:23).

This seemed to satisfy him to some extent, but then he said: "Bob, many of my fellow Christians have noted how hard it is to figure out what Mormons believe. They say it's like trying to nail Jell-O to the wall! What *do* you people believe? How do you decide what *is* your doctrine and what is not?" I sensed that we were in the midst of a very important conversation, one that was pushing me to the limits and requiring that I do some of the deepest thinking I had done for a long time. His questions were valid and in no way mean-spirited. They were not intended to entrap or embarrass me or the Church. He simply was seeking information. I said, "You've asked some excellent questions. Let me see what I can do to answer them." I suggested that he consider the following three ideas:

1. The teachings of the Church today have a rather narrow focus, range, and direction; central and saving doctrine is what we are called upon to teach and emphasize, not tangential and peripheral teachings.

2. Very often what is drawn from Church leaders of the past is, like the matter of blood atonement mentioned above, either misquoted, misrepresented, or taken out of context. Further, not everything that was ever spoken or written by a past Church leader is a part of what we teach today. Ours is a living constitution, a living tree of life, a dynamic Church (see D&C 1:30). We are commanded to pay heed to the words of living oracles (see D&C 90:3–5).
3. In determining whether something is a part of the doctrine of the Church, we might ask, Is it found within the four standard works? Within official declarations or proclamations? Is it discussed in general conference or other official gatherings by general Church leaders today? Is it found in the general handbooks or approved curriculum of the Church today? If it meets at least one of these criteria, we can feel secure and appropriate about teaching it.

A significant percentage of anti-Mormonism focuses on Church leaders' statements of the past that deal with peripheral or noncentral issues. No one criticizes us for a belief in God, in the divinity of Jesus Christ or His atoning work, in the literal bodily resurrection of the Savior and the eventual resurrection of mankind, in baptism by immersion, in the gift of the Holy Ghost, in the sacrament of the Lord's Supper, and so forth. But we are challenged regularly for statements in our literature on such matters as the following:

- God's life before He was God
- How Jesus was conceived
- The specific fate of sons of perdition
- Teachings about Adam as God
- Details concerning what it means to become like God hereafter
- That plural marriage is essential to one's exaltation
- Why blacks were denied the priesthood prior to 1978

Loyalty to Men Called as Prophets

While we love the scriptures and thank God regularly for them, we believe that anyone can have sufficient confidence and even reverence for holy writ without believing that every word between Genesis 1:1 and Revelation 22:21 is the word-for-word dictation of the Almighty or that the Bible now reads as it has always read. Indeed, the Book of Mormon and other scriptures attest that plain and precious truths and many covenants of the Lord were taken away or kept back from the Bible before it was compiled (see 1 Nephi 13:20–29; Moses 1:40–41; Articles of Faith 1:8).[10]

But we still cherish the sacred volume, recognize and teach the doctrines of salvation within it, and seek to pattern our lives according to its timeless teachings.

In like manner, we can sustain with all our hearts the prophets and apostles without believing that they are perfect or that everything they say or do is exactly what God wants said and done. In short, we do not believe in apostolic or prophetic infallibility. Moses made mistakes, but we love and sustain him and accept his writings nonetheless. Peter made mistakes, but we still honor him and study his words. Paul made mistakes, but we admire his boldness and dedication and treasure his epistles. James pointed out that Elijah "was a man subject to like passions as we are" (James 5:17), and the Prophet Joseph Smith taught that "a prophet [is] a prophet only when he [is] acting as such."[11]

On another occasion, the Prophet declared, "I told them I was but a man, and they must not expect me to be perfect; if they expected perfection from me, I should expect it from them; but if they would bear with my infirmities and the infirmities of the brethren, I would likewise bear with their infirmities."[12]

"I can fellowship the President of the Church," said Lorenzo Snow, "if he does not know everything I know. . . . I saw the . . . imperfections in [Joseph Smith]. . . . I thanked God that He would put upon a man who had those imperfections the power and authority He placed upon him . . . for I knew that I myself had weakness, and I thought there was a chance for me."[13]

As we have been reminded again and again, whom God calls, God qualifies. That is, God calls His prophets. He empowers and strengthens the individual, provides an eternal perspective, loosens his tongue, and enables him to make divine truth known. But being called as an Apostle or even as President of the Church does not remove the man from mortality or make him perfect. President David O. McKay explained that "when God makes the prophet He does not unmake the man."[14]

"I was this morning introduced to a man from the east," Joseph Smith stated. "After hearing my name, he remarked that I was nothing but a man, indicating by this expression, that he had supposed that a person to whom the Lord should see fit to reveal His will, must be something more than a man. He seemed to have forgotten the saying that fell from the lips of St. James, that [Elijah] was a man subject to like passions as we are, yet he had such power with God, that he, in answer to his prayers, shut the heavens that they gave no rain for the space of three years and six months."[15]

"With all their inspiration and greatness," Elder Bruce R. McConkie declared, "prophets are yet mortal men with imperfections common to mankind in general. They have their opinions and prejudices and are left to work out their problems without inspiration in many instances."[16]

"Thus the opinions and views, even of a prophet, may contain error, unless those opinions and views were inspired by the Spirit."[17]

"There have been times," President Harold B. Lee pointed out, "when even the President of the Church has not been moved upon by the Holy Ghost. There is, I suppose you'd say, a classic story of Brigham Young in the time when Johnston's army was on the move. The Saints were all inflamed, and President Young had his feelings whetted to fighting pitch. He stood up in the morning session of general conference and preached a sermon vibrant with defiance at the approaching army, declaring an intention to oppose them and drive them back. In the afternoon, he rose and said that Brigham Young had been talking in the morning but the Lord was going to talk now. He then delivered an address in which the tempo was the exact opposite of the morning sermon. Whether that happened or not, it illustrates a principle: that the Lord can move upon His people but they may speak on occasions their own opinions."[18]

In 1865 the First Presidency counseled the Latter-day Saints as follows:

> We do not wish incorrect and unsound doctrines to be handed down to posterity under the sanction of great names to be received and valued by future generations as authentic and reliable, creating labor and difficulties for our successors to perform and contend with, which we ought not to transmit to them. The interests of posterity are, to a certain extent, in our hands. Errors in history and in doctrine, if left uncorrected by us who are conversant with the events, and who are in a position to judge of the truth or falsity of the doctrines, would go to our children as though we had sanctioned and endorsed them. . . . We know what sanctity there is always attached to the writings of men who have passed away, especially

> to the writings of Apostles, when none of their contemporaries are left, and we, therefore, feel the necessity of being watchful upon these points.[19]

President Gordon B. Hinckley stated: "I have worked with seven Presidents of this Church. I have recognized that all have been human. But I have never been concerned over this. They may have had some weaknesses. But this has never troubled me. I know that the God of heaven has used mortal men throughout history to accomplish His divine purposes."[20]

On another occasion, President Hinckley pleaded with the Saints that "as we continue our search for truth . . . we look for strength and goodness rather than weakness and foibles in those who did so great a work in their time. We recognize that our forebears were human. They doubtless made mistakes. . . . There was only one perfect man who ever walked the earth. The Lord has used imperfect people in the process of building his perfect society. If some of them occasionally stumbled, or if their characters may have been slightly flawed in one way or another, the wonder is the greater that they accomplished so much."[21]

Prophets are men called of God to serve as covenant spokesmen for His children on earth, and thus we should never take lightly what they say. The early Brethren of this dispensation were the living prophets for their contemporaries, and much of what we believe and practice today rests upon the doctrinal foundation they laid. But the work of the Restoration entails a gradual unfolding of divine truth in a line-upon-line fashion. Some years ago, my colleague Joseph McConkie remarked to a group of religious educators:

> We have the scholarship of the early brethren to build upon; we have the advantage of additional history; we have inched our way up the mountain of our destiny and now stand in a position to see some things with greater clarity than did they. . . . We live in finer houses than did our pioneer forefathers, but this does not argue that we are better or that our rewards will be greater. In like manner our understanding of gospel principles should be better housed, and we should constantly be seeking to make it so. There is no honor in our reading by oil lamps when we have been granted better light.[22]

Thus, it is important to note that ultimately the Lord will hold us responsible for the teachings, direction, and focus provided by the living oracles of our own day, both in terms of their commentary upon canonized scripture as well as the living scripture that is delivered through them by the power of the Holy Ghost (see D&C 68:3–4).

Facing Hard Issues

My experience suggests that anti-Mormonism will probably continue to increase in volume, at least until the Savior returns and shuts down the presses. Because we believe in the Apostasy and the need for a restoration of the fulness of the gospel, we will never be fully accepted by those who claim to have all the truth they need in the Bible. But I want to note two things about anti-Mormonism: First, anti-Mormon material definitely affects more than those who are not Latter-day Saints. Not only does it in some cases deter or frighten curious or interested investigators but it also troubles far more members of the Church than I had previously realized. I must receive ten phone calls, letters, or e-mails per week from members throughout the Church asking hard questions that have been raised by their neighbors or some literature they read. A short time ago a young man (married, with a family) phoned me in late afternoon, excused himself for the interruption, and then proceeded to tell me that he was teetering on the edge of leaving the Church because of his doubts. He posed several questions, and I responded to each one and bore my testimony. After about a half-hour chat, he offered profound thanks and indicated that he felt he would be okay now. Such an experience is not uncommon. I guess what I am saying is that antagonistic materials are here to stay and are affecting adversely both Latter-day Saints and the attitudes of those of other faiths.

Second, very often the critics of the Church simply use our own "stuff" against us. They do not need to create new material; they simply dig up and repackage what some of our own Church leaders have said in the past that would not be considered a part of the doctrine of the Church today. Latter-day Saints are eager to sustain and uphold their leaders. Consequently, we are especially hesitant to suggest that something taught by President Brigham Young or Elders Orson Pratt or Orson Hyde might not be in harmony with the truth as God has made it known to us "line upon line, precept upon precept" (Isaiah 28:10; 2 Nephi 28:30).

Some time ago a colleague and I were in southern California speaking to a group of about five hundred people, both Latter-day Saints and Protestants. During the question-and-answer phase of the program, someone asked the inevitable: "Are you really Christian? Do you, as many claim, worship a different Jesus?" I explained that we worship the Christ of the New Testament, that we believe wholeheartedly in His virgin birth, His divine sonship, His miracles, His transforming teachings, His atoning sacrifice, and His bodily resurrection from the dead. I added that we also believe in the teachings of and about Christ found in the Book of Mormon and modern revelation. After the meeting, a Latter-day Saint woman came up to me and said, "You didn't tell the truth about what we believe!"

Startled, I asked, "What do you mean?"

She responded, "You said we believe in the virgin birth of Christ, and you know very well that we don't believe that."

"Yes, we do," I retorted.

She then said with a great deal of emotion, "I want to believe you, but people have told me for years that we believe that God the Father had sexual relations with Mary and thereby Jesus was conceived."

I looked her in the eyes and said, "I'm aware of that teaching, but that is not the doctrine of the Church; that is not what we teach in the Church today. Have you ever heard the Brethren teach it in conference? Is it in the standard works, the curricular materials, or the handbooks of the Church? Is it a part of an official declaration or proclamation?" I watched as a five-hundred-pound weight seemed to come off her shoulders, as tears came into her eyes, and she simply said, "Thank you, Brother Millet."

Not long ago, Pastor Greg Johnson and I met with an Evangelical Christian church in the Salt Lake area. The minister there asked us to come and make a presentation ("An Evangelical and a Latter-day Saint in Dialogue") that Greg and I have made several times before in different parts of the country. The whole purpose of our presentation is to model the kind of relationships people with differing religious views can have. This kind of presentation has proven, in my estimation, to be one of the most effective bridge-building exercises in which I have been involved.

On this particular night, the first question asked by someone in the audience was on DNA and the Book of Mormon. I made a brief comment and indicated that a more detailed (and informed) response would be forthcoming in a journal article from a BYU biologist. There were many hands in the air at this point. I called on a woman close to the front of the church. Her question was, "How do you deal with the Adam-God doctrine?"

I responded, "Thank you for that question. It gives me an opportunity to explain a principle early in our exchange that will lay the foundation for other things to be said." I took a few moments to address the questions, "What is our doctrine? What do we teach today?" I indicated that if some teaching or idea was not in the standard works, not among official declarations or proclamations, was not taught currently by living apostles or prophets in general conference or other official gatherings, or was not in the general handbooks or official curriculum of the Church, it is probably *not* a part of the doctrine or teachings of the Church.

I was surprised when my pastor friend then said to the group: "Are you listening to Bob? Do you hear what he is saying? This is important! It's time for us to stop criticizing Latter-day Saints on matters they don't even teach today." At this point in the meeting, two things happened: first, the number of hands went down, and second, the tone of the meeting changed quite dramatically. The questions were not baiting or challenging ones but rather were efforts to clarify. For example, the last question asked was by a middle-aged man: "I for one would like to thank you, from the bottom of my heart, for what you have done here tonight. This thrills my soul. I think this is what Jesus would do. I have lived in Utah for many years, and I have many LDS friends. We get along okay; we don't fight and quarrel over religious matters. But we really don't talk with one another about the things that matter most to us—that is, our faith. I don't plan to become a Latter-day Saint, and I'm certain my Mormon friends don't plan to become Evangelical, but I would like to find more effective ways to talk heart to heart. Could you two make a few suggestions on how we can deepen and sweeten our relationships with our LDS neighbors?"

At that point, I sensed that we had somehow gotten through to some of the audience. Richard Mouw, one of my Evangelical friends, has suggested the need for "convicted civility," the challenge to be true to our own faith and not compromise one whit of our doctrine and way of life, and at the same time strive to better understand and respect our neighbors who are of another religious persuasion.[23]

These experiences highlight for me the challenge we face. I have no hesitation telling an individual or a group "I don't know" when I am asked why men are ordained to the priesthood and women are not; why blacks were denied the blessings of the priesthood for almost a century and a half; and several other matters that have neither been revealed nor clarified by those holding the proper keys. The difficulty comes when someone in the past has spoken on these matters, has put forward ideas that are out of harmony with what we know and teach today, and when those teachings are still available, either in print or among the everyday conversations of the members, and have never been corrected or clarified. The underlying questions are simply, "What is our doctrine? What are the teachings of the Church today?" If we could somehow help the Saints (and the larger religious world) know the answers to those questions, it would no doubt enhance our missionary effort, our convert retention, our activation, and the image and overall strength of the Church. If presented properly, it need not weaken faith or create doubts. It could do much to focus the Saints more and more on the central, saving verities of the gospel.

Further Illustrations

We discussed earlier that one of the ways to keep our doctrine pure is to present the gospel message the way the prophets and apostles today present it. Similarly, our explanations of certain "hard doctrines" or deeper doctrines should not go beyond what the prophets believe and teach today. Let us take two illustrations. The first is an extremely sensitive matter, one that currently affects and will continue to affect the quantity and quality of convert baptisms in the Church. I speak of the matter of the blacks and the priesthood. I was raised in the Church, just as many readers were, and was well aware of the priesthood restriction. For as long as I can remember, the explanation for why our black brethren and sisters were denied the full blessings of the priesthood (including the temple) was some variation of the theme that they had been less valiant in the premortal life and thus had come to earth under a curse, an explanation that has been perpetuated as doctrine for most of our Church's history. I had committed to memory the article of our faith that states that men and women will be punished for their own sins and not for Adam's transgression (see Articles of Faith 1:2) and later read that "the sins of the parents cannot be answered upon the heads of the children" (Moses 6:54), but I had assumed that somehow these principles did not apply to the blacks.

In June of 1978 everything changed—not just the matter of who could or could not be ordained to the priesthood but also the nature of the explanation for *why* the restriction had been in place from the beginning. Elder Dallin H. Oaks, in a 1988 interview, was asked: "As much as any doctrine the Church has espoused, or controversy the Church has been embroiled in, this one [the priesthood restriction] seems to stand out. Church members seemed to have less to go on to get a grasp of the issue. Can you address why this was the case, and what can be learned from it?" In response, Elder Oaks stated that

> if you read the scriptures with this question in mind, "Why did the Lord command this or why did he command that," you find that in less than one in a hundred commands was any reason given. It's not the pattern of the Lord to give reasons. We can put reason to revelation. We can put reasons to commandments. When we do we're on our own. Some people put reasons to the one we're talking about here, and they turned out to be spectacularly wrong. There is a lesson in that. The lesson I've drawn from that [is that] I decided a long time ago that I had faith in the command and I had no faith in the reasons that had been suggested for it.

Then came a follow-up question: "Are you referring to reasons given even by General Authorities?" Elder Oaks answered: "Sure. I'm referring to reasons given by General Authorities and reasons elaborated upon that reason by others. The whole set of reasons seemed to me to be unnecessary risk taking. . . . Let's don't make the mistake that's been made in the past, here and in other areas, trying to put reasons to revelation. The reasons turn out to be man-made to a great extent. The revelations are what we sustain as the will of the Lord and that's where safety lies."[24]

In other words, we really do not know why the restriction on the priesthood existed. "I don't know" is the correct answer when we are asked "Why?" The priesthood was restricted "for reasons which we believe are known to God, but which he has not made fully known to man."[25]

I have come to realize that this is what Elder McConkie meant in his August 1978 address to the Church Educational System when he counseled us to:

> forget everything that I have said, or what President Brigham Young or President George Q. Cannon or whosoever has said in days past that is contrary to the present revelation. We spoke with a limited understanding and without the light and knowledge that now has come into the world.

> We get our truth and our light line upon line and precept upon precept. We have now had added a new flood of intelligence and light on this particular subject, and it erases all the darkness and all the views and all the thoughts of the past. They don't matter any more. . . . It is a new day and a new arrangement, and the Lord has now given the revelation that sheds light out into the world on this subject. As to any slivers of light or any particles of darkness of the past, we forget about them.[26]

It seems to me, therefore, that we as Latter-day Saints have two problems to solve in making the restored gospel available more extensively to people of color. First, we need to have our hearts and minds purified of all pride and prejudice. Second, we need to dismiss all previous explanations for the restriction and indicate that while we simply do not know why the restriction existed before, the fulness of the blessings of the restored gospel are now available to all who prepare themselves to receive them. Elder M. Russell Ballard observed that "we don't know all of the reasons why the Lord does what he does. We need to be content that someday we'll fully understand it."[27]

Now to the second illustration. When I open the discussion to questions before a group of persons not of our faith, I am always asked about our doctrine of God and the Godhead, particularly concerning the teachings of Joseph Smith and Lorenzo Snow. I generally do not have too much difficulty explaining our view of how through the Atonement man can eventually become like God, become more and more Christlike. For that matter, Orthodox Christianity, a huge segment of the Christian world, still holds to a view of human deification. The Bible itself teaches that men and women may become "partakers of the divine nature" (2 Peter 1:4), "joint-heirs with Christ" (Romans 8:17), gain "the mind of Christ" (1 Corinthians 2:16), and become perfect, even as our Father in heaven is perfect (see Matthew 5:48). The Apostle John declared, "Beloved, now are we the [children] of God, and it doth not yet appear what we shall be: but we know that, when he shall appear, we shall be like him; for we shall see him as he is" (1 John 3:2). Perhaps more important, this doctrine is taught powerfully in modern revelation (see D&C 76:58; 132:19–20).

The tougher issue for other Christians to deal with is the accompanying doctrine set forth in the King Follett sermon[28] and the Lorenzo Snow couplet[29]—namely, that God was once a man. Latter-day scriptures state unequivocally that God is a man, a Man of Holiness (see Moses 6:57) who possesses a body of flesh and bones (see D&C 130:22). These concepts are clearly a part of the doctrinal restoration. We teach that man is not of a lower order or different species than God. This, of course, makes many of our Christian friends extremely nervous (if not angry), for it appears to them that we are lowering God in the scheme of things and thus attempting to bridge the Creator/creature chasm.

I suppose all we can say in response is that we know what we know as a result of modern revelation and that from our perspective the distance between God and man is still tremendous, almost infinite. Our Father in Heaven is indeed omnipotent, omniscient, and, by the power of His Holy Spirit, omnipresent. He is a gloried, exalted, resurrected being, "the only supreme governor and independent being in whom all fullness and perfection dwell; . . . in him every good gift and every good principle dwell; . . . he is the Father of lights; in him the principle of faith dwells independently, and he is the object in whom the faith of all other rational and accountable beings center for life and salvation."[30]

Modern revelation attests that the Almighty sits enthroned "with glory, honor, power, majesty, might, dominion, truth, justice, judgment, mercy, and an infinity of fulness" (D&C 109:77).

And what do we know beyond the fact that God is an exalted man? What do we know of His mortal existence? What do we know of the time before He became God? Nothing. We really do not know more than what was stated by the Prophet Joseph Smith, and that is precious little. Insights concerning God's life before Godhood are not found in the standard works, in official declarations or proclamations, in current handbooks, or in curricular materials, nor are doctrinal expositions on the subject delivered in general conference today. This topic is not what we would call a central and saving doctrine, one that must be believed (or understood) to hold a temple recommend or be in good standing in the Church.

This latter illustration highlights an important point: a teaching may be true and yet not a part of what is taught and emphasized in the Church today. Whether it is true or not may, in fact, be irrelevant, if indeed the Brethren do not teach it today or it is not taught directly in the standard works or found in our approved curriculum. Let's take another question: Was Jesus married? The scriptures do not provide an answer. "We do not know anything about Jesus Christ being married," President Charles W. Penrose stated. "The Church has no authoritative declaration on the subject."[31]

So whether He was or was not is not part of the doctrine of the Church. It would be well for us to apply the following lesson from President Harold B. Lee: "With respect to doctrines and meanings of scriptures, let me give you a safe counsel. It is usually not well to use a single passage of scripture [or, I would add, a single sermon] in proof of a point of doctrine unless it is confirmed by modern revelation or by the Book of Mormon. . . . To single out a passage of scripture to prove a point, unless it is [so] confirmed . . . is always a hazardous thing."[32]

Conclusion

There is a very real sense in which we as Latter-day Saints are spoiled. We have been given so much, have had so much knowledge dispensed from on high relative to the nature of God, Christ, man, the plan of salvation, and the overall purpose of life here and the glory to be had hereafter, that we are prone to expect to have all the answers to all the questions of life. Elder Neal A. Maxwell pointed out that

> the exhilarations of discipleship exceed its burdens. Hence, while journeying through our Sinai, we are nourished in the Bountiful-like oases of the Restoration. Of these oases some of our first impressions may prove to be more childish than definitive. . . . In our appreciation, little wonder some of us mistake a particular tree for the whole of an oasis, or a particularly refreshing pool for the entirety of the Restoration's gushing and living waters. Hence, in our early exclamations there may even be some unintended exaggerations. We have seen and partaken of far too much; hence, we "cannot [speak] the smallest part which [we] feel" (Alma 26:16)[33]

We have much, to be sure, but there are indeed "many great and important things pertaining to the Kingdom of God" yet to come forth (Articles of Faith 1:9). The Lord stated to Joseph Smith in Nauvoo: "I deign to reveal unto my church things which have been kept hid from before the foundation of the world, things that pertain to the dispensation of the fulness of times" (D&C 124:41; compare 121:26; 128:18). As Elder Oaks observed, we have been given many of the commands but not all of the reasons why, many of the directives but not all of the explanations. I regularly state to my classes that it is as important for us to know *what we do not know* as it is for us to know what we know. Far too many things are taught or discussed or even argued about that fit into the realm of the unrevealed and thus the unresolved. Such matters, particularly if they do not fall within the range of revealed truth we teach today, do not edify or inspire. Often, very often, they lead to confusion and sow discord.

This does not in any way mean that we should not seek to study and grow and expand in our gospel understanding. Peter explained that there needs to be a reason for the hope within us (see 1 Peter 3:15). Our knowledge should be as settling to the mind as it is soothing to the heart. Elder Maxwell taught that some "Church members know just enough about the doctrines to converse superficially on them, but their scant knowledge about the deep doctrines is inadequate for deep discipleship (see 1 Corinthians 2:10). Thus uninformed about the deep doctrines, they make no deep change in their lives."[34]

President Hugh B. Brown once observed: "I am impressed with the testimony of a man who can stand and say he knows the gospel is true. What I would like to ask is 'But, sir, do you know the gospel?' . . . Mere testimony can be gained with but perfunctory knowledge of the Church and its teachings. . . . But to retain a testimony, to be of service in building the Lord's kingdom, requires a serious study of the gospel and knowing what it is."[35]

On another occasion, President Brown taught that we are required only to "defend those doctrines of the Church contained in the four standard works. . . . Anything beyond that by anyone is his or her own opinion and not scripture. . . . The only way I know of by which the teachings of any person or group may become binding upon the church is if the teachings have been reviewed by all the brethren, submitted to the highest councils of the church, and then approved by the whole body of the church."[36]

Again, the issue is one of focus, one of emphasis—where we choose to spend our time when we teach the gospel to both Latter-day Saints and to those of other faiths.

There is a valid reason why it is difficult to "tie down" Latter-day Saint doctrine, one that derives from the very nature of the Restoration. The fact that God continues to speak through His anointed servants; the fact that He, through those servants, continues to reveal, elucidate, and clarify what has already been given; and the fact that our canon of scripture is open, flexible, and expanding—all of these things militate against what many in the Christian world would call a systematic theology.

It is the declaration of sound and solid doctrine, the doctrine found in scripture and taught regularly by Church leaders, that builds faith and strengthens testimony and commitment to the Lord and His kingdom. Elder Maxwell explained that "deeds do matter as well as doctrines, but the doctrines can move us to do the deeds, and the Spirit can help us to understand the doctrines as well as prompt us to do the deeds."[37]

He also noted that "when weary legs falter and detours and roadside allurements entice, the fundamental doctrines will summon from deep within us fresh determination. Extraordinary truths can move us to extraordinary accomplishments."[38]

The teaching and the application of sound doctrine are great safeguards to us in these last days, shields against the fiery darts of the adversary. Understanding true doctrine and being true to that doctrine can keep us from ignorance, from error, and from sin. The Apostle Paul counseled Timothy: "If thou put the brethren [and sisters] in remembrance of these things, thou shalt be a good minister of Jesus Christ, nourished up in the words of faith and of good doctrine, whereunto thou hast attained. . . . till I come, give attendance to reading, to exhortation, to doctrine" (1 Timothy 4:6, 13).

Notes

1. *Holman Bible Dictionary*, ed. Trent C. Butler (Nashville: Holman Bible Publishers, 1991), 374.
2. Bruce R. McConkie, *Mormon Doctrine*, 2nd ed. (Salt Lake City: Bookcraft, 1966), 204.
3. Joseph Smith, *Teachings of the Prophet Joseph Smith*, comp. Joseph Fielding Smith (Salt Lake City: Deseret Book, 1976), 121.
4. Boyd K. Packer, in Conference Report, April 1977, 80; emphasis added.
5. Boyd K. Packer, in Conference Report, October 1986, 20.
6. Neal A. Maxwell, *One More Strain of Praise* (Salt Lake City: Bookcraft, 1999), x.
7. Gordon B. Hinckley, *Teachings of Gordon B. Hinckley* (Salt Lake City: Deseret Book, 1997), 620.
8. Smith, *Teachings*, 392.
9. Joseph F. Smith, *Gospel Doctrine* (Salt Lake City: Deseret Book, 1971), 9.
10. Compare Smith, *Teachings*, 9–10, 61, 327.
11. Smith, *Teachings*, 278.

12. Smith, *Teachings*, 268.
13. Cited by Neal A. Maxwell, in Conference Report, October 1984, 10.
14. David O. McKay, in Conference Report, April 1907, 11–12; see also October 1912, 121; April 1962, 7.
15. Smith, *Teachings*, 89.
16. McConkie, *Mormon Doctrine*, 608.
17. Bruce R. McConkie, "Are the General Authorities Human?" address delivered at the Institute of Religion Forum at the University of Utah, October 28, 1966.
18. Harold B. Lee, *The Teachings of Harold B. Lee*, ed. Clyde J. Williams (Salt Lake City: Bookcraft, 1996), 542.
19. Brigham Young, Heber C. Kimball, and Daniel H. Wells, in *Messages of the First Presidency*, comp. James R. Clark (Salt Lake City: Bookcraft, 1965–75), 2:232.
20. Gordon B. Hinckley, in Conference Report, April 1992, 77.
21. Gordon B. Hinckley, "The Continuous Pursuit of Truth," *Ensign*, April 1986, 5.
22. Joseph Fielding McConkie, "The Gathering of Israel and the Return of Christ," the Sixth Annual Church Educational System Religious Educators' Symposium, August 1982, Brigham Young University, typescript, 3, 5.
23. See Richard Mouw, *Uncommon Decency* (Downers Grove, IL: InterVarsity Press, 1992).
24. Dallin H. Oaks, *Provo Daily Herald*, 5 June 1988, 21.
25. David O. McKay, Hugh B. Brown, and N. Eldon Tanner, First Presidency Message, January 1970.
26. Bruce R. McConkie, "The New Revelation on Priesthood," in *Priesthood* (Salt Lake City: Deseret Book, 1981), 132.
27. M. Russell Ballard, remarks at Elijah Abel memorial service; reported in *Church News*, October 5, 2002, 12.
28. Smith, *Teachings*, 345–46.
29. Lorenzo Snow, *Teachings of Lorenzo Snow*, ed. Clyde J. Williams (Salt Lake City: Bookcraft, 1996), 1.
30. Joseph Smith, comp., *Lectures on Faith* (Salt Lake City: Deseret Book, 1985), 10.
31. Charles W. Penrose, "Editor's Table," *Improvement Era*, September 1912, 1042.
32. Lee, *Teachings*, 157.
33. Neal A. Maxwell, in Conference Report, April 1996, 94–95.
34. Neal A. Maxwell, *Men and Women of Christ* (Salt Lake City: Bookcraft, 1991), 2.
35. Hugh B. Brown to Robert J. Matthews, January 28, 1969; cited in Matthews, "Using the Scriptures," *1981 Brigham Young University Fireside and Devotional Speeches* (Provo, UT: Brigham Young University Press, 1981), 124.

36. Hugh B. Brown, *An Abundant Life: The Memoirs of Hugh B. Brown*, ed. Edwin B. Firmage (Salt Lake City: Signature Books, 1988), 124.
37. Neal A. Maxwell, *That My Family Should Partake* (Salt Lake City: Deseret Book, 1974), 87.
38. Neal A. Maxwell, *All These Things Shall Give Thee Experience* (Salt Lake City: Deseret Book, 1979), 4.

Abinadi offered a stirring defense of
Christ's ability to perform the Atonement.

The Role of Christ as the Father in the Atonement

Paul Y. Hoskisson

***Paul Y. Hoskisson** is a professor of ancient scripture at BYU.*

As a former student and I were discussing Mosiah 15:1–8, one of the more puzzling sections of Abinadi's speech before King Noah and his court of priests, it occurred to me that Abinadi was not giving a discourse on the Godhead, but rather the Atonement. Specifically, as part of his defense before Noah's court and at the same time as part of his responsibility to deliver his prophetic message to Noah's people, Abinadi was explaining the role that Christ would play and the reason that He could perform the Atonement. In the course of this discourse, Abinadi also explained why Christ would be called the "Father"[1] and the "Son" and what the relationship is between His fatherhood, His sonship, and the Atonement.

Abinadi's explanation of the Atonement was prompted when one of his interrogators, near the beginning of his trial, posed the question, "What meaneth the words which are written" by Isaiah when he said, among other things, "How beautiful upon the mountains are the feet of him that bringeth good tidings?" (12:20–21).[2] To answer the question, Abinadi reminded Noah and his priests that all the prophets had declared that "God himself should come down among the children of men, and take upon him the form of man, and go forth in mighty power upon the face of the earth" (13:34). Then, after quoting Isaiah 53, which explains through the Suffering Servant motif what will befall God during His sojourn on the earth, Abinadi bore his own personal witness that "God himself shall come down among the children of men, and shall redeem his people" (15:1).

What follows next, in verses 2–8, is a succinct and sublime exposition of why Christ, the God who will "come down among the children of men," was capable of atoning for "their iniquity and their transgressions, having redeemed them, and satisfied the demands of justice" (15:9). Because Abinadi uses expressions that can easily be misunderstood, it will be helpful to fill out the following table, based on 15:2–8.

Christ's dual titles:		
Christ's parentage:		
Christ's dual nature:		
Christ's dual capacity:		

This God, the Jehovah of the Old Testament, will be called the Father and the Son (15:2). He will be called the Son "because he dwelleth in flesh" (15:2) and because He "subjected [that] flesh to the will of the Father" (15:2). When Abinadi mentions the Father and the Son in verse 2, he is quick to forestall any misunderstanding that he is talking about different members of the Godhead by immediately stating that the personage of whom he is speaking, namely, the Messiah, is "the Father and the Son" (15:2). Thus, the first row of the table can be filled in as follows.

Christ's dual titles:	Father	Son
Christ's parentage:		
Christ's dual nature:		
Christ's dual capacity:		

Abinadi explained that the Savior is called "the Father, because he was conceived by the power of God" (15:3), that is, the title "Father" was given to Christ because He was begotten of God the Father.[3] He is called "the Son, because of the flesh" (15:3), that is, the title "Son" was given to him because He was conceived by Mary. And thus the Messiah, or the Savior, became "the Father and Son" (15:3). Luke phrased it only somewhat differently in his Gospel, "And the angel answered and said unto [Mary], The Holy Ghost shall come upon thee, and the power of the Highest shall overshadow thee: therefore also that holy thing which shall be born of thee shall be called the Son of God" (Luke 1:35).[4]

Abinadi wanted there to be no confusion that, when he used the titles "Father" and "Son," he was talking, almost exclusively, about only one member of the Godhead. And just to make sure there was no confusion, he again stated that the single person he was talking about and who carries the titles "Father" and "Son" was "one God, yea, the very Eternal Father of heaven and of earth" (15:4). Thus, the table can be expanded in the following manner:

Christ's dual titles:	Father	Son
Christ's parentage:	Begotten by God	Conceived by Mary
Christ's dual nature:		
Christ's dual capacity:		

The Messiah was called the Son of God because He "dwelleth in flesh" (15:2). This aspect of Christ's nature allowed him to be a part of mortality in every way that we are a part of it, suffering "temptation," though He did not yield "to the temptation" (15:5). He even "descended below all things" (D&C 88:6).[5] In order for Christ to accomplish the Atonement, He had to "subject the flesh to the will of the Father," that is, He had to overcome the mortal nature He inherited from Mary by submitting that mortal nature to the will of His divine nature which He inherited from God the Father. Using a tidy little couplet, Abinadi paralleled the "flesh" with the "Son" and the "spirit" with the "Father," namely, "The Father, because he was conceived by the power of God; and the Son, because of the flesh" (15:3). This allows the chart to be filled in as follows.

Christ's dual titles:	Father	Son
Christ's parentage:	Begotten by God	Conceived by Mary
Christ's dual nature:	Spirit	Flesh
Christ's dual capacity:		

Though Abinadi does not explicitly draw the following conclusion concerning Christ's dual abilities, the conclusion nevertheless can be extrapolated from his short treatise. Because Christ was begotten by God and conceived by Mary, He also inherited the abilities He would need to perform the Atonement. Through His mother, Mary, He inherited all the abilities of mortality, including the possibility of dying. Through His Father, Elohim, He inherited many traits of divinity, including the possibility of not dying. The first ability is one that He shares with all mankind (see especially Alma 7:10–13);[7] the second ability is unique to Himself. Thus, His ability to die and His ability not to be subject to death make Him unique among all those born on the earth.[8] Truly, He is the only person born into this life who could choose whether or not He would die. As Christ Himself expressed it, "No man taketh [my life] from me, but I lay it down of myself. I have power to lay it down, and I have power to take it again" (John 10:18).[9] Thus, the chart may be completed:[10]

Christ's dual titles:	Father	Son
Christ's parentage:	Begotten by God	Conceived by Mary
Christ's dual nature:	Spirit	Flesh
Christ's dual capacity:	He did not have to die.	He could die.

This God, who is called the Father and Son, "shall come down among the children of men" (15:1) and dwell on the earth. He will suffer "temptation" but will not yield "to the temptation" (15:5). He will allow Himself, as the Suffering Servant passage prophesied, "to be mocked, and scourged, and cast out, and disowned by his people. And after all this, after working many mighty miracles among the children of men, he shall be led, yea, even as Isaiah said, as a sheep before the shearer is dumb, so he opened not his mouth. Yea, even so he shall be led, crucified, and slain" (15:5–7).

In this final act of self-sacrifice, in allowing Himself to "be led, crucified, and slain," when at any moment He could have walked away from it, He made the ultimate submission. He subjected the "flesh" (which He inherited from Mary) "even unto death." In so doing, "the will of the Son" (the mortal desire to live) became "swallowed up in the will of the Father" (in the will of the Savior's divine spirit, which He inherited from His Father) (15:7). Thus He completed the temporal requirements of the Atonement, that is, as the final act of the earthly Atonement, Christ, who did not have to die, freely and voluntarily offered up His life on the cross[11] so that we might also, after our inevitable temporal death, be raised to everlasting life with Him. "The death of Christ," as Amulek concisely put it, "shall loose the bands of this temporal death, that all shall be raised from this temporal death" (Alma 11:42).

In summary, Abinadi's unique and beautiful explanation of the Atonement may be outlined as follows:

1. God Himself will come down and live on the earth. He will be tempted but will yield to no temptation, and in the process He will be mocked, oppressed, scourged, and eventually crucified.
2. Christ inherited from His mother, Mary, the same mortal nature that all the children of Adam possess, including the ability to die.
3. Christ inherited from His Father, Elohim, a divine nature that no other children of Adam possess, including the capability of not dying.
4. On the cross Christ freely chose to submit His mortal self to His immortal self, that is, of His own free will He subjected Himself to death and accomplished the Atonement. Just as Adam made death possible for all of Heavenly Father's children by freely submitting to the conditions that brought about mortal life, so Christ, by freely submitting to mortal death, brought about the conditions that made everlasting life possible to all of God's children.

Certainly, many of the prophets knew the doctrine that Abinadi taught.[12] But no other scripture combines these elements together the way Abinadi did. There can be no doubt that Abinadi knew the Savior, that he knew about the Savior, and that he understood the unique role and nature of the Savior many years before Christ would condescend to be born among the children of Adam.

I cannot leave the subject of Abinadi without making one more observation. It seems to me that Abinadi must have been aware of some partial but commanding parallels between himself and the Savior, as there is with nearly all of God's prophets. Like Christ, Abinadi experienced much of the same rejection and persecution expressed in the Suffering Servant motif of Isaiah 53 (see also Mosiah 14). For example, nowhere in Abinadi's speech does he mention the fact that Christ succeeded in converting anyone during His time on the earth. In fact, several of the statements from Isaiah quoted in

Mosiah 14 could be interpreted to mean that Christ would have little or no success in converting people during His mortal ministry. For example, "He is despised and rejected of men; . . . we hid as it were our faces from him; he was despised, and we esteemed him not" (v. 3); "we did esteem him stricken, smitten of God" (v. 4); and "all we, like sheep, have gone astray; we have turned every one to his own way" (v. 6). Abinadi must have wondered if he also would be killed without achieving even modest success. Indeed, as far as his finite knowledge was concerned, he could easily have thought that he had not succeeded in converting a single person.

Like the Savior, Abinadi was executed by people unworthy to sit in judgment on him. And yet it seems likely that he was aware that he would be executed when he returned the second time to preach to Noah and his people. During the course of his trial, Abinadi said, "I will not recall the words which I have spoken unto you concerning this people, for they are true; and that ye may know of their surety I have suffered myself that I have fallen into your hands. Yea, and I will suffer even until death, and I will not recall my words, and they shall stand as a testimony against you. And if ye slay me ye will shed innocent blood" (17:9–10). It would appear that Abinadi, in a manner not unlike his Savior, also freely chose to expose himself to temporal death, thereby sealing "the truth of his words" (17:20). Abinadi was, as almost all prophets have been, a type and shadow of the path the Savior would tread.

This powerful testimony of Abinadi, given as it was to an apostate and wicked people, contains information about the Savior expressed in a way like no other passage in scripture. Truly, how beautiful upon the mountains were the feet of Abinadi.

Notes

1. Traditionally, as Elder Bruce R. McConkie has stated, there are three reasons that Christ the Son also bears the title Father: (1) He is the "Creator . . . of the heavens and of the earth," (2) "He is the Father of all those who are born again," and (3) He is the Father because of "divine investiture" (*Mormon Doctrine*, 2nd ed. [Salt Lake City: Bookcraft, 1966], 130). See also the important and more thorough statement dated June 30, 1916, by the First Presidency and Council of the Twelve Apostles recorded in James R. Clark, ed., *Messages of the First Presidency* (Salt Lake City: Bookcraft, 1971), 5:25–34. Sometimes I have heard a fourth reason (similar to Elder McConkie's second reason), that Christ is the Father because He is the Father of the Atonement, just as George Washington

is the father of the United States. The reason Abinadi applied the title Father to Christ in this passage is different than these four, making this a fifth reason. This paper will make the fifth reason clear.

2. This and all subsequent scriptural references refer to Mosiah in the Book of Mormon unless specifically noted otherwise.
3. For other references to Christ as the Only Begotten Son of God, see Jacob 4:5 and 11; John 1:14 and 18.
4. See also D&C 93:4, where Christ states that He is "the Father because he gave me of his fulness, and the Son because I was in the world and made flesh my tabernacle, and dwelt among the sons of men."
5. See also Joseph Smith, comp., *Lectures on Faith* (Salt Lake City: Deseret Book, 1985), 59. Christ "is called the Son because of the flesh, and descended in suffering below that which man can suffer; or, in other words, suffered greater sufferings, and was exposed to more powerful contradictions than any man can be." See also 3 Nephi 1:14 and Ether 4:12, where Christ talks about Himself in His roles as Father and Son.
6. "Spirit" here does not refer to the spirit person that we were in the premortal life. It refers rather to a characteristic or an aspect of Christ's divine nature which He inherited as the Only Begotten. Another way of stating this would be "spiritual nature" versus "mortal nature." This distinction is obvious for "spiritually" versus "naturally" in Moses 3:5. Compare Bruce R. McConkie, *Mormon Doctrine*, 756–61, and Joseph F. Smith, *Gospel Doctrine*, 14th ed. (Salt Lake City: Deseret Book, 1971), 432.
7. That is why Amulek could say "there should be a great and last sacrifice; yea, not a sacrifice of man, neither of beast, neither of any manner of fowl; for it shall not be a human sacrifice; but it must be an infinite and eternal sacrifice" (Alma 34:10). Christ, if He were only a mortal like all other mortals, could not have performed a sacrifice to atone for mankind. It was because of His immortal nature that His sacrifice was infinite and eternal.
8. See also Russell M. Nelson, in Conference Report, October 1993, 46; "The Savior was the only one who could accomplish [the Atonement]. From His mother He inherited power to die. From His Father He obtained power over death." On the same page, Elder Nelson speaks of a paradisiacal creation by God, a mortal creation caused by the Fall, and an immortal creation brought about by the Atonement.

9. A colleague in Religious Education at Brigham Young University reminded me of this passage. Note also Christ's words on the cross, "Father, into thy hands I commend my spirit: and having said thus, he gave up the ghost" (Luke 23:46).
10. For a similar listing, see Jeffrey R. Holland, *Christ and the New Covenant* (Salt Lake City: Deseret Book, 1997), 192.
11. The Atonement, if it is to be effected by a valid sacrifice, must be freely given (as all sacrifices must be freely given to be valid). If the Savior's life could be taken from Him by force, then His death would be involuntary and not a sacrifice. Thus He said, "Therefore doth my Father love me, because I lay down my life, that I might take it again" (John 10:17). President John Taylor said, "The Father gave [Christ] power to have life in himself: 'For as the Father hath life in himself, so hath he given to the Son to have life in Himself' (John 5:26). And further, He had power, when all mankind had lost theirs, to restore life to them again; and hence He is the resurrection and the life, which power no other man possesses" ("The Mediation and Atonement of Christ," *The Gospel Kingdom*, ed. G. Homer Durham [Salt Lake City: Bookcraft, 1964], 114–15). It was not enough that He had the ability to simply walk away from captivity and death. It was not enough that He allowed Himself to be placed in the hands of the executioners. He also had to choose, He had to will, temporal death. For this reason, crucifixion, though we are repulsed by the vile aspects of this form of execution, was probably the only type of execution that gave the Savior the choice of whether to die or not to die. To the casual observer, it would have appeared that Christ had been executed by crucifixion. However, to those like Abinadi who understood the nature of Christ's sacrifice, His death on the cross was an act of His own will and not of the executioners. This recognition is hinted at in Mark 15:39 by the Roman centurion attending the Crucifixion when he stated, "Truly this man was the Son of God." There may be other forms of execution that would fulfil the requirements just outlined, but I am unaware of any.
12. See King Benjamin's delivery of the words of an angel of God on the Atonement in Mosiah 3. Verses 8 and 9 especially reveal a knowledge of the doctrine Abinadi taught. See also Nephi's vision in 1 Nephi 11, Alma's speech in Alma 7, Amulek's understanding in Alma 34:9–10, and Alma's explanation of the Atonement to his son in Alma 42, especially verse 15. It should be noted that Abinadi may not have had access to any of these discourses, with the exception of 1 Nephi 11. But he could have drawn upon the same source of inspiration for this doctrine that was available to Alma and Amulek.

The Sanctity of Food: A Latter-day Saint Perspective

Paul H. Peterson

***Paul H. Peterson** is a former professor of Church history and doctrine at BYU.*

One hesitates to begin a paper by issuing disclaimers, but issue them I must.[1] From my vantage point, most Latter-day Saints do not approach food and drink in the same sanctifying sense that many observant Jewish people do. The Jewish approach to diet includes an elaborate, highly detailed web of regulations that comprise a complete, ethical system. For reasons largely having to do with holiness rather than health or hygiene, many Jews follow this intricate and complex dietary system—one they consider to be divinely sanctioned and one that closely governs and limits what foods they eat.[2]

Why must observant Jews practice such dietary discipline? Why would God be so concerned about the food people eat? The reasons, many Jews will admit, are not altogether clear. The Torah gives only one reason for God's requiring such observance: the dietary laws will help Israel become holy.[3]

In short, Jews believe that obeying such laws promotes holy living. "Jews who keep these laws," as noted by scholar Louis Jacobs, "introduce a spiritual element into their lives, even into the satisfaction of hunger, the most basic and animal-like of all human appetites. By means of the dietary laws one's everyday life becomes nobler and purer."[4]

The position of The Church of Jesus Christ of Latter-day Saints on food and drink (and it may be presumptuous to assume a position exists) is different. Many Latter-day Saints regard food and drink as a means to an end. The Church's emphasis has always been on the importance, or even sacredness, of the body and the necessity of treating it properly. We hold, as do many Jews, that the body is sacred. As Jacobs observed, most Jews believe that the "human body is given to a person in trust by God."[5]

We are not uncomfortable with that observation. Our founding prophet, Joseph Smith, said, "We came to this earth that we might have a body and present it pure before God in the celestial kingdom. The great principle of happiness consists in having a body."[6]

According to Latter-day Saint theology, the soul of man or woman consists of both the spirit and the body (see D&C 88:15). In emphasizing the importance of the body, Latter-day Saints often quote 1 Corinthians 3:16–17. It reads, "Know ye not that ye are the temple of God, and that the Spirit of God dwelleth in you? If any man defile the temple of God, him shall God destroy; for the temple of God is holy, which temple ye are."

Because we hold the body sacred, we take certain precautions to maintain its purity, strength, and integrity. Like many others, members of the Church believe in chastity before marriage and fidelity afterward. Because we hold the body sacred, we maintain that certain foods are especially important to eat and that certain substances or foods and drinks should be avoided. The Word of Wisdom, a revelation given to Joseph Smith, serves as a general guide in this respect.

The Coming Forth of the Word of Wisdom

The Word of Wisdom was given at a meeting of the School of the Prophets in Kirtland, Ohio, in February 1833. According to President Brigham Young's later recollection, it came about largely as a result of Joseph and Emma's concerns about frequent tobacco use by school participants:

> I think I am as well acquainted with the circumstances which led to the giving of the Word of Wisdom as any man in the Church, although I was not present at the time to witness them. The first school of the prophets was held in a small room situated over the Prophet Joseph's kitchen, in a house which belonged to Bishop Whitney, and which was attached to his store, which store probably might be about fifteen feet square. In the rear of this building was a kitchen, probably ten by fourteen feet, containing rooms and pantries. Over this kitchen was situated the room in which the Prophet received revelations and in which he instructed his brethren. The brethren

> came to that place for hundreds of miles to attend school in a little room probably no larger than eleven by fourteen. When they assembled together in this room after breakfast, the first thing they did was to light their pipes, and while smoking, talk about the great things of the kingdom, and spit all over the room, and as soon as the pipe was out of their mouths a large chew of tobacco would then be taken. Often when the Prophet entered the room to give the school instructions he would find himself in a cloud of tobacco smoke. This, and the complaints of his wife at having to clean so filthy a floor made the Prophet think upon the matter, and he inquired of the Lord relating to the conduct of the Elders in using tobacco, and the revelation known as the Word of Wisdom was the result of his inquiry.[7]

About twenty-two people were in attendance the day Joseph walked into the room and read the revelation. One of them, Zebedee Coltrin, recalled that Joseph's reading of the revelation had an immediate impact on the assembled brethren: "The Prophet Joseph was in an adjoining room . . . and came in with that Revelation in his hand. Out of the twenty two members that were there assembled, all used tobacco more or less, except two. Joseph read the Revelation and when they heard it they all laid aside their pipes and use of tobacco."[8]

The revelation Joseph read on that occasion became canonized scripture in 1835. Today, it is known as section 89 of the Doctrine and Covenants. As almost all members of the Church know, section 89 contains far more than just a single prohibition against tobacco. It contains other proscriptions, some prescriptions, and a series of promises involving increased vitality and knowledge for those who adhere to the instructions contained in the revelation.

In terms of prescriptions, Saints were advised to eat herbs (including vegetables) and fruits, especially fresh ones. Grains were to serve as the staff of life. Meat was to be eaten sparingly—more specifically, only in times of winter or famine.

The proscriptions listed in section 89 were fewer in number but more pointed. Saints were instructed to use wine only of their "own make" for sacramental purposes. They were enjoined not to partake of or use internally any strong drink, tobacco, or hot drinks. Interestingly, with all these admonitions, there was an important qualification. Unlike other revelations Joseph received, this one was to be received "not by commandment or constraint." In other words, when initially given, compliance with the instructions given in the revelation was advocated or recommended—but not necessarily mandated.

How unique was the Word of Wisdom? It was not as novel as many have supposed. As Lester Bush has demonstrated, most physicians in the United States in the 1830s, both orthodox and botanic or herbal, would have agreed with much of the counsel given in Doctrine and Covenants 89. In that era, many doctors felt disease was a result of the overstimulation of one's energy source. Ardent spirits were deemed a major cause of overstimulation, and, to a lesser extent, so was meat. Thus, many medical practitioners recommended they be used sparingly. There was more ambivalence about the stimulating effects of tea and coffee. Tobacco would have weighed in somewhere between ardent spirits and tea and coffee on the "stimulation scale."[9]

What was novel about the revelation, of course, at least for Church members, was the prophetic authority that was attached to it. Although many other Americans may have agreed with much of the counsel contained in section 89, there is no evidence such belief translated into lifestyle changes. The fact that Church members felt it was given by God rather than by man made a considerable difference in terms of overall acceptance. In large part, because of this divine stamp of approval, Latter-day Saints, collectively speaking, came to embrace the counsel contained in section 89—at least some portions of it—with a fair amount of willingness and, in some cases, enthusiasm.

The Interpretation of the Word of Wisdom in the Joseph Smith Era

How did Church members come to interpret the Word of Wisdom in the years immediately following its reception? What parts of the revelations were deemed most important? Not surprisingly, because the revelation was in its infancy and because Joseph never precisely delineated the relative importance of the various prescriptions and proscriptions, some lack of uniformity existed in early obedience patterns. In other words, different Saints embraced different parts of the revelation. For example, some took seriously the passage indicating that "all wholesome herbs God hath ordained for the constitution, nature, and use of man" (D&C 89:10). Botanic physician Willard Richards, among others, advocated the use of herbs.[10]

But despite Willard's advocacy of herbs, herb usage never took hold among the general populace of Saints; it never became a criterion for fellowship. In addition to herb usage, there is limited evidence that at least two other notions, derived from various passages in the revelation, held some attraction for some Saints for a limited period. Regarding the injunction limiting meat eating to times of winter or famine, Joseph instructed some participants on the Zion's Camp march in 1834 that "fish was much healthier for us to eat than meat, and the use of fish in warm weather was not prohibited in the Word of Wisdom."[11]

And William W. Phelps was possibly alluding to avoiding drinks of extreme temperature as well as tea and coffee when he noted in correspondence to his wife that the Kirtland Saints were unified in keeping the Word of Wisdom. "They drink cold water," Phelps said, "and dont [*sic*] even mention tea and coffee."[12]

But like herbs, neither eating fish or any other kind of meat, in winter or whatever season, nor avoiding drinks of extreme temperature caught on. Nor did any other of the various prescriptions gain ascendency. Indeed, it is interesting, perhaps instructive, just how quickly the overwhelming majority of leaders and lay members identified exclusively with the proscriptive stipulations dealing with alcohol, tobacco, and hot drinks (meaning tea and coffee). And, almost from the onset, there was a certain pecking order regarding these items. Alcohol, and more especially distilled liquor as opposed to fermented drinks like wine, was considered most objectionable. Tobacco use closely followed alcohol consumption as a transgression of consequence, with tea and coffee lagging somewhat behind. The identification of hot drinks with tea and coffee was in place by the mid-1830s. Church member Joel Hills Johnson recalled that about four months following the reception of section 89, Joseph Smith said to the Saints: "I understand that some of the people are excusing themselves in using tea and coffee, because the Lord only said 'hot drinks' in the revelation of the Word of Wisdom. The Lord was showing us what was good for man to eat and drink. Now, what do we drink when we take our meals? Tea and Coffee is it not? Yes! tea and coffee then, they are what the Lord meant when he said 'hot drinks.'"[13]

In less than a decade following its reception, the contours of the revelation were in place. For nearly all Church members, observance of the Word of Wisdom implied either nonuse or sparing use of alcohol, tobacco, tea, and coffee. These were the only items that became criteria of Church fellowship.

Why, it may be fairly asked, did the proscriptions prevail while the prescriptions were largely shoved aside? Probably, at least in part, because Church leaders felt the social and moral results of disobedience to the proscriptive counsel (especially with regard to alcohol and tobacco) were of far greater consequence.

How closely was the Word of Wisdom lived in its infancy? In all likelihood, more diligently than many historians have supposed. In February 1834 the high council of the Church resolved that "No official member in this Church is worthy to hold an office, after having the Word of Wisdom properly taught him, and he, the official member, neglecting to comply with or obey it."[14]

Most Church leaders and many Church members took this declaration at its word and emphasized adherence to the proscriptive portions of the revelation with some vigor through at least 1837, especially at Church headquarters in Ohio.[15]

But the relatively strict approach to Word of Wisdom observance that characterized many Ohio Saints in the 1830s did not prevail for long. For reasons difficult to discern but probably in part having to do with the varied challenges of establishing and maintaining a church amid hostile surroundings, Word of Wisdom considerations assumed secondary status. This comparatively relaxed approach was in place by at least 1842 when the Saints lived in Nauvoo, Illinois.

Word of Wisdom Observance in Territorial Utah

By and large, the comparatively liberal attitude toward Word of Wisdom observance that existed in Nauvoo prevailed in Utah Territory for the rest of the nineteenth century. It is true that Brigham Young asked Latter-day Saints in the September general conference of 1851 to covenant to keep the Word of Wisdom; it is also true that, for whatever reason, President Young chose not to require Latter-day Saints to keep that particular covenant.[16] Perhaps, he reasoned, that with all the challenges inherent in settling and colonizing their Great Basin kingdom, it made little sense to quibble about a cup of coffee. As late as 1861, President Young indicated that although observance should be a worthy goal, he did not desire to make adherence to the Word of Wisdom a test of fellowship.[17]

In 1883, President John Taylor initiated the most zealous, widespread Word of Wisdom reform movement in the half century following the inception of the revelation. Following President Taylor's lead, at general conference in October 1883, Wilford Woodruff, President of the Quorum of the Twelve, preached Word of Wisdom observance to assembled Saints and indicated "the time was at hand when it would be necessary to keep the whole law of God."[18]

Two months later, Elder Woodruff told members of the newly formed St. George School of the Prophets that the time had come for Church members to observe the Word of Wisdom.[19]

Unfortunately, the antipolygamy legislation and resultant persecution disrupted Latter-day Saint society and largely sapped the vigor of President Taylor's Word of Wisdom crusade.[20]

What then, in summary, constituted Word of Wisdom observance in the nineteenth century? At least three general patterns of adherence can be identified: (1) moderation, rather than abstinence, was the major concern; (2) drunkenness was not tolerated; and (3) wine was generally not categorized as a "strong drink."

A Twentieth-Century Test of Fellowship

From 1901 until 1945, two men, Joseph F. Smith and Heber J. Grant, directed the Church. Presidents Smith and Grant had very similar views on the Word of Wisdom—essentially, that abstinence rather than moderation should constitute the primary criterion for Word of Wisdom compliance. The path to our current interpretation of the Word of Wisdom can be traced to their administrations.[21]

President Grant probably emphasized Word of Wisdom compliance more than any other General Authority, before or since. At general conference in October 1935, President Grant announced he was going to read the revelation to the congregation. "It may be that it will be the fifty-third time in the past fifty-three years," he declared to the congregation. "I think that I have read it at least once a year if not a half a dozen times."[22]

By the 1920s, abstinence became a requirement for a temple recommend.[23] By that same period, Word of Wisdom adherence had clearly replaced plural marriage as the Latter-day Saint badge of identification. Certainly, the Word of Wisdom did not escape nineteenth-century non-Mormon detection—various travelers through Utah often commented on the overall orderliness and sobriety that prevailed in Latter-day Saint communities.[24]

But nineteenth-century non-Mormon emphasis on distinctive Latter-day Saint Word of Wisdom patterns paled in significance compared to the deluge of twentieth-century gentile commentary. To outsiders, Mormons became known primarily as the people who wouldn't smoke, consume alcohol, or drink coffee or tea.[25]

A Temporal and Spiritual Guide

Although the differences and distinctions between Latter-day Saint and Jewish attitudes to food and diet will probably always be greater than the similarities, it is possible that in the future, many Latter-day Saints, of their own volition, will adopt attitudes and assume patterns toward food and drink that are somewhat analogous to the Jewish approach. I predict (some would say, with unwarranted temerity) that some alteration of attitudes will take place along two fronts. The first such front has to do with the broadening of Word of Wisdom considerations to include more than just the present list of proscriptions. In short, in all likelihood, more and more Latter-day Saints will come to view Doctrine and Covenants 89 not only as a delineator of forbidden items but also as an indicator of what one should eat.

The second front where some alteration might occur has to do with perspective or viewpoint. I suspect that in this present age of environmental sensitivity and holistic living, a good many Church members might begin to view the entire revelation in a larger and more holistic sense—as a guide not only to physical well-being but also to spiritual growth.

Are there legitimate reasons or precedents to believe that such lifestyle changes will occur among some in the Latter-day Saint community in the future? I believe there are. Certainly there are strong scriptural precedents—both in canonized scripture and in the statements of presiding brethren whom Church members revere as prophets and revelators.

Regarding precedents contained in canonized scripture, I noted earlier that Doctrine and Covenants 89 included both prescriptions as well as proscriptions. In truth, the prescriptions actually take up more scriptural space. Among other things, Saints were advised in holy writ to eat herbs and fruits, regard grain as the "staff of life," and eat meat sparingly. And, of course, the concluding verses of the revelation indicate "spiritual blessings" await those Saints who comply—presumably with both proscriptions and prescriptions.

The first latter-day prophet to emphasize a so-called expanded view of the Word of Wisdom—that is, to emphasize the importance of the prescriptions as well as the proscriptions—was Brigham Young. As early as 1855, President Young complained of the food he was fed when visiting Saints. "The only thing I crave," he said, "is milk." On this occasion, he also noted that he wished Latter-day Saints could become more of "a natural people."[26] In 1860, President Young observed that the Lord has given us wheat, beef, and herbs (probably including vegetables) for our benefit. Regarding herbs, he asked rhetorically that if they were useless, why did the Lord make them available?[27] At the April 1868 general conference, both Brigham Young and George Q. Cannon advised Latter-day Saints to avoid eating pork.[28]

Other General Authorities who have emphasized Word of Wisdom prescriptions are Lorenzo Snow, Heber J. Grant, John A. Widtsoe, Joseph F. Merrill, Joseph Fielding Smith, and Ezra Taft Benson. In the 1890s, Apostle Lorenzo Snow expressed surprise that so many of the brethren who preached on the Word of Wisdom avoided commenting on the passage advocating the use of meat sparingly. Elder Snow suggested, seemingly for humane reasons, that the time was not far distant when the eating of animal flesh would be prohibited.[29] At one time, Heber J. Grant also apparently believed that the day would come when meat eating would be forbidden.[30] John A. Widtsoe coauthored with his wife, Leah, *The Word of Wisdom: A Modern Interpretation,* a widely read book that advocated the use of grains and the use of meat sparingly, among other things. *A Modern Interpretation* was used as the Melchizedek Priesthood study manual in 1938.[31]

In April general conference of 1948, Elder Joseph F. Merrill of the Quorum of the Twelve lamented that "all over the Church the belief is general that the Word of Wisdom is practically observed if the individual abstains from the use of tea, coffee, liquor, and tobacco. But a careful reading of the revelation," cautioned Elder Merrill, "shows this belief to be erroneous." Brother Merrill then proceeded to emphasize the injunction advocating the sparing use of meat.[32]

In more recent times, Presidents Joseph Fielding Smith and Ezra Taft Benson have advised Church members to heed the prescriptive portion of section 89. President Smith noted:

> We seldom hear of the things mentioned which are "ordained for the constitution, nature, and use of man." The Lord has given us all good herbs, fruits and grains. These are to be the main foods of men, beast, and fowls. But we should not overlook the fact that they are to be used with "prudence and

> thanksgiving." . . . The difficulty with most of the human family, is eating too much, and failing to heed this counsel. There would be less disease and mankind would live longer if all would also heed the counsel of the Lord concerning the use of wholesome foods. Many a man thinks he keeps the Word of Wisdom, who knows only the "don'ts" which is [are] but a part of its great meaning.[33]

Most recently, we are aware that at various times in his ministry, President Benson promoted the advantages of eating food in its natural state and partaking heartily of grains, fruits, and vegetables.[34] I also understand that President Benson, in his personal life, was sparing in his use of meat and generous in his use of fresh vegetables and grains.[35]

Clearly then, there are both scriptural and prophetic precedents for members of the Church—if they so desire to expand their own personal list of Word of Wisdom considerations. There are also scriptural and prophetic models for viewing the entire revelation in a more holistic way by our combining the physical with the spiritual—by our viewing the eating of foods that God has prescribed as a spiritual act or event. Indeed, if Latter-day Saints chose to pursue this path, it would be somewhat analogous to Jewish attitudes.

In his introduction to Jewish belief, Louis Jacobs indicated that "in Judaism everything must be brought into contact with the spiritual domain."[36] Latter-day Saints could identify with that notion. In the Doctrine and Covenants, the Lord told Joseph Smith, "Wherefore verily I say unto you that all things unto me are spiritual, and not at any time have I given unto you a law which was temporal; neither any man, nor the children of men; neither Adam, your father, whom I created" (D&C 29:34). Mormonism, then, postulates a blending of the spiritual and temporal domains.

Church members, if they so chose, could regard eating and drinking as temporal-spiritual events. Orthodox Jews, by eating some foods and refraining from others in obedience to their religion, actually elevate the act of eating to a level of godliness. As Jacob Milgrom observed, "The dietary laws are rungs on the ladder of holiness, leading to a life of pure thought and deed, characteristic of the nature of God."[37]

Although such a view is hardly widespread in the Latter-day Saint community, it is scripturally supportable. For example, why couldn't Latter-day Saints, by avoiding the food and drink God has placed off limits and by eating only those foods they believe God has singled out as being especially good for mankind, gain greater reverence for life and increased appreciation for the Lord? My suspicion is that in the future, some Church members will do so and thus come to regard eating as much more than just a practical necessity.

To concern oneself with eating foods the Lord has prescribed and to consider eating prescribed foods as an act of holiness are both attitudes that could be understood as logical results of living in divine harmony with the earth God has created. Latter-day Saints believe that men and women are God's superior creations but not His only creations. Many also believe they are to respect, not abuse, the earth they are placed on and live in divine harmony with it.[38]

The Lord indicates that "the good things which come of the earth, whether for food or for raiment, . . . are made for the benefit and the use of man." But the revelation also stipulates that such things are "to be used, with judgment, not to excess, neither by extortion" (D&C 89:17–18).

Brigham Young, who respected and even revered the earth that God created, taught: "Man cannot control the heavens; he cannot control the earth, nor the elements; he can fertilize and prepare the ground for the reception of seed; he can plant, water, till, and reap, . . . but, until his mind is opened by the Spirit of God, he cannot see that it is by a superior power that corn, wheat, and every kind of vegetation spring into life, and ripen for the sustenance of man and beast."[39]

I conclude with two very different observations. First, I want to make plain my intentions. I have no hidden agenda. I am not crusading for change in Word of Wisdom emphasis—that is hardly my province. My motivation for writing this paper came when I was asked to compare Latter-day Saint attitudes toward food and drink with those of Jewish people. I have indicated that at present, the similarities are not striking; and I have speculated that in the future, at least for some Latter-day Saints, the similarities (in attitude rather than detail) will become more obvious. I wouldn't be surprised if, in the future, some of the presiding leaders of the Church occasionally emphasize some of the prescriptive portions of section 89. I will be surprised, however, if such an emphasis ever assumes fellowship proportions. For social, moral, and practical reasons, I expect that adherence to the proscriptive elements of the Word of Wisdom will remain the only criteria for Church fellowship.

Second, it should be mentioned that one important similarity between Jewish and Latter-day Saint dietary approaches has not been discussed.

Herman Wouk observed that Jewish dietary laws serve as both "a community bond and a reminder of personal identity that comes whenever a man gets hungry. It is a daily commitment in action to one's faith, a formal choice, a quiet self-discipline." Such laws are, Wouk concludes, "social instruments for keeping the Jewish nation alive, and psychological instruments for preserving the identity of individuals."[40]

Possibly to a lesser but still a highly meaningful extent, the Word of Wisdom has served a similar function among Latter-day Saints. Every time a Church member politely says "no thank you" to the generous offer of an acquaintance or stranger to partake of coffee or alcohol, the action has the effect of reminding everyone involved that Latter-day Saints are a "separate people," that they made covenants with the Lord, and that because of their "peculiarity," there are things they can and cannot do. Indeed, it is difficult to conceive of a more suitable vehicle to remind us of our covenantal responsibilities and embed them into our self-consciousness than to require certain patterns of eating and drinking—something that is usually done openly and daily.[41]

In this very functional sense, Jews and Mormons—peculiar peoples both—can readily identify with one another.

Notes

1. This article is adapted from a paper given on October 5, 1995, as part of a lecture series featuring Jewish and Latter-day Saint scholars. The lecture series, "Jews and Mormons—A Common Heritage," was held at Utah Valley State College during fall semester 1995.
2. Jacob Milgrom, "The Biblical Diet Laws as an Ethical System," in *Studies in Cultic Theology and Terminology*, ed. Jacob Milgrom (Leiden: E. J. Brill, 1983), 104–18.
3. Herman Wouk, *This Is My God: The Jewish Way of Life*, rev. ed. (New York: Pocket Books, 1974), 99.
4. Louis Jacobs, *The Book of Jewish Practice* (West Orange, NJ: Behrman House, 1987), 68.
5. Louis Jacobs, *The Book of Jewish Belief* (West Orange, NJ: Behrman House, 1984), 38.
6. Joseph Smith, *Teachings of the Prophet Joseph Smith*, comp. Joseph Fielding Smith (Salt Lake City: Deseret Book, 1977), 181.
7. Brigham Young, in *Journal of Discourses* (Liverpool: Latter-day Saints' Book Depot, 1854–86), 12:158.

8. Minutes of the St. George School of the Prophets, December 23, 1883, Church History Library, Salt Lake City.
9. Lester E. Bush Jr., "The Word of Wisdom in Early Nineteenth-Century Perspective," *Dialogue* 14, no. 3 (Autumn 1981): 48–58.
10. Willard Richards to "Sister Hepsy," January 28, 1837, Church History Library.
11. George A. Smith, "My Journal," *The Instructor* 81, no. 5 (May 1946): 323.
12. William W. Phelps to Sally Waterman Phelps, May 26, 1835, Journal History of the Church, Church History Library.
13. Joel Hills Johnson, Excerpts from Autobiography, typescript made by Norman E. Wright, January 25, 1952, L. Tom Perry Special Collections, Harold B. Lee Library, Brigham Young University, Provo, UT.
14. Joseph Smith, *History of the Church of Jesus Christ of Latter-day Saints*, ed. B. H. Roberts, 2nd ed. rev. (Salt Lake City: Deseret Book, 1957), 2:35.
15. I am not suggesting that Saints in the 1830s matched the levels of obedience their twentieth-century descendants reached. If for no other reason, two common perceptions preclude such a possibility. First, like many other nineteenth-century Americans, most early Saints genuinely believed the prohibited substances had legitimate medicinal and fatigue-removing properties that justified occasional use. Second, most Church members did not categorize occasional wine drinking, especially at sacramental or festive events, as an infringement of the Word of Wisdom.
16. *Millennial Star*, February 1, 1852, 35; James R. Clark, ed., *Messages of the First Presidency of The Church of Jesus Christ of Latter-day Saints* (Salt Lake City: Bookcraft, 1965), 2:90; Paul H. Peterson, "An Historical Analysis of the Word of Wisdom" (master's thesis, Brigham Young University, 1972), 49–53; Robert J. McCue, "Did the Word of Wisdom Become a Commandment in 1851?" *Dialogue* 14, no. 3 (Autumn 1981): 66–77.
17. Brigham Young, in *Journal of Discourses*, 9:35.
18. Journal History of the Church, October 6, 1883, 8, Church History Library.
19. Minutes of the St. George School of the Prophets, December 23, 1883, Church History Library.
20. Peterson, "An Historical Analysis of the Word of Wisdom," 76–77.
21. Thomas G. Alexander, *Mormonism in Transition: A History of the Latter-day Saints, 1890–1930* (Urbana: University of Illinois Press, 1986), 261.
22. Heber J. Grant, in Conference Report, October 1935, 8.
23. Alexander, *Mormonism in Transition*, 264–65.

24. See, for example, the accounts of Solomon Nunes Carvalho, *Incidents of Travel and Adventure in the Far West* (New York: Derby and Jackson, 1857), 209; and William Hepworth Dixon, *New America,* 9th ed. (London: Hurst and Blackett, 1869), 117.
25. Peterson, "An Historical Analysis of the Word of Wisdom," 101–2.
26. Thomas Bullock Minutes, 1848–56, loose papers, April 15, 1855, Church History Library.
27. Brigham Young Office Journal, Book D, March 12, 1860, Church History Library.
28. Brigham Young Manuscript History, April 6, 1868, Church History Library; *Journal of Discourses*, 12:221.
29. Heber J. Grant Diary, October 1, 1895, Church History Library; Journal History, May 5, 1898, 2.
30. Heber J. Grant to Anna Grant, September 16, 1901, Church History Library.
31. John A. Widtsoe and Leah D. Widtsoe, *The Word of Wisdom: A Modern Interpretation* (Salt Lake City: Deseret Book, 1937).
32. Joseph F. Merrill, "Eat Flesh Sparingly," *Improvement Era*, May 1948, 279, 314.
33. Joseph Fielding Smith, *Church History and Modern Revelation* (Salt Lake City: Deseret Book, 1953), 1:385.
34. Ezra Taft Benson, *The Teachings of Ezra Taft Benson* (Salt Lake City: Bookcraft, 1988), 476–77.
35. Personal conversation with Reed A. Benson, son of President Ezra Taft Benson, October 3, 1995.
36. Jacobs, *The Book of Jewish Belief*, 132.
37. Milgrom, "The Biblical Diet Laws as an Ethical System," 111.
38. Hugh Nibley opined that "man's dominion is a call to service, not a license to exterminate" (*Brother Brigham Challenges the Saints*, ed. Don E. Norton and Shirley S. Ricks [Salt Lake City: Deseret Book and FARMS, 1994], 18). Nibley's four essays on Brigham Young and the environment in this volume make for insightful reading.
39. Brigham Young, in *Journal of Discourses*, 3:119.
40. Wouk, *This Is My God*, 108.
41. Edwin B. Firmage, "The Word of Wisdom: Mark of a Peculiar People," *Ensign*, October 1972, 18–19.

"And I Saw the Hosts of the Dead, Both Small and Great": Joseph F. Smith, World War I, and His Visions of the Dead

Richard E. Bennett

Richard E. Bennett *is a professor of Church history and doctrine at BYU.*

> "As I pondered over these things which are written, the eyes of my understanding were opened, and the Spirit of the Lord rested upon me, and I saw the hosts of the dead, both small and great" (D&C 138:11).

Joseph F. Smith's discourses on life, death, and war are revered today by Latter-day Saints as profoundly important contributions to Mormon doctrine. Sixth President of The Church of Jesus Christ of Latter-day Saints (he served from 1901 to 1918) and nephew of Joseph Smith, the founder of the Church, President Smith proclaimed some of his most comforting and most important discourses on the topics of death and suffering during the waning months of World War I. His final sermon, his "Vision of the Redemption of the Dead," now canonized as revelation by the Church, stands as the authoritative Mormon declaration of its time.

A thorough study of the historical process that brought this doctrinal statement out of obscurity and into the realm of modern Mormon scripture begs to be written. However, the purpose of this paper is to place this and his other wartime sermons in their historical context, to suggest their place in the wider tapestry of Christian thought, and to argue for their fuller application as commentary on temple work, war, and several other critical issues of the day. Just as it took Church leaders years to rediscover the full significance of President Smith's visions of the redemption of the dead and their full significance as a vital assist to modern temple work, so also Latter-day Saint historians have been slow to view them as essential documents, pointers, and commentaries of the age. To the views and comments of other religionists of the day who were sharing their own important visions at war's end, Joseph F. Smith's must now be added.[1]

At a time when prayers in schools are discouraged, if not denied, at the "eleventh hour of the eleventh day of the eleventh month," school children across Canada and throughout much of the British Commonwealth of Nations are asked to bow their heads in grateful remembrance for those who died in war. To this day, Remembrance Day, November 11, is a Sabbath-like observance, a tolling bell in honor of those who gave their last true measure of devotion to the cause of God, king, and country. Canadians wear scarlet poppies on their lapels and gather respectfully at public war memorials across the land, sing hymns, honor mothers who lost sons in battle, and listen reverently to the following poem, penned by John McCrae during the frightful battle of Ypres where men by the tens of thousands died in the blooming poppy fields of Belgium:

In Flanders fields the poppies blow
Between the crosses, row on row,
That mark our place; and in the sky
The larks, still bravely singing, fly
Scarce heard amid the guns below.
We are the Dead. Short days ago
We lived, felt dawn, saw sunset glow;
Loved and were loved, and now we lie
In Flanders fields.
Take up our quarrel with the foe;
To you from failing hands we throw
The torch; be yours to hold it high.
If ye break faith with us who die
We shall not sleep, though poppies grow
In Flanders fields.[2]

Indeed, "lest we forget," more than nine million men in uniform and countless legions of civilians perished in the battlefields, battleships, and bombed-out byways of World War I. Another twenty-one million were permanently scarred and disfigured. Whatever the causes of that conflict, they have long been overshadowed by the "sickening mists of slaughter" that, like a pestilence, hung over the world for four and a half years. The terrible battles of the Marne, Ypres, Verdun, the Somme, Vimy Ridge, Jutland, Passchendaele, Gallipoli, and many others are place names synonymous with unmitigated human slaughter in what some have described as a nineteenth-century war fought with twentieth-century weaponry. This was the conflict, remember, that witnessed the awful stalemate of protracted trench warfare and pitched hand-to-hand combat in the "no-man's lands" of western Europe, the introduction of Germany's lethal submarine attacks, chemical-gas mass killings, and aerial bombings on a frightening scale. Yet the Great War, that "war to end all wars," became but the catalyst and springboard for an even deadlier conflict a generation later. And with its long-prayed-for conclusion on November 11, 1918, came prayers for a lasting peace, hopes for a League of Nations that would guarantee future world peace, and sermons and visions that spoke of new hopes and new dreams for a blighted world.

Joseph F. Smith's Responses to War

Compared to the other great religions of the time, The Church of Jesus Christ of Latter-day Saints, with a membership then of only a few hundred thousand, most of whom lived in Utah and surrounding states, may seem like a very small voice in a vastly overcrowded cathedral. Though as many as fifteen thousand Latter-day Saints saw battle, mainly as enlisted men in the United States Army, Mormonism as a religion was spared the tragedy of killing its own, as opposed to Catholic shooting Catholic and of Lutheran gunning down Lutheran on the distant battlefields of Europe. Headquartered far away in the tops of the Rocky Mountains of the American West, the Church remained relatively unscathed from the intimate hell and awful horror of war, much as it had done during America's Civil War fifty years before. Nevertheless, the Church's leaders held definite positions toward the war, some of which were modified over time.

With the sudden, unexpected outbreak of the war and in response to President Woodrow Wilson's request for prayers of peace, Joseph F. Smith, himself a confirmed Republican, and his counselors in the First Presidency, the highest ecclesiastical body in the Church, called upon the entire membership to support the nation's president and to pray for peace. "We deplore the calamities which have come upon the people in Europe," he declared, "the terrible slaughter of brave men, the awful sufferings of women and children, and all the disasters that are befalling the world in consequence of the impending conflicts, and earnestly hope and pray that they may be brought to a speedy end."[3]

His counselor, Charles W. Penrose, speaking further on President Smith's behalf, condemned neither side in the war, "We ask Thee, O Lord, to look in mercy upon those nations. No matter what may have been the cause which has brought about the tumult and the conflict now prevailing, wilt Thou grant, we pray Thee, that it be overruled for good, so that the time shall come when, though thrones may totter and empires fall, liberty and freedom shall come to the oppressed nations of Europe, and indeed throughout the world."[4] This spirit of the entire Church praying for peace lasted throughout the war.[5]

Speaking in the general conference of the Church just one month after the outbreak of war, President Smith expressed, for the first time, his public interpretation of the war and of its causes. Still stunned by news of the enormously high numbers of casualties so soon inflicted, he reiterated his desire for peace, pointed to the "deplorable" spectacle of war, and blamed it not upon God but squarely upon man's inhumanity to man, on dishonest politics, on broken treaties, and, above all, on the apostate conditions he believed were endemic to modern Christianity. "God did not design or cause this," he preached. "It is deplorable to the heavens that such a condition should exist among men."[6]

Choosing not to interpret the conflict in economic, political, or even nationalist tones, he ever saw it, at base, as the result of moral decline, of religious bankruptcy, and of the world's refusal to accept the full gospel of Jesus Christ. "Here we have nations arrayed against nations," he said, "and yet in every one of these nations are so-called Christian peoples professing to worship the same God, professing to possess belief in the same divine Redeemer . . . and yet these nations are divided against the other, and each is praying to his God for wrath upon and victory over his enemies."[7] Loyal in every way to the message of the Book of Mormon and the Restoration of the gospel of Jesus Christ, he saw it this way: "Would it be possible—could it be possible, for this condition to exist if the people of the world possessed really the true knowledge of the Gospel of Jesus Christ? And if they really possessed the Spirit of the living God—could this condition exist? No; it could not exist, but war would cease, and contention and strife would be at an end. . . . Why does it exist? Because they are not one with God, nor with Christ. They have not entered into the true fold, and the result is they do not possess the spirit of the true Shepherd sufficiently to govern and control their acts in the ways of peace and righteousness."[8]

The only real and lasting antidote to the sin of war, he believed, was the promulgation of the restored gospel of Jesus Christ "as far as we have power to send it forth through the elders of the Church."[9]

Though the war was not the work of God, the Church leader was nonetheless quick to see in it a fulfilment of divine prophecy, both ancient and modern. "The newspapers are full of the wars and the rumors of wars," he wrote in a private family letter of November 1914, "which seem to be literally poured out upon all nations as foretold by the Prophet [Joseph Smith] in 1832. The reports of the carnage and destruction going on in Europe are sickening and deplorable, and from the latest reports the field of carnage is greatly enlarging instead of diminishing."[10]

A few weeks later, in his annual Christmas greeting to the Church for December 1914, he returned to this same theme. "The sudden 'outpouring' of the spirit of war upon the European nations which startled the whole world and was unexpected at the time of its occurrence, had long been expected by the Latter-day Saints, as it was foretold by the Prophet Joseph Smith on Christmas Day, December 25th, 1832."[11]

Yet no one took pleasure in seeing such foreboding prophecy fulfilled. Nor could predictions be made tantamount to divine imposition on the affairs of men. At stake was the agency—and the evil—of man. As the cold calamity of war spread across the battlefields of Europe, President Smith continually stressed this point. "God, doubtless, could avert war," he said in December of 1914, "prevent crime, destroy poverty, chase away darkness, overcome error, and make all things bright, beautiful and joyful. But this would involve the destruction of a vital and fundamental attribute of His sons and daughters that they become acquainted with evil as well as good, with darkness as well as light, with error as well as truth and with the results of the infraction of eternal laws."[12] Thus, the war, among so many other things, was a schoolmaster, a judgment of man's own doing, a terrible lesson of what inevitably transpires when hate and greed rule the day.

Despite these broken laws and with them the inevitable fulfillment of calamitous prophecy, there can be found, like a stream of clear water running throughout his teachings, the doctrine of ultimate redemption and resolution: "Therefore [God] has permitted the evils which have been brought about by the acts of His creatures, but will control their ultimate results for His own glory and the progress and exaltation of His sons and daughters, when they have learned obedience by the things they suffer. . . . The foreknowledge of God does not imply His action in bringing about that which He foresees."[13]

Vowing initially not to take sides in the struggle, President Smith found it increasingly challenging, however, to remain neutral. The sinking of the *Lusitania* in May 1915 struck an ominous chord in America, intent as the country was in staying clear of the conflict. His colleague Elder James E. Talmage, then a member of the Church's Quorum of the Twelve Apostles, described the sinking as "one of the most barbarous developments of the European war," charging Germany for staining its hands "with innocent blood never to be washed away."[14]

Despite such wartime atrocities, President Smith clung to the hope that America could somehow remain detached from the war. "I am glad that we have kept out of war so far, and I hope and pray that we may not be under the necessity of sending our sons to war, or experience as a nation the distress, the anguish and sorrow that come from a condition such as exists upon the old continent."[15]

Nevertheless, as America lurched reluctantly toward war, President Smith saw America's involvement as a necessity. News of the zeppelin bombing raids over England and his consequent fear for the safety of his own mission president son and missionaries then serving in England particularly bothered him and led him to question ever further Germany's wartime tactics. "It seems to me that the only object of such raids is the wanton and wicked destruction of property and the taking of defenseless lives," he wrote. "It appears that the spirit of murder, the shedding of blood, not only of combatants but of anyone connected with the enemy's country seems to have taken possession of the people, or at least the ruling powers in Germany. What they gain by it, I do not know. It is hardly possible that they expect to intimidate the people by such actions, and it surely does not diminish the forces of the opposition. By such unnecessary and useless raids in the name of warfare, they are losing the respect of all the nations of the earth."[16]

A staunch patriot, he was soon to admit the obvious: "I have a feeling in my heart that the United States has a glorious destiny to fulfil, and that part of that glorious destiny is to extend liberty to the oppressed, as far as it is possible to all nations, to all people." Gradually, he forged a cautious, nonpacifist view in behalf of the entire Church: "I do not want war; but the Lord has said it shall be poured out upon all nations, and if we escape, it will be 'by the skin of our teeth.' I would rather the oppressors should be killed, or destroyed, than to allow the oppressors to kill the innocent."[17]

If Latter-day Saints must fight—and thousands of them soon enlisted in the cause—their attitude must ever be that of "peace and good will toward all mankind, . . . that they will not forget that they are also soldiers of the Cross, that they are ministers of life and not of death; and when they go forth, they may go forth in the spirit of defending the liberties of mankind rather than for the purpose of destroying the enemy. . . . Let the soldiers that go out from Utah be and remain men of honor."[18]

Eager to demonstrate Mormon loyalty to an America still suspicious of the Church and of some of its teachings and to support President Wilson's entry into the war, President Smith led active campaigns to enlist Latter-day Saints in the ranks of the military and to involve the Church and its membership in the various Liberty Bond drives of the time, raising hundreds of thousands of dollars in the process.[19]

Significantly, his writings bear an absence of malice or a spirit of vengeance toward the aggressor. Less critical than other younger leaders, such as Elder James E. Talmage who, although not given to retribution, felt Germany had a debt to pay, President Smith was ever slow to condemn. Said he, "Let the Lord exercise vengeance where vengeance is needed. And let me not judge my fellow men, nor condemn them lest I condemn them wrongly."[20]

Meanwhile, until the war ended, Latter-day Saints joined with others in praying for peace and in taking up arms in the cause of victory over the enemy. America's involvement eventually turned the tide of war, ultimately bringing a defeated Germany and the other Axis powers to Versailles. And though half a world away, news of the pending peace was as jubilantly received in Utah as it was most everywhere else in the free world.[21]

The Armistice

The Latter-day Saints were, of course, not alone in proclaiming a vision of the war and of peace. A sampling of what others saw as the war wore away may be instructive. Randall Thomas Davidson, Archbishop of Canterbury, was trying earnestly to see meaning out of a senseless war, to see divine purpose in man's malignancy, and to bring vision to a groping world. He said in his war-closing sermon of gratitude preached at Westminster Abbey in London on November 10, 1918:

> There, then, with all that the war has brought us of darkened homes and of shattered hopes for those we loved, with all its hindering and setting back of our common efforts and energies to promote things peaceable and lovely and of good report, [the war] has, beyond any doubt, been our schoolmaster to bring us to a larger vision of the world as God sees it. It is one of the great things which our sons, our dear sons, have wrought for us by their dauntless sacrifice. . . . Just now, this week, when the whole life—I do not think I am exaggerating—the whole life of the world is being re-conditioned, re-established, re-set for good. This is that crisis-hour. Something has happened, is happening, which can best find description in . . . the living word or message of God to man. It cuts right to the centre of our being.[22]

He closed a later sermon with his particular vision of a new Christian way: "Jesus Christ is the real centre and strength of the best hopes and efforts man can make for the bettering and the brightening of the world. Only we must quietly, determinedly, thoughtfully, take His law and His message as our guide. . . . The task is hardest perhaps when we are dealing with life's largest relationship—the relationship between peoples. Can we carry the Christian creed and rule there? Who shall dare to say we cannot? It needs a yet larger outlook. . . . Surely it is a vision from on high."[23]

Pope Benedict XV, in his first encyclical immediately following the end of the war, rejoiced that "the clash of arms has ceased," allowing "humanity [to] breathe again after so many trials and sorrows." Next only to gratitude, his sentiment was one of profound regret, bordering on apology, that a leading cause of the war had been the "deplorable fact that the ministers of the Word" had not more courageously taught true religion rather than the politics of accommodation from the pulpit. The conscience of Christianity had been scarred by its own advocates. "The blame certainly must be laid on those ministers of the Gospel," he lamented. He went on to chastise the pulpit and called for a new vision, a new order of valiant, righteous Christian spokesmen who would declare peace and the cross fearlessly. "It must be Our earnest endeavor everywhere to bring back the preaching of the Word of God to the norm and ideal to which it must be directed according to the command of Christ Our Lord, and the laws of the Church."[24]

The official American Catholic response may best be seen in the pastoral letters of its bishops. At its base, the war showed a deep "moral evil" in man where "spiritual suffering" and "sin abounded." Despite all of mankind's progress—"the advance of civilization, the diffusion of knowledge, the unlimited freedom of thought, the growing relaxation of moral restraint— . . . we are facing grave peril." Scientific and materialistic progress notwithstanding, a world without moral discipline and faith will lead only to destruction. The only true vision of hope is "the truth and the life of Jesus Christ," and the Catholic Church must uphold the dignity of man, defend the rights of the people, relieve distress, consecrate sacrifice, and bind all classes together in the love of the Savior.[25]

James Cardinal Gibbons of Baltimore, the leading American Catholic spokesman, in calling upon Americans to "thank God for the victory of the allies and to ask him for grace to 'walk in the ways of wisdom, obedience and humility,'" ordered his priests to substitute the prayer of thanksgiving in the Mass in place of the oration.[26]

He instructed them further that a solemn service be held in all the churches of the archdiocese on November 28, 1918, at which the Church's official prayer of thanksgiving, the *Te Deum*, should be sung.[27]

Written as early as AD 450, the words to one of Catholicism's most famous hymns speak of man's immortality, of Christ's divinity, and of His redemption of the dead:

> We praise Thee, O God: we
> acknowledge Thee to be the Lord
> Thee, the Eternal Father, all
> the earth doth worship. . . .
> Thou, O Christ, art the King of glory.
> Thou art the Everlasting Son of the Father.
> Thou didst not abhor the Virgin's
> womb, when Thou tookest upon
> Thee human nature to deliver man.
> When Thou hadst overcome the
> sting of death, Thou didst open
> to believers the kingdom of heaven.
> Thou sittest at the right hand of
> God, in the glory of the Father.
> Thou, we believe, art the Judge to come.[28]

The American Protestant view of the war, and more especially of its postwar opportunities, are varied and diverse and defy simple categorization and analysis. There were almost as many "visions" as there were denominations. While most, like Bishop Charles P. Anderson of the Protestant Episcopal Church, spoke in terms of gratitude, many others soon were speaking jingoistically, calling for immediate punishment and retribution.[29] "*The Christian Century*, which was representative of a great portion of Christendom, believed in the thorough chastisement of Germany."[30] Likewise, the *Congregationalist* editorialized that "Germany is a criminal at the bar of justice."[31] Reverend Dr. S. Howard Young of Brooklyn called "retribution upon the war lords" as "divine," "the first world lesson to be derived from the German downfall."[32]

Meanwhile, Billy Sunday, "God's Grenadier" and by far the most popular patriot-evangelist of his day, saw the war as good against evil, God against Satan, "America and Christ, indissolubly linked, forging ahead in a glorious struggle."[33] Though some others shared his view, Billy characteristically always went a step or two further. "Hey, Jesus, you've gotta send a country like that to damnation," he once said. "I'll raise enough of an army myself to help beat the dust off the Devil's hordes."[34] He also saw the end of the war as a window, a God-given opportunity to revitalize the evangelical cause of Christian revivalism and of individual spiritual rebirth, a time to confront the anti-Christ of such foreign-inspired teachings as evolution, social Darwinism, higher criticism, and every other philosophical evil of the age.

Other more moderate clergymen like the positive-minded Presbyterian, Robert E. Speer, saw a moral victory stemming out of the war, a new vision rising out of the ashes of Europe. "The war also has unmistakably set in the supreme place those moral and spiritual principles which constitute the message of the Church," he declared. "The war has shown that these values are supreme over personal loss and material interest. . . . We succeeded in the war whenever and wherever this was our spirit. . . . The war says that what Christ said is forever true."[35]

Rabbi Silverman, speaking in Chicago's Temple Beth-El synagogue, mirrored Speer's sentiments. "The world was nearer its millennium today than ever before," he is reported to have said. "War had brought mankind nearer to brotherhood than had centuries of religious teachings. . . . War had brought religion back to its original task of combating bigotry, fighting sin, and uplifting mankind."[36]

Both Reverend Speer and Henry Emerson Fosdick, professor of the Union Theological Seminary in New York, along with other leading religious leaders, welcomed the end of war as an opportunity to launch "the Church Peace Union," a new united religious order funded, in part, by Andrew Carnegie and his Carnegie Endowment for International Peace to unite multiple Protestant faiths marching under one grand united banner—"the new political heaven [to] regenerate earth," as Bishop Samuel Fallows of the Reformed Episcopal Church liked to describe it. Though destined to failure because of oppressive debts, internal disagreements, and opposition from Protestant fundamentalism, for a brief moment, this Interchurch World Movement of Protestants, Catholics, and Jewish leaders in America became "the principal voice of institutional religion on behalf of peace-keeping and peace-making" and appeared to hold enormous promise for church unity, social reform, and economic improvement.[37]

Fosdick, one of the most eloquent American Protestant statesmen of his time, had grudgingly supported America's entry into the war but came out of it a confirmed pacifist. Reflecting the utter disillusionment the war wrought on many religionists, Fosdick listed several elements in his vision of warning for the future: "There is nothing glamorous about war any more," "war is not a school for virtue any more," "there is no limit to the methods of killing in war any more," "there are no limits to the cost of war any more," "there is no possibility of sheltering any portion of the population from the direct effect of war any more," and "we cannot reconcile Christianity and war any more."[38] Every effort must be made to avoid such a future calamity. He, like many others, was bitterly disappointed by America's refusal to ratify the Versailles Peace Treaty and enter the League of Nations. As one commentary said, "God won the war and the devil won the peace."[39]

Joseph F. Smith's Visions of the Dead

Worn out by a long life of devoted Church service and worn down in sorrow with the recent deaths of several members of his immediate family, Joseph F. Smith, though a loving soul, knew all about grief. "I lost my father when I was but a child," he once said. "I lost my mother, the sweetest soul that ever lived, when I was only a boy. I have buried one of the loveliest wives that ever blessed the lot of man, and I have buried thirteen of my more than forty children. . . . And it has seemed to me that the most promising, the most helpful, and, if possible, the sweetest and purest and the best have been the earliest called to rest."[40]

Speaking of the loss of one of his former polygamist wives, Sarah E., and, shortly thereafter, of his daughter Zina, he said: "I cannot yet dwell on the scenes of the recent past. Our hearts have been tried to the core. Not that the end of mortal life has come to two of the dearest souls on earth to me, so much as at the sufferings of our loved ones, which we were utterly powerless to relieve. Oh! How helpless is mortal man in the face of sickness unto death!"[41]

His daughter's death triggered four of the most revealing discourses ever given by a Latter-day Saint leader on the doctrines of death, the spirit world, and the resurrection. As one noted scholar put it: "It is doubtful if in any given period of like duration in the entire history of The Church of Jesus Christ of Latter-day Saints so much detail as to the nature of the life after death has been given to any other prophet of this dispensation."[42]

All were well received by the membership and extended hope and comfort to those who had lost loved ones or who might be asked to sacrifice family members in times of peace or of conflict. The war, raging loud and cruel, served as a vivid backdrop to these emerging doctrines.

On April 6, 1916, with the battles of Verdun and the Somme very much dominating the daily news, he gave a talk entitled "In the Presence of the Divine." In it he spoke of the very thin veil separating the living and the dead. Speaking of Joseph Smith, Brigham Young, Wilford Woodruff, and his other predecessors, he preached the doctrine that the dead, those who have gone on before, "are as deeply interested in our welfare today, if not with greater capacity, with far more interest, behind the veil, than they were in the flesh. I believe they know more. . . . Although some may feel and think that it is a little extreme to take this view, yet I believe that it is true." He went on to say, "We cannot forget them; we do not cease to love them; we always hold them in our hearts, in memory, and thus we are associated and united to them by ties that we cannot break."[43]

President Smith taught that death was neither sleep nor annihilation; rather, death involved a change into another world where the spirits of those once here can be solicitous of our welfare, "can comprehend better than ever before, the weaknesses that are liable to mislead us into dark and forbidden paths."[44]

Two years later, speaking at a meeting in Salt Lake City in February 1918, he spoke additional words of comfort and consolation, particularly to those who had lost children or whose youthful sons were dying overseas. He said,

> The spirits of our children are immortal before they come to us, and their spirits after bodily death are like they were before they came. They are as they would have appeared if they had lived in the flesh, to grow to maturity, or to develop their physical bodies to the full stature of their spirits. . . . [Furthermore,] Joseph Smith taught the doctrine that the infant child that was laid away in death would come up in the resurrection as a child; and, pointing to the mother of a lifeless child, he said to her: "You will have the joy, the pleasure and satisfaction of nurturing this child, after its resurrection, until it reaches the full stature of its spirit." . . . It speaks volumes of happiness, of joy and gratitude to my soul.[45]

Two months later, having recovered from illness sufficiently to speak at the April 1918 general conference of the Church, he gave a talk entitled "A Dream That Was a Reality." In it, he recounted a particularly poignant and unforgettable dream he had experienced sixty-five years earlier as a very young missionary in Hawaii, a dream-vision that dramatically influenced the rest of his life. He spoke of seeing his father, Hyrum, his mother, Mary, Joseph Smith, and several others who had ushered him into a mansion after he had bathed and cleansed himself. "That vision, that manifestation and witness that I enjoyed that time has made me what I am," he confessed. "When I woke up I felt as if I had been lifted out of a slum, out of despair, out of the wretched condition that I was in. . . . I know that that was reality, to show me my duty, to teach me something, and to impress upon me something that I cannot forget."[46]

Just weeks before, on January 23, his Apostle son, Hyrum, then only forty-five years of age, was struck down in his prime by a ruptured appendix. It was a devastating blow from which Joseph F. never fully recovered, compounded as it was with the further sorrowful news of the death of his daughter-in-law and Hyrum's wife, Ida Bowman Smith, just a few months thereafter. Wrote Talmage in behalf of the Twelve: "Our great concern has been over the effect the great bereavement will have upon President Joseph F. Smith, whose health has been far from perfect for months past. This afternoon he spent a little time in the office of the First Presidency, and we find him bearing up under the load with fortitude and resignation."[47]

Sick and intermittently confined to bed rest for several months afterwards, he had rallied sufficiently to speak briefly in the October general conference of the Church, long enough to proclaim his particular message of peace to a war-weary world.[48]

He spoke of having lately received, while pondering on the biblical writings of the Apostle Peter, another, ultimately his final, vision of the dead. While meditating upon these things, he said he "saw the hosts of the dead, both small and great," those who had died "firm in the hope of a glorious resurrection," waiting in a state of paradise for their ultimate redemption and resurrection. Suddenly, the "Son of God appeared, declaring liberty to the captives who had been faithful." Choosing not to go Himself to the wicked and unfaithful dead who waited in the more nether realms of the spirit world, Christ organized a great missionary force among His most faithful followers, dispatching them to minister and teach the gospel of Jesus Christ to "all the spirits of men," those who had been less faithful and obedient in their mortal lives, including, as Peter writes, "those who were sometime disobedient" in the days of Noah and the great flood. In addition, he saw many of the ancient prophets, including Adam and Eve, involved in this spirit prison ministry of redemption. Likewise, "the faithful elders of this dispensation" were called to assist. His vision closed with the declaration that the dead "who repent will be redeemed, through obedience to the ordinances of the house of God . . . after they have paid the penalty of their transgressions."[49]

Whereas his earlier discourses have remained memorable sermons, this sixty-verse document was immediately sustained, in the words of James E. Talmage, as "the word of the Lord" by his counselors in the First Presidency and by the Quorum of the Twelve.[50]

For reasons not entirely clear, though widely read in the Church, the document was not formally accepted as canonized scripture for almost sixty years. Then, in 1976, President Spencer W. Kimball directed that it be added to the Pearl of Great Price.[51]

Later, in June 1979, the First Presidency announced it would become section 138 of the Doctrine and Covenants. Considered an indispensable contribution to a fuller understanding of temple work—especially in an age of very active temple construction—the performances of proxy ordinances for the dead, including baptism for the dead and confirmation, and of the relationship between the living and the dead, it has been heralded as "central to the theology of the Latter-day Saints because it confirms and expands upon earlier prophetic insights concerning work of the dead."[52] Others have written elsewhere about the contributions of this document to temple work.[53]

Because this document is far more than a mere sermon to the faithful Latter-day Saint and because it is regarded as the word and will of the Lord—in fact, it is the only canonized revelation of the twentieth century—it bears careful scrutiny. And, as a wartime document, it may have other meanings and applications not plumbed before.

For instance, although a discourse on the dead, it owed nothing to spiritualism. It is a matter of record that public interest in the dead and in communicating with the dead peaked during and immediately following the war. In 1918, Arthur Conan Doyle of Sherlock Holmes fame published his book *New Revelation* on the subject of psychical research and phenomena, bemoaning the decline in church attendance in England and of Christianity generally and proclaiming a new religion, a new revelation. He urged a belief not in the fall of man or in Christ's redemption as the basis of faith but in the validity of "automatic writings," seances, and other expressions of spiritualism as a new universal religion and of communicating with lost loved ones—or, as he put it, "the one provable thing connected with every religion, Christian or non-Christian, forming the common solid basis upon which each raises, if it must needs raise, that separate system which appeals to the varied types of mind."[54]

In contrast, President Smith's vision was very much Christ centered, a reiteration of the Savior's Atonement for a fallen world. Though he certainly believed that "we move and have our being in the presence of heavenly messengers and heavenly beings" and though the dead may even transcend the veil and appear unto loved ones, if so authorized, he steered the Church away from any hint of spiritualism.[55] Latter-day Saints were to seek *after* the dead—that is, their spiritual welfare—rather than to seek the dead.

His revelation also reaffirmed the Christian belief in Adam and Eve and in a divine creation, for, in President Smith's words, he saw "Father Adam, the Ancient of Days, and father of all" as well as "our glorious Mother Eve" (D&C 138:38–39). Though nothing is said specifically about evolution and the caustic, contemporary debates of the time over the origin of the species, these verses very simply restated the doctrines of the Church on this subject without argument or ambiguity.

Likewise, in an age of higher criticism with its attack on the authenticity and authority of the Bible, the revelation reestablished, for Latter-day Saints at least, a twentieth-century belief in the primacy and authority of scripture, a belief in the writings of Peter, a belief in Noah and the flood not as allegory but as actual event, and, by extension, a renewed belief in the entire Old and New Testaments. For a church ofttimes criticized for its belief in additional scripture, if nothing else, section 138 is a classic declaration of biblical authority for modern times.[56]

The vision may also be important for what it does not say. There is no discussion of peace treaties, no references to ecumenism or the interchurch movements of the times, no calls for social repentance and the social gospel. Neither prowar nor pacifist, it says nothing about cultural or nationalistic superiorities. The problem of evil is reduced to redeemable limits; and although man will always reap what he sows, there is still hope and redemption. Meanwhile, the Church retains its own mission as the gospel of Jesus Christ upon the earth as preestablished in its restoration a century earlier.

Finally, it proclaimed God's intimate involvement in the affairs of humankind and His benevolent interest in His children. Steering the Church away from the yawning secularism that stood to envelope many other faiths in the postwar era, President Smith spoke confidently, above all, about Christ and His triumphant victory over sin and death.[57]

To the utter waste and sheer terror of the just-concluded catastrophe, there was ultimate redemption. To those who had lost faith in God and in their fellowmen, there was certain restoration. To the soldier lost in battle, to the sailor drowned at sea, and to a prophet-leader mourning the deaths of his own family, there was the reality of the resurrection.

Notes

I thank my research assistant, Keith Erekson, for his valuable assistance in helping me prepare this work.

1. The definitive biography of President Joseph F. Smith remains to be written. Joseph Fielding Smith, one of his sons, wrote *Life of Joseph F. Smith, Sixth President of the Church of Jesus Christ of Latter-day Saints* (Salt Lake City: Deseret News Press, 1938; Deseret Book, 1969) in praise of his father. Since then, Francis M. Gibbons has written *Joseph F. Smith: Patriarch and Preacher, Prophet of God* (Salt Lake City: Deseret Book, 1984). See also Scott Kenney, "Joseph F.

Smith," in *The Presidents of the Church*, ed. Leonard J. Arrington (Salt Lake City: Deseret Book, 1986), 179–211.

2. John McCrae, "In Flanders Fields," *One Hundred and One Famous Poems*, ed. Roy J. Cook (Chicago: Contemporary Books, 1958), 11. Lieutenant-Colonel John McCrae, a member of the first Canadian contingent, died in France on January 28, 1918, after four years of service on the western front.
3. "Special Announcement" of the First Presidency, September 8, 1914, in *Messages of the First Presidency of The Church of Jesus Christ of Latter-day Saints*, ed. James R. Clark (Salt Lake City: Bookcraft, 1970), 4:311.
4. Charles W. Penrose, "A Prayer for Peace," in Conference Report, October 1914, 9.
5. See Conference Report, April 1915, 3; and Conference Report, April 1916, 3.
6. Joseph F. Smith, in Conference Report, October 1914, 7.
7. Smith, in Conference Report, 7.
8. Smith, in Conference Report, 7.
9. Smith, in Conference Report, 8. In a letter to his son, Hyrum, then a mission president in Liverpool, England, President Smith said: "We still see from the papers that the war in Europe is going on, the whole thing is a sad comment upon the civilization and Christian spirit of the age" (Joseph F. Smith to Hyrum Smith, November 7, 1914, Correspondence Files, Joseph F. Smith Collection, Church History Library, The Church of Jesus Christ of Latter-day Saints, Salt Lake City, Utah).
10. Joseph F. Smith to Hyrum Smith, November 7, 1914, Joseph F. Smith Papers, Church History Library.
11. "A Christmas Greeting from the First Presidency," in *Messages of the First Presidency,* 4:319. The prophecy alluded to, commonly referred to as the "Civil War Prophecy," spoke of the pending Civil War and its commencement in South Carolina. Later, the South would be compelled to call upon Great Britain for assistance. Great Britain, in turn, "shall also call upon other nations, in order to defend themselves against other nations, and thus war shall be poured out upon all nations" (D&C 87:3).
12. "A Christmas Greeting from the First Presidency," December 19, 1914, in *Messages of the First Presidency*, 4:325–26.
13. "A Christmas Greeting," 4:326.
14. Journal of James E. Talmage, May 7 and 13, 1915, James E. Talmage Collection, L. Tom Perry Special Collections, Harold B. Lee Library, Brigham Young University, Provo, Utah. For a thorough study of Elder Talmage's corresponding views of the war, see the author's "'How Long, Oh Lord, How Long?' James E.

Talmage and the Great War," a paper delivered at "The Church Meets the Twentieth Century" symposium, sponsored by the Joseph Fielding Smith Institute for Latter-day Saint History, March 18, 2000.

15. Joseph F. Smith, in Conference Report, April 1915, 6. Writing in an editorial of December 1915, he said much the same: "We pray that [America's] leaders may receive wisdom of our Father in Heaven, to so direct the affairs in their charge that we may continue in the enjoyment of peace and prosperity throughout the land" (Joseph F. Smith to the editor of the *Liahona, The Elders' Journal*, December 18, 1915, Joseph F. Smith Papers, Church History Library).
16. Joseph F. Smith to his son, Hyrum Smith, February 19, 1916, Joseph F. Smith Papers, Church History Library.
17. Joseph F. Smith, in Conference Report, October 1916, 154.
18. Joseph F. Smith, in Conference Report, April 1917, 3–4.
19. The Church itself participated in the war effort by purchasing $850,000 in liberty bonds. In addition, it strongly encouraged its membership to participate in the bond drive, with the result that the people of Utah far exceeded the state's quota of $6.5 million. One reason the Church was so eager to participate in the war effort was to shed the negative publicity cast upon it during and immediately following the Reed Smoot Senate hearing in Washington DC. Elected in 1903, Smoot, a Mormon Apostle, had been barred from taking his seat until 1907 because of acrimonious debates over Mormon plural marriage and Mormon loyalties. President Smith and many other prominent Church leaders traveled to Washington on several occasions to testify on behalf of the Church. In 1907, the First Presidency issued a special address to the world explaining the Church's stand on these and many other topics, including its loyalty to America. For a fine summary of the Reed Smoot hearings and their impact upon the Church, see Thomas G. Alexander, *Mormonism in Transition: A History of the Latter-day Saints, 1890–1930* (Urbana: University of Illinois Press, 1986), 16–36.
20. "Status of Children in the Resurrection," May 1918, in *Messages of the First Presidency*, 5:97.
21. Official word reached Salt Lake City very early in the morning of November 11, 1918. Despite the late hour and the curfews imposed because of the influenza epidemic, the city seemed to spring into life. In the words of James E. Talmage, "Bells were tolled, whistles blown, and within an incredibly short time hundreds of automobiles were dashing about the streets, most of them having tin cans, sheet iron utensils and other racket-making appendages attached to the rear." Later in the day, "Flags and bunting appeared in abundance everywhere, tons of

confetti were thrown from the tops of high buildings, every available band was pressed into service, and during the afternoon and well on into the night dancing was indulged in on Main Street." Talmage enthusiastically concluded: "Such a day as this has never before been witnessed in the world's history" (James E. Talmage Journal, November 11, 1918).

22. Randall Thomas Davidson, "The Armistice," in *The Testing of a Nation* (London: Macmillan, 1919), 159–60.
23. Davidson, "The Dayspring," in *The Testing of a Nation*, 176–77, 180.
24. Benedict XV, "Quod Iam Diu," in *The Papal Encyclicals 1903–1939*, comp. Claudia Carlen (Wilmington, NC: McGrath, 1981), 1:153–54.
25. *Pastoral Letter of the Archbishops and Bishops of the United States Assembled in Conference at the Catholic University of America* (Washington DC: National Catholic Welfare Council, 1920), 39–40.
26. *The Chicago Daily Tribune*, November 11, 1918, 3.
27. John Tracy Ellis, *The Life of James Cardinal Gibbons, Archbishop of Baltimore 1834–1921* (Milwaukee: Bruce, 1952), 258.
28. "Te Deum," in *The Catholic Encyclopedia for School and Home* (New York: McGraw-Hill, 1965), 10:563.
29. *The Chicago Daily Tribune*, November 15, 1918, 4.
30. Ray H. Abrams, *Preachers Present Arms: The Role of the American Churches and Clergy in World Wars I and II, with Some Observations on the War in Vietnam* (Scottsdale, PA: Herald Press, 1969), 232–33.
31. Abrams, *Preachers Present Arms*, 233.
32. *The Chicago Daily Tribune*, November 11, 1918, 11.
33. Roger A. Bruns, *Preacher: Billy Sunday and Big-Time American Evangelism* (New York: Norton, 1922), 249.
34. Bruns, *Preacher*, 252.
35. R. E. Speer, *The New Opportunity of the Church* (New York: Macmillan, 1919), 48–49, as quoted in *A Documentary History of Religion in America since 1865*, ed. Edwin S. Gaustad (Grand Rapids, MI: Eerdmans, 1983), 148.
36. *Chicago Daily Tribune*, November 11, 1918, 11. The editor of the *Methodist Review* called for the regeneration of the family and of motherhood and for reenshrining the teachings of Christ. "Without this light the world must stumble along in darkness. Is it not evident then that it is the bounden duty of the Church to seek a fresh Pentecost? The times, wild and disturbed as they are, are not unripe for a baptism of power from within the veil" ("What the World Is Facing," *Methodist Review* 68, no. 4 [October 1919]: 590).

37. Gaustad, *Documentary History of Religion*, 148. This interchurch vision continued to a lesser extent as the Federal Council of Churches, Reverend Robert E. Speer playing an active part.
38. Henry Emerson Fosdick, "'Shall We End the War,' A Sermon Preached at the First Presbyterian Church, New York, June 5, 1921" (New York: Clearing House for the Limitation of Armament), 3–12.
39. Eldon G. Ernst, *Moment of Truth for Protestant America: Interchurch Campaigns Following World War One*, Dissertation Series, no. 3 (Missoula, MT: American Academy of Religion and Scholars Press, 1974), 139.
40. *Messages of the First Presidency*, 5:92.
41. Joseph F. Smith to Hyrum Smith, November 3, 1915, Joseph F. Smith Papers, Church History Library.
42. James R. Clark, editorial note in *Messages of the First Presidency*, 5:5.
43. *Messages of the First Presidency*, 5:6–7.
44. *Messages of the First Presidency*, 5:7.
45. "Status of Children in the Resurrection," in *Messages of the First Presidency*, 5:94–95.
46. "A Dream That Was a Reality," in *Messages of the First Presidency*, 5:100–101. It is interesting to note that this was not the first unique dream he had of his beloved mother. On July 21, 1891, he had dreamed that his "precious mother came to live with him. It seemed that she had been gone for a long time." In this dream, he "fixed her up a room all for herself and made it as comfortable as I could. . . . This is the third time I have seemed to put [up] my mother since she left us" (Joseph F. Smith to "My Dear Aunt Thompson," July 21, 1891, Letters of Joseph F. Smith, as cited in the Scott G. Kenney Collection, L. Tom Perry Special Collections, Harold B. Lee Library, Brigham Young University).
47. James E. Talmage Journal, January 25, 1918.
48. Because of his frail condition, President Smith did not actually read this document in conference but had it delivered in writing to the leadership of the Church shortly after the conference had concluded.
49. See Doctrine and Covenants 138 to read the vision in its entirety.
50. Elder Talmage wrote for October 31, 1918: "Attended meeting of the First Presidency and the Twelve. Today President Smith, who is still confined to his home by illness, sent to the Brethren the account of a vision through which, as he states, were revealed to him important facts relating to the work of the disembodied Savior in the realm of departed spirits, and of the missionary work in progress on the other side of the veil. By united action the Council of the

Twelve, with the Counselors in the First Presidency, and the Presiding Patriarch accepted and endorsed the revelation as the Word of the Lord. President Smith's signed statement will be published in the next issue (December) of the Improvement Era" (James E. Talmage Journal, October 31, 1918).

51. From time to time, General Authorities referred to the vision before 1976. See, for example, Joseph L. Wirthlin, April 1945 general conference; Marion G. Romney, April 1964 general conference; Spencer W. Kimball, October 1966 general conference; Boyd K. Packer, October 1975 general conference. For this information, I am indebted to Robert L. Millet, "The Vision of the Redemption of the Dead," in *Hearken, O Ye People: Discourses on the Doctrine and Covenants* (Sandy, UT: Randall Book, 1984), 268. Latter-day Saints accept the messages of their living prophets as scripture. "Whatsoever they shall speak when moved upon by the Holy Ghost shall be scripture, shall be the will of the Lord, shall be the mind of the Lord, shall be the word of the Lord, shall be the voice of the Lord, and the power of God unto salvation" (D&C 68:4). However, there are degrees of scripture within the Church. Once Joseph F. Smith's vision had been presented to the Church membership and voted upon and accepted as scripture, it shifted in significance from *scripture* to *canonized* scripture. As Robert L. Millet said, "Prior to 3 April 1976 it represented a theological document of inestimable worth to the Saints, one that deserved the study of those interested in spiritual things; on that date it was circumscribed into the standard works, and thus its message—principles and doctrines—became binding upon the Latter-day Saints, the same as the revelations of Moses or Jesus or Alma or Joseph Smith. The Vision of the Redemption of the Dead became a part of the canon, the rule of faith and doctrine and practice—the written measure by which we discern truth from error" (Robert L. Millet, "The Vision of the Redemption of the Dead," in *Hearken O Ye People*, 265).
52. Millet, "The Vision of the Redemption of the Dead," 259.
53. See *The Doctrine and Covenants Student Manual* (Salt Lake City: The Church of Jesus Christ of Latter-day Saints, 1981), 356–61; see also Michael J. Preece, *Learning to Love the Doctrine & Covenants* (Salt Lake City: MJP Publishing, 1988), 409–13. It should be noted in passing, however, that Joseph F. Smith's vision was not a sudden extension of his sickness or sorrows. For instance, as early as 1882, he had spoken of Christ's preaching in the spirit prison (*Gospel Doctrine: Selections from the Sermons and Writings of Joseph F. Smith* [Salt Lake City: Deseret Book, 1961], 437–38). Likewise, he had previously taught of ancient prophets and modern-day missionaries teaching to the spirits in prison

(*Gospel Doctrine*, 430, 460). His funeral sermons are replete with this doctrine. For example, see his talk given in Logan, Utah, October 27, 1907, at the quarterly conference of the Logan Stake, typed manuscripts, 16, Papers of Joseph F. Smith, Church History Library. Although a careful analysis of President Smith's developing doctrines of death and the resurrection remains to be done, what he said in October 1918 was entirely consistent with what he had been preaching for almost forty years.

54. Arthur Conan Doyle, *The New Revelation* (New York: George H. Doran, 1918), 52. Doyle visited Salt Lake City in May 1923, lecturing one night in the Salt Lake Tabernacle to more than five thousand people. Spiritualism was not an unknown phenomenon to the Latter-day Saints. Years before, the Godbeite movement in Salt Lake had proclaimed it part of their new religion, claiming former Apostle Amasa Lyman in the process (see Ronald W. Walker, *Wayward Saints: The Godbeites and Brigham Young* [Urbana: University of Illinois Press, 1998], 254–57).
55. *Gospel Doctrine*, 430. For more on this topic, see Michael W. Homer, "Spiritualism and Mormonism: Some Thoughts on Similarities and Differences," *Dialogue: A Journal of Mormon Thought* 27, no. 1 (Spring 1994): 171–91.
56. Joseph F. Smith knew all about how divisive the debate over modernism and higher criticism could become. In 1913, after a series of prolonged hearings and debates, Brigham Young University dismissed four professors because of their tendency to accommodate the theory of evolution and to "de-mythologize" the Bible. For a full discussion of this controversy, see Ernest L. Wilkinson, ed., *Brigham Young University: The First One Hundred Years* (Provo, UT: Brigham Young University Press, 1975), 1:412–32.
57. For more on the rising secularism after the war, see Alan D. Gilbert, *The Making of Post-Christian Britain: A History of the Secularization of Modern Society* (London: Longman Group, 1980) and Burnham P. Beckwith, *The Decline of U.S. Religious Faith 1912–1984 and the Effects of Education and Intelligence on Such Faith* (Palo Alto, CA: P. A. Beckwith, 1985). According to one study, the decline in church attendance in England since World War I has been precipitous. Between 1885 and 1928, the proportion of the population in England of the age of fifteen and over who were Easter Day communicants in the Church of England never fell below 84 per 1,000. In 1925, it was 90 per 1,000. But since the early 1930s, that number has steadily declined: by 1939 the proportion had dropped to 73 per 1,000, 63 per 1,000 by 1958, and 43 per 1,000 by 1973 (Alan Wilkinson, *The Church of England and the First World War* [London:

Society for Promoting Christian Knowledge, Holy Trinity Church, 1978], 292). In contrast, Latter-day Saint membership has grown from four hundred thousand to eleven million, and activity rates are higher now than ever before (see Rodney Stark, "The Basis of Mormon Success: A Theological Application," in *Latter-day Saint Social Life: Social Research on the LDS Church and Its Members*, ed. James T. Duke [Provo, UT: Religious Studies Center, Brigham Young University, 1998]: 29–70).

Moses 1:1–19 on Old Testament Manuscript 1, page 1, "A Revelation given to Joseph the Revelator." This is the beginning of Joseph Smith's New Translation of the Bible. Dated June 1830, in Oliver Cowdery's handwriting, Courtesy of Library-Archives, Community of Christ, Independence, Missouri.

How We Got the Book of Moses

Kent P. Jackson

***Kent P. Jackson** is a professor of ancient scripture at BYU.*

The Book of Moses is an extract from Joseph Smith's New Translation of the Bible. It was revealed to the Prophet in 1830 and in early 1831, beginning not long after the organization of the Church. This article is a brief introduction to the origin of the Book of Moses and the Bible translation from which it derives.

Beginning in June 1830, Joseph Smith began a careful reading of the Bible to revise and make corrections in accordance with the inspiration he would receive. The result was the revelation of many important truths and the restoration of many of the "precious things" that Nephi had foretold would be taken from the Bible (see 1 Nephi 13:23–29). In a process that took about three years, the Prophet made changes, additions, and corrections as were given him by divine inspiration while he filled his calling to provide a more correct translation for the Church.[1] Today the Prophet's corrected text is usually called the Joseph Smith Translation (JST), but Joseph Smith and his contemporaries referred to it as the New Translation.[2] The title *Inspired Version* refers only to the edited, printed edition, published in Independence, Missouri, by the Community of Christ (formerly the Reorganized Church of Jesus Christ of Latter Day Saints). The Book of Moses in the Pearl of Great Price is the very beginning of the New Translation, corresponding to Genesis 1:1–6:13 in the Bible.

The Translation

The first revelation of the JST was what we now have as Moses 1. It is the preface to the book of Genesis. It begins the earliest manuscript of the New Translation, designated Old Testament Manuscript 1 (OT1).[3] Serving as scribes for what is now in the Book of Moses were:

Oliver Cowdery	Moses 1:1–5:43	Beginning June 1830
John Whitmer	Moses 5:43–6:18	October 21, November 30, 1830
Emma Smith	Moses 6:19–52	December 1, 1830
John Whitmer	Moses 6:52–7:1	December 1830
Sidney Rigdon	Moses 7:2–8:30	December 1830, February 1831

Dictating the text of the New Translation to these scribes, the Prophet progressed to Genesis 24:41, when he set aside Genesis to begin translating the New Testament as he was instructed by the Lord on March 7, 1831 (see D&C 45:60–62). He and his scribes worked on the New Testament until it was finished in July 1832, when they returned to work on the Old Testament.[4]

A second Old Testament manuscript, designated Old Testament Manuscript 2 (OT2), started as a copy of the first manuscript (OT1). John Whitmer had made the copy in March 1831 while Joseph Smith was working on the New Testament with Sidney Rigdon. After OT2 was started, it became the manuscript of the continuing translation through the rest of the Old Testament. The earlier manuscript (OT1) remained essentially unused, as a backup copy. The translation of the Old Testament began anew in July 1832 and continued for about a year. At the end of the Old Testament manuscript, after the book of Malachi, the following words are written in large letters: "Finished on the 2d day of July 1833" (OT2, p. 119). That same day the Prophet wrote to Church members in Missouri and told them, "We this day finished the translating of the Scriptures for which we returned gratitude to our heavenly father."[5]

During the course of the Prophet's work with the Bible, changes were made in about thirteen hundred Old Testament verses and in about twenty-one hundred verses in the New Testament.[6] Most of the changes are rewordings of the existing King James Version. But other changes involve the addition of new material—in some cases substantial amounts. Presumably, every book in the Bible was examined, but no changes were made in fifteen of them (Ruth, Ezra, Esther, Ecclesiastes, Song of Solomon, Lamentations, Obadiah, Micah, Nahum, Habakkuk, Zephaniah, Haggai, Malachi, 2 John, and 3 John). The books with no corrections are identified on the manuscripts with brief notations like "Micah—Correct" (OT2, p. 118). Ecclesiastes is the only book not mentioned at all. Regarding another book, the manuscript notes, "The Songs of Solomon are not Inspired writings" (OT2, p. 97).

Most passages in the New Translation were revealed in clarity the first time and show little need for later refining. But some passages show that the Prophet struggled with the wording until he was satisfied it was acceptable to the Lord. His careful effort was in harmony with the instruction he had received previously that we should "study it out in [our] mind" as we listen to the Spirit and apply our best efforts, after which a confirmation will come if it is correct (D&C 9:8; see also D&C 9:7–9).

On many of the manuscript pages, there are revisions that were made some months after the original dictation, when the Prophet went through parts of the Bible again to add words to the text or revise existing wording.[7] Some of these changes simply correct errors in the original recording, such as when his eyes skipped words while he was dictating or when his scribe recorded words incorrectly. But some insertions revise the writing or add words or phrases to produce new meanings not recorded in the original dictation. Many important revisions were made to the Book of Moses in this process. Joseph Smith called this second pass through the text the "reviewing." He finished the reviewing of the New Testament in February 1833, and he probably finished all, or virtually all, of his work on the text of the Old Testament that summer.[8]

Was the translation finished? The best answer is yes, but this requires some explanation. The Bible, even in its purest and fullest form, never contained the complete records of those who are mentioned in it. The book of Genesis, for example, was a revelation to Moses that provided mere summaries of important lives and events. Certainly there are other truths from ancient times that *could have been* revealed in the New Translation and other additions that *could have been* inserted to make it more complete. But from July 1833 on, the contemporary sources show that Joseph Smith considered it finished. He no longer spoke of translating the Bible but of printing it,[9] which he wanted and intended to accomplish "as soon as possible."[10] He sought to find the means to publish it as a book, and he and other Church leaders encouraged the Saints to donate money for the project. Excerpts were printed in the Church's newspapers and elsewhere, so some sections of it were available for the early Saints.[11] But because of poverty, continuing persecutions and relocations, and the other priorities of members of the Church, when the Prophet was martyred in 1844, he had not seen the realization of his desire to have the entire New Translation appear in print.

In the decades after Joseph Smith's death, Latter-day Saints in Utah lacked access to the manuscripts of the New Translation and had only limited knowledge about how it was produced. None of the participants in the translation process were with the Church when the Saints moved west in 1846.[12] This and related circumstances resulted in many misconceptions about it that eventually made their way into our culture. Among those misconceptions are the beliefs that the Prophet did not finish the translation and that it was not intended to be published. Careful research by BYU professor Robert J. Matthews shows that these ideas are refuted in Joseph Smith's own words.[13] But was the New Translation ready to go to the printer the day Joseph Smith died? The manuscripts show that after the translation was completed, much work was done to get it ready for printing. Joseph Smith or his assistants went through the text and inserted punctuation and verse breaks and corrected the capitalization. By today's standards, we might say that more work was needed to make the punctuation and spelling more consistent, and a few of the Prophet's changes to the text had resulted in uneven wording that had not yet been smoothed out. But the translation was finished, and there is every indication that the Prophet believed that the text was ready to go to press. Perhaps he felt that any remaining refinements would be worked out during the typesetting and proofing.

Types of Changes

Joseph Smith had the authority to make changes in the Bible as God directed. In one revelation, he is called "a seer, a revelator, a translator" (D&C 107:92), and in several other Doctrine and Covenants passages, his work with the translation is endorsed by the Lord (see D&C 35:20; 43:12–13; 73:3–4; 90:13; 93:53; 94:10). The Prophet called his Bible revision a "translation," though it did not involve creating a new rendering from Hebrew or Greek manuscripts. He never claimed to have consulted any text other than his English Bible for the translation, but he "translated" it in the sense of conveying it in a new form.

It appears that several different kinds of changes were involved in the process, but it is difficult to know with certainty the nature or origin of any particular change. I propose the following categories of revisions:

1. Restoration of original text. Because Nephi tells us that "many plain and precious things" would be "taken away" from the Bible (1 Nephi 13:28), we can be certain that the JST includes the restoration of content that was once in original manuscripts. To Moses, the Lord foretold the removal of material from his record and its restoration in the latter days: "Thou shalt write the things which I shall speak. And in a day when the children of men shall esteem my words as naught and take many of them from the book which thou shalt write, behold, I will raise up another like unto thee; and they shall be had again among the children of men—among as many as shall believe" (Moses 1:40–41). Joseph Smith was the man like Moses whom the Lord raised up to restore lost material from the writings of Moses, as well as lost material from the words of other Bible writers. But Joseph Smith did not restore the very words of lost texts because they were in Hebrew or Greek (or other ancient languages) and because the New Translation was to be in English. Thus, his translation, in the English idiom of his own day, would restore the meaning and the message of original passages but not necessarily the words and the literary trappings that accompanied them when they were first put to writing. This is why the work can be called a "translation." Parts of the Book of Moses—including Moses's vision in chapter 1 and Enoch's visions in chapters 6 and 7—have no counterparts in the Bible. It is likely that those passages are restoration of material that was once in ancient manuscripts.

2. Restoration of what was once said or done but was never in the Bible. Joseph Smith stated, "From what we can draw from the scriptures relative to the teachings of heaven we are induced to think, that much instruction has been given to man since the beginning which we have not."[14] Perhaps the New Translation includes teachings or events in the ministries of prophets, apostles, or Jesus Himself that were never recorded anciently. It may include material of which the biblical writers were unaware, which they chose not to include, or which they neglected to include (see 3 Nephi 23:6–13).

3. Editing to make the Bible more understandable for modern readers. Many of the individual New Translation changes fall into this category. There are numerous instances in which the Prophet rearranged word order to make a text read more easily or modernized its language. Examples of modernization of language include the many changes from *wot* to *know*,[15] from *an* to *a* before words that begin with *h,* from *saith* to *said,* from *that* and *which* to *who,* and from *ye* and *thee* to *you.*[16] In many instances, Joseph Smith added short expansions to make the text less ambiguous. For example, there are several places where the word *he* is replaced by a personal name, thus making the meaning more clear, as in Genesis 14:20 (KJV "And he gave" = JST "And Abram gave"), and in Genesis 18:32 (KJV "And he said. . . . And he said" = JST "And Abraham said. . . . And the Lord said").

4. Editing to bring biblical wording into harmony with truth found in other revelations or elsewhere in the Bible. Joseph Smith said, "[There are] many things in the Bible which do not, as they now stand, accord with the revelation of the Holy Ghost to me."[17] Where there were inaccuracies in the Bible, regardless of their source, it was well within the scope of the Prophet's calling to change what needed to be changed. Where modern revelation had given a clearer view of a doctrine preserved less adequately in the Bible, it was appropriate for Joseph Smith to add a correction—whether or not that correction reflects what was on ancient manuscripts. The Prophet also had authority to make changes when a passage was inconsistent with information elsewhere in the Bible itself. Perhaps the following example will illustrate this kind of correction: The Gospel of John records the statement, "No man hath seen God at any time" (John 1:18), which contradicts the experience of Joseph Smith (Joseph Smith—History 1:17–20) as well as several examples in the Bible itself of prophets seeing God (e.g., Exodus 24:9–11; 33:11; Numbers 12:6–8; Isaiah 6:1; Amos 9:1). The JST change at John 1:18 clarifies the text and makes it consistent with what we know from other revealed sources.

Later History

When Joseph Smith died, the manuscripts of the New Translation were not in the possession of the Church but of his family, who remained in Illinois when the leaders of the Church and the majority of the Saints moved to the West. In 1867, the Reorganized Church of Jesus Christ of Latter Day Saints (RLDS) published the New Translation under the title *The Holy Scriptures, Translated and Corrected by the Spirit of Revelation, By Joseph Smith, Jr., the Seer.* The name *Inspired Version,* by which it is commonly known, was added in an edition of 1936, but it is not inappropriate to refer to it by that name in earlier contexts. The RLDS publication committee undertook substantial editing for punctuation and spelling.[18]

In 1851, Elder Franklin D. Richards of the Quorum of the Twelve Apostles was serving as president of the British mission in Liverpool. Sensing a need to make available for the British Saints some of Joseph Smith's revelations that had been published already in America, he compiled a mission pamphlet entitled *The Pearl of Great Price.*[19] His intent was that his "little collection of precious truths" would "increase [the Saints'] ability to maintain and to defend the holy faith."[20] In it he included, among other important texts, excerpts from the Prophet's New Translation of the Bible that had been published already in Church periodicals and elsewhere: the first five and one-half chapters of Genesis and Matthew 24. Elder Richards did not have access to the original manuscripts of the New Translation, and the RLDS *Inspired Version* had not yet been published. For the Genesis chapters, he took the text primarily from excerpts that had been published in Church newspapers in the 1830s and 1840s. But those excerpts had come from OT1 and did not include Joseph Smith's final revisions that were recorded on OT2. The Genesis material was in two sections: "Extracts from the Prophecy of Enoch" (Moses 6:43–7:69) and "The Words of God, which He Spake unto Moses" (Moses 1:1–5, 16, 19–40; 8:13–30).[21]

In the late 1870s, the decision was made to prepare the Pearl of Great Price for Churchwide distribution at Church headquarters in Salt Lake City. Elder Orson Pratt of the Quorum of the Twelve Apostles was assigned to prepare the edition, which was published in 1878. Knowing that Joseph Smith had made later corrections to the New Translation, Elder Pratt drew the Genesis chapters not from the original Liverpool *Pearl of Great Price* but from the printed RLDS *Inspired Version,* which he copied exactly for the Book of Moses. Again, the material was in two sections, this time called "Visions of Moses" (Moses 1) and "Writings of Moses" (Moses 2–8).

The Genesis text in the 1867 *Inspired Version,* though more accurate than the Liverpool version of 1851, was not always consistent with Joseph Smith's intentions. The RLDS publication committee apparently did not understand the relationship between OT1 and OT2 and excluded a significant number of the Prophet's corrections from the *Inspired Version.* As a result, our Book of Moses today still lacks important corrections that were made by Joseph Smith.[22]

In the October 1880 general conference, the new Pearl of Great Price was presented to the assembled membership for a sustaining vote and was canonized as scripture and accepted as binding on the Church. Since then, the

Pearl of Great Price has been one of the standard works, and the few chapters of the Joseph Smith Translation in it (the Book of Moses and Joseph Smith—Matthew) have been recognized not only as divine revelation—which they always were—but also as integral parts of our scripture and doctrine.

Later editions of the Pearl of Great Price made changes to the Genesis material to make the Book of Moses as it is today. The 1902 edition was the first to use the name "The Book of Moses," and it was the first to add chapters, verses, and cross-reference footnotes. Revisions were made in the text, but the Church did not have the original manuscripts to guide the process. The 1921 edition was the first to be printed in double-column pages. The current name, "Selections from the Book of Moses," was added in the edition of 1981. This name acknowledges that the Pearl of Great Price does not contain all of Moses's record.

Because the Saints in Utah knew little about the Joseph Smith Translation and did not have access to its original manuscripts, for many years the translation was not widely used within the Church, except for the excerpts that are part of the Pearl of Great Price. During the 1960s and 1970s, Professor Robert Matthews conducted exhaustive research on the manuscripts.[23] His study confirmed the general integrity of the printed *Inspired Version* and taught us many things about the New Translation and how it was produced.[24] In the process, Professor Matthews brought the JST to the attention of members of the Church.[25]

In 1979, when the Church published a Latter-day Saint edition of the Bible in the English language, it included generous amounts of material from the New Translation in footnotes and in an appendix. In subsequent years, JST excerpts were included in the "Guide to the Scriptures," a combination concordance–Bible dictionary published with the LDS scriptures in languages other than English. And in 2004, the Religious Studies Center at Brigham Young University published a typographic transcription of all the original manuscript pages, complete with original spelling, cross-outs, and insertions.[26] A significant aspect of these publications is the fact that they have made the JST accessible to an extent that it never had been before. Now General Authorities, curriculum writers, scholars, and students can draw freely from it in their research and writing, bringing the JST to its rightful place alongside the other great revelations of the Prophet Joseph Smith. Latter-day Saints know that Joseph Smith was appointed by God to provide a corrected translation of the Bible (see D&C 76:15). God endorsed it in strong language: "And the scriptures shall be given, even as they are in mine own bosom, to the salvation of mine own elect" (D&C 35:20). The New Translation is, as Elder Dallin H. Oaks of the Quorum of the Twelve Apostles observed, "a member of the royal family of scripture" that "should be noticed and honored on any occasion when it is present."[27]

Notes

1. See Scott H. Faulring, Kent P. Jackson, and Robert J. Matthews, eds., *Joseph Smith's New Translation of the Bible: Original Manuscripts* (Provo, UT: Religious Studies Center, Brigham Young University, 2004); Kent P. Jackson, *The Book of Moses and the Joseph Smith Translation Manuscripts* (Provo, UT: Religious Studies Center, Brigham Young University, 2005). In 1975 Robert J. Matthews published *"A Plainer Translation": Joseph Smith's Translation of the Bible—A History and Commentary* (Provo, UT: Brigham Young University Press, 1975). These newer studies have clarified many matters discussed in Matthews's book, including scribal identifications, dates, and the process of the Prophet's work.
2. See Doctrine and Covenants 124:89; *Times and Seasons* 1, no. 9 (July 1840): 140; Joseph Smith, *History of the Church of Jesus Christ of Latter-day Saints*, ed. B. H. Roberts, 2nd ed. rev. (Salt Lake City: Deseret Book, 1957), 1:341, 365; 4:164.
3. The original JST manuscripts are located in the Library-Archives of the Community of Christ in Independence, Missouri. Note that in Matthews's *"A Plainer Translation"* and other early publications, an old archival numbering system was used for the manuscripts, resulting from an early misunderstanding of the order in which the manuscripts were written. OT1 was previously designated OT2, and OT2 was previously designated OT3. Matthews was the first to question the accuracy of the numbering system (see Matthews, *"A Plainer Translation,"* 67–72; Richard P. Howard, *Restoration Scriptures: A Study of Their Textual Development,* rev. and enl. [Independence, MO: Herald, 1995], 63n1).
4. In a letter dated July 31, 1832, the Prophet stated, "We have finished the translation of the New testament . . . , we are making rapid strides in the old book [Old Testament] and in the strength of God we can do all things according to his will" (Joseph Smith to W. W. Phelps, July 31, 1832, Joseph Smith Collection, Church History Library, Salt Lake City; published in Dean C. Jessee, ed., *The Personal Writings of Joseph Smith*, rev. ed. [Salt Lake City: Deseret Book, 2002], 274).

5. Sidney Rigdon, Joseph Smith, and Frederick G. Williams to the Brethren in Zion, July 2, 1833, Joseph Smith Collection, Church History Library; published in Joseph Smith, *History of the Church*, 1:368.
6. Matthews, *"A Plainer Translation,"* 425.
7. Some of these insertions required more room than was available between the lines of the text and were written on small pieces of paper and attached in place with straight pins—the nineteenth-century equivalent of paper clips or staples.
8. "This day completed the translation and the reviewing of the New Testament" (Kirtland High Council Minute Book, February 2, 1833, 8, Church History Library; published in Joseph Smith, *History of the Church*, 1:324).
9. The evidence is collected in Matthews, "Joseph Smith's Efforts to Publish His Bible Translation," *Ensign*, January 1983, 57–64; see also Matthews, *"A Plainer Translation,"* 40–48, 52–53.
10. "You will see by these revelations that we have to print the new translation here at kirtland for which we will prepare as soon as possible" (Joseph Smith, Sidney Rigdon, and Frederick G. Williams to Edward Partridge, August 6, 1833, Joseph Smith Collection, Church History Library).
11. *The Evening and the Morning Star* 1, no. 3 (August 1832): 2–3 (Moses 7); 1, no. 10 (March 1833): 1 (Moses 6:43–68); 1, no. 11 (April 1833): 1 (Moses 5:1–16); 1, no. 11 (April 1833): 1–2 (Moses 8:13–30); *Doctrine and Covenants of the Church of the Latter Day Saints* (Kirtland, OH: F. G. Williams and Co., 1835), "Lecture First," 5 (Heb. 11:1); "Lecture Second," 13–18 (Moses 2:26–29; 3:15–17, 19–20; 4:14–19, 22–25; 5:1, 4–9, 19–23, 32–40); *Times and Seasons* 4, no. 5 (January 16, 1843): 71–73 (Moses 1); Peter Crawley, *A Descriptive Bibliography of the Mormon Church, Volume One, 1830–1847* (Provo, UT: Religious Studies Center, Brigham Young University, 1997), 60–61 (Matthew 24).
12. Joseph Smith (died 1844), Oliver Cowdery (excommunicated 1838), John Whitmer (excommunicated 1838), Emma Smith (did not go west), Sidney Rigdon (excommunicated 1844), Jesse Gause (excommunicated 1832), and Frederick G. Williams (excommunicated 1839, died 1842).
13. See Matthews, "Joseph Smith's Efforts."
14. *The Evening and the Morning Star* 2, no. 18 (March 1834): 143.
15. The manuscript at Exodus 32:1 revises *wot* to *know* with a note that *know* "should be in the place of 'wot' in all places."
16. These changes are not universally consistent in the manuscripts.
17. Andrew F. Ehat and Lyndon W. Cook, eds., *The Words of Joseph Smith: The Contemporary Accounts of the Nauvoo Discourses of the Prophet Joseph* (Provo, UT:

Religious Studies Center, Brigham Young University, 1980), 211; spelling and capitalization modernized.

18. See Jackson, *Book of Moses,* 20–33.
19. *The Pearl of Great Price: Being a Choice Selection from the Revelations, Translations, and Narrations of Joseph Smith, First Prophet, Seer, and Revelator to the Church of Jesus Christ of Latter-day Saints* (Liverpool: F. D. Richards, 1851).
20. Preface, 1851 *Pearl of Great Price,* page [v].
21. See Jackson, *Book of Moses,* 18–20.
22. Some of these are noted in Matthews, *"A Plainer Translation,"* 145–61. For a full discussion, see Jackson, *Book of Moses,* 20–36.
23. Robert J. Matthews, "A Study of the Doctrinal Significance of Certain Textual Changes Made by the Prophet Joseph Smith in the Four Gospels of the Inspired Version of the New Testament" (master's thesis, Brigham Young University, 1960), and "A Study of the Text of the Inspired Revision of the Bible" (PhD dissertation, Brigham Young University, 1968). *"A Plainer Translation"* was published in 1975.
24. See Matthews, *"A Plainer Translation,"* 141–61.
25. See Thomas E. Sherry, "Changing Attitudes Toward Joseph Smith's Translation of the Bible," in *Plain and Precious Truths Restored: The Doctrinal and Historical Significance of the Joseph Smith Translation,* ed. Robert L. Millet and Robert J. Matthews (Salt Lake City: Bookcraft, 1995), 187–226.
26. Faulring, Jackson, and Matthews, *Joseph Smith's New Translation of the Bible: Original Manuscripts.*
27. Dallin H. Oaks, "Scripture Reading, Revelation, and Joseph Smith's Translation of the Bible," in Millet and Matthews, eds., *Plain and Precious Truths Restored,* 13.

Stuart P. Heimdal, *Abraham in Pharaoh's Court*

Encircling Astronomy and the Egyptians: An Approach to Abraham 3

Kerry Muhlestein

Kerry Muhlestein *is an assistant professor of ancient scripture at BYU.*

> I have long held the view that the universe is built upon symbols, whereby one thing bespeaks another; the lesser testifying of the greater, lifting our thoughts from man to God, from earth to heaven, from time to eternity. . . . God teaches with symbols; it is his favorite method of teaching.
>
> —Orson F. Whitney[1]

Abraham 3 is one of the most enigmatic sections of the Pearl of Great Price. Teacher and student together sense there is something more to the text than the meaning they are drawing out of it. Each thorough exploration gently nudges another layer of understanding from the text, but we always feel we have unraveled only the smallest portion of what it has to offer. Though I do not pretend to have a great key to unlock this revelation, I believe there are some apperceptive principles that cast light on Abraham's night vision.

Certainly teachers can take a variety of approaches when teaching Abraham 3. Most students will be curious about the exotic names provided in verses 3 and 13, and it is worth time to address these questions.[2] Investigations into the Egyptians' astronomical abilities and how Abraham may have contributed to these abilities are also worthwhile. Undoubtedly, the Egyptians of Abraham's day conceived of a geocentric cosmos with particular emphasis on that "which the sun encircles (*šnnt ỉtn*),"[3] denoting the earth. In many aspects, Abraham's vision appears to be geocentric.[4] Yet Abraham also gains a "Kolob-centric" view of the universe.[5] However, some aspects of Egyptian astronomical thought are not "centric" at all. It is even possible that the vision fits no known astronomic approach because the Lord may have shown Abraham a model not yet understood by modern astronomers. However, I think we stumble when we attempt to understand Abraham's vision in terms of astronomic paradigms.[6] It is quite likely that the Lord was describing astronomy and the heavens allegorically in order to teach doctrinal, not astronomical, principles. While attempting to understand astronomical principles has merit (though inconclusive attempts have certainly been used against us[7]), and while there may be an understandable cosmic paradigm to be teased out of the narrative, it seems that the allegorical teachings are the weightier matters as far as the gospel classroom is concerned.

Abraham was no beginner in astronomy. He tells us he has the records of the fathers and these records contain "a knowledge of the beginning of the creation, and also of the planets, and of the stars, as they were made known unto the fathers"; Abraham continues by making it clear that the information he records is "for the benefit of [his] posterity" (Abraham 1:31). As such, we must not only ask ourselves what the knowledge provided in Abraham 3 meant to those in Abraham's time, but also what he meant for us, his latter-day posterity, to derive from it. This requires both an intensive investigation into Abraham's era and into the ramifications of the vision for our day.

It is interesting to note that Abraham appears to have two distinct visions, one via the Urim and Thummim and recorded in the first part of chapter 3, and the second as he speaks with the Lord face to face, beginning somewhere between verses 10 and 12 (it is unclear when Abraham goes from hearing the Lord via the Urim and Thummim to talking with Him face to face). In fact, the first part of the chapter may not have been a vision but may have consisted of Abraham viewing the stars with his naked eye and conversing with the Lord about what he saw by means of the Urim and Thummim.[8] The second part is surely a vision. In each of these visions, Abraham sees something of the cosmic system, which the Lord then uses apperceptively to teach doctrinal principles.[9] In both visions, the principles taught are similar, but the first vision seems to discuss these principles on a more general level, and the second on a more specific level. To elucidate the lessons the Lord is teaching Abraham—and teaching us through Abraham—we must first ask some questions.

Purposes of Astronomy

To understand the symbols the Lord is using in this revelation to Abraham, we must ask ourselves, why is the Lord talking to Abraham about the stars? While the Lord often teaches His prophets about the heavens, He does not always teach the same thing in each encounter. For example, when Moses learns of God's many creations, it is to help him understand the vastness of God's great work and mankind's centrality to that work (see Moses 1:32–39). While we do not know what Joseph Smith learned about the heavens from God, it is clear he learned something that helped him understand the degrees of glory to which mankind is headed (see D&C 76:70–71, 96–98). But why was Abraham shown a vision of the stars and planets? What was the point?

The Lord Himself partially answers this question: "Abraham, I show these things unto thee before ye go into Egypt, that ye may declare all these words" (Abraham 3:15). What words did the Lord want Abraham to declare? If the Lord is referring to the words He uses to describe the rotations of Kolob, the earth, the moon, and other celestial bodies, it is possible the Lord simply wanted Abraham to teach the Egyptians astronomy. The Genesis account of Abraham's visit to Egypt emphasizes that Abraham was enriched there (see Genesis 13:2). Perhaps the Lord used Abraham's astronomic awareness to introduce him to Pharaoh's court, where he would be made wealthy and thus return to the promised land in a position of power. However, the phrase "all these words" indicates that Abraham was to teach not only astronomy but also gospel principles the Lord explained through astronomic means.

Egyptian Symbols

If this is the case, why did the Lord choose astronomy as the symbolic medium of His message? Why subscribe to this set of symbols? Of course, the Lord has not given us a direct answer to this question, yet there are some things we can reason out with a certain degree of confidence. While this is not the place for a detailed investigation into Egyptian astronomy, some ideas are worth highlighting so we may understand the magnitude of the symbolic language Abraham was to employ in Egypt.

It is indisputable that the Egyptians set significance to the movements and domains of celestial bodies. For instance, after the annual disappearance of Sirius (*Sopdet*), the Egyptians knew that the rerising of the Dog Star generally coincided with the annual flood of the Nile. The flood of the Nile was a type of rebirth, and thus the rebirth of the star was a harbinger of the rebirth that Egypt experienced each year. Sirius was also believed to serve as a guide to the deceased as they journeyed through the stars.[10]

The Egyptians designated Sirius as one of thirty-six stars known as *decans* because of the heliacal role they played in a complex calendar system in which one decan replaced another every ten days. Our knowledge of this system stems from astronomic paintings on a series of coffins from just before Abraham's time. These paintings make it clear that in Abraham's day the Egyptians placed significance on the movement of the stars.[11] This is further reflected in one of the long-standing titles of the head priest of Heliopolis (biblical On), who was known as the chief observer.

Many planets and stars played a particularly important role in Egyptian culture. Their gods were believed to have left the earth to reside in the sky;[12] the moon was associated with the god Thoth, the sun with Ra, and Orion with the god Osiris. Of particular import to the king, who was associated with Horus, were the planets Jupiter, Saturn, and Mars, which were also associated with Horus. Moreover the king would have paid particular attention to what Abraham had to say about the "greater light which is set to rule the day" (Abraham 3:6) because the king was integrally tied to Ra, the sun, and its journey.[13]

Information about the stars was also important to the king. Stars such as Gemini and Deneb were seen as significant markers in the known course of the sun through the stars. One of the most prolific of early kingship images was the belief that the king was destined to become one of the circumpolar stars (the *i͗ḫmw-sk*, the stars "that did not know destruction" because they did not disappear).[14] In the afterlife the king could also become Sirius.[15] Additionally, Sirius was seen as his sister,[16] which may be explained by references in which Sirius is also identified with Isis[17] (whereas the dead king is Osiris). Furthermore, Sirius was associated with the king's daughter[18] and the king's father.[19] Orion was described both as the king[20] and as the king's brother,[21] and Venus as his daughter[22] and his guide.[23] Amenemhet III, a likely contemporary of Abraham, wrote on the top of his pyramid that he was "higher than the heights of Orion."[24]

These few references amply illustrate the point: the Egyptian king and his court were aware of and keenly interested in the movements of the sun, moon, planets, and stars. In our era of large cities and electric lights, it is hard to picture how much these celestial bodies were part of Egyptian life. Most students do not regularly see starry nights because of light pollution.

The natural nocturnal luminaries were particularly striking in Egypt, where most nights were cloudless and very clear. The lustrous bodies of the night sky were overlarge; they dominated the night landscape and forced their way into the minds and visions of every Egyptian soul. They were a much greater and pressing presence for these ancient inhabitants than most of us would naturally assume. Because of this powerful, intrusive sight, the stars spoke loudly to the Egyptians, whether they wanted them to or not. Their movements and power were an inescapable noise raining upon the eyes of our ancient counterparts.

In my estimation, this is why Abraham would find the language of the stars to be a meaningful mode of communication with the Egyptians. In modern missionary parlance, astronomy enabled Abraham to build on common ground, and his expertise in this area helped him build a relationship of trust. If the Lord wanted to find ground that was both common and persuasive as a vehicle for teaching Pharaoh and his people about the gospel, astronomy was an effective choice not only because the Egyptians would be interested, nor solely because they were accustomed to celestial bodies carrying symbolic teachings, but also because the movements and principles of the stars and planets lend themselves to a powerful message.

Essentially the Lord was teaching Abraham and the Egyptians by symbolism as He so often does. As we recognize and understand these symbols, we not only unlock information regarding this specific revelation to Abraham, but we also become more familiar with the language of symbolism. Working through *these* symbols equips our students to work through *others* on their own; it should help students develop both scriptural abilities and confidence in those abilities.

There is another lesson to be learned. When we see the pains to which the Lord goes to help one of His greatest prophets be prepared to share the gospel among a strange people, we realize how important this is to Him. In recording this experience for his posterity, Abraham emphasizes to us how much the Lord wants him to be prepared to keep the charge within the Abrahamic covenant to make the Lord's name known throughout the earth. Here we see Abraham going through the Lord's missionary training center; he is motivated to share the gospel, and he is equipped with both a message and tools (such as building on common ground) as he shares that message.

Governing Points of the Universe

To elucidate the principles taught by this astronomical message, I have created concentric circle models as visual aids (though we do not know if the Egyptians employed the idea of concentric circles at this time). Creating these models forces one to ask whether the governing body should be drawn at the center or as the outermost sphere. A good case can be made for both models. As noted, astronomy at the time was viewed geocentrically. This would put the earth at the center of the model with the greater bodies in the outer orbits. This model would have been particularly meaningful to the Egyptians. With our modern astronomical viewpoint, we tend to think of the center as the point of control or governance. The sun is the center of our solar system, governing the system by its gravitational pull. The sun is revolving around a central gravitational point in our galaxy (likely a black hole), and even the galaxies are revolving around a central gravitational pull in our supercluster of galaxies.[25] And yet, in the Lord's analogy given to the Egyptians through Abraham, if the earth is at the center, then it is not the central point that governs, but the outermost point that encircles all else. This is aligned with Egyptian thinking in many respects, though it seems contrary to a geocentric point of view. For the Egyptians, encircling something was a powerful symbol of controlling or ruling over it, often including an element of protecting what was encircled. Power over creation was shown by Ra, who encircled the earth. The deceased wished to have such power by "going about (*dbn*) the two heavens, encircling (*pẖr*) the two lands."[26] The deceased king is pictured as more powerful than even the gods by describing him as one who has "encircled (*šn.n=k*) every god in your arms, their lands and all their possessions. O King, you are great, you are wrapped around (*dbn*) like the circle which encircles (*pẖr*) the great rulers."[27] In Egyptian thought, it is that which encircles that controls, not that which is in the center. Thus in a geocentric model, the vision given Abraham places God at the outer orbits.

On the other hand, there is some evidence that we would do best to draw Kolob, or the governing point, at the center of our model. Michael Rhodes has suggested an etymology for Kolob as coming from the "Semitic root *QLB*, which has the basic meaning of 'heart, center, middle.'"[28] This is corroborated by Joseph Smith's explanation of the center figure of the hypocephalus in facsimile 2 as Kolob. These ideas indicate a model with Kolob at the center. The central point of any model is completely a matter of perspective. The earth orbits the sun, but from our perspective it appears that the sun circles the earth.

Because Pharaoh already conceived of the sun circling the earth and other significant bodies moving in cyclical journeys around the earth and sun, he would have easily understood the concept that heavenly orbs revolved around each other in concentric circles. Thus the information given to Abraham in verses 3 through 7 would have made perfect sense. For each known orb there was another above it until the governing body was reached. Pharaoh could easily picture a cosmos which looked thus:

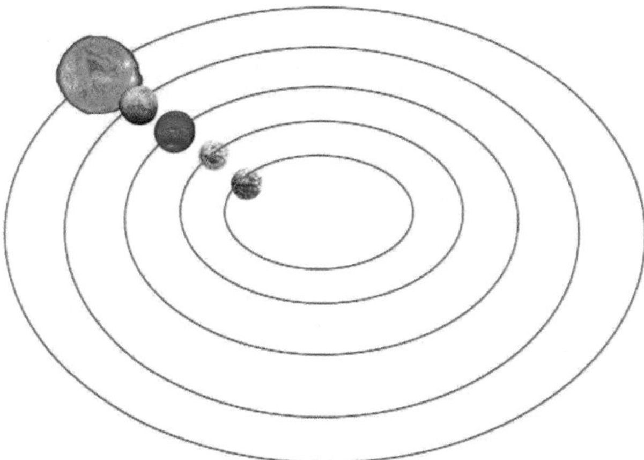

Fig. 1. Pharaoh's concept of cosmos

In the end, we cannot know which way Abraham or the Egyptians would have drawn their models, with the governing point at the center or as the body which encircles all else. I have chosen to make my illustrations with the governing point at the center because it is the most intuitive model. For us, saying that God is at the center means He is the focal, governing point, and pedagogically this is preferable. Thus for our purposes, the cosmos Abraham was explaining could look like Figure. 2.

This picture of the cosmos helps us visualize what Abraham was teaching Pharaoh. The crucial information came in verses 8 and 9: "And where these two facts exist, there shall be another fact above them, that is, there shall be another planet whose reckoning of time shall be longer still; and thus there shall be the reckoning of the time of one planet above another, until thou come nigh unto Kolob, which Kolob is after the reckoning of the Lord's time;

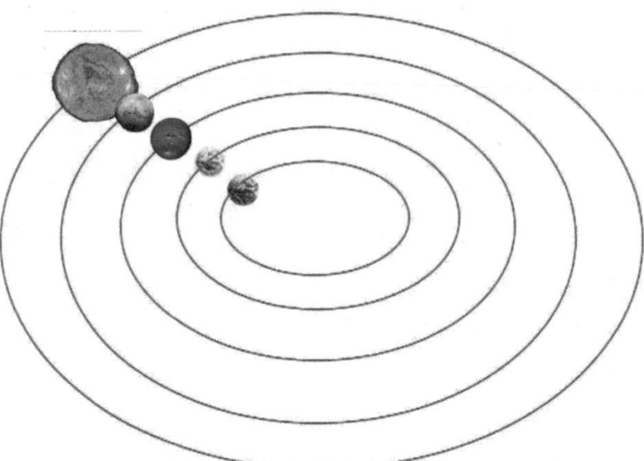

Fig. 2. Abraham's concept of cosmos

which Kolob is set nigh unto the throne of God, to govern all those planets which belong to the same order as that upon which thou standest." Here the concept of orbiting planets and their governing times was used as apperception to explain that a being—not a planet—was the governing source. This would give the glorious Egyptian king something to think about.

He would have clearly understood that there were many rulers upon the earth and that they possessed differing magnitudes of power. For example, the Egyptians knew of a Canaanite ruler in Jerusalem but considered him subservient to Egypt, and thus he would have been considered to be on one of the lesser orbits of rulers. Pharaoh probably also knew of Mesopotamian

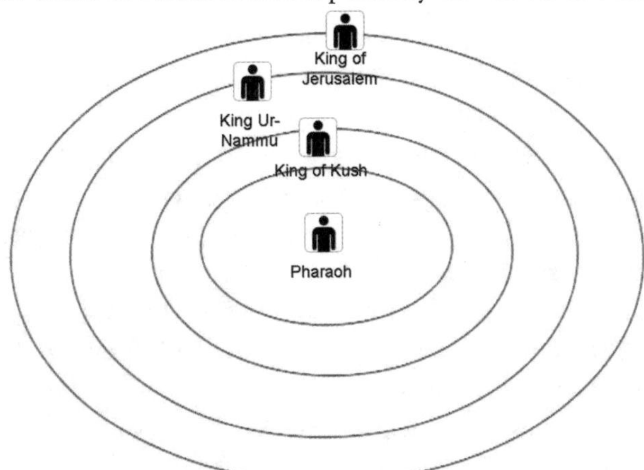

Fig. 3. Pharaoh-centered universe

kings, perhaps King Ur-Nammu of the city of Ur. This leader would likely have been viewed as occupying an orbit closer to the Egyptian ruler. The Nubian kingdom of Kush had become powerful by this time, but again the Egyptians dominated this group. The probability is great that the Egyptian king considered himself to be the body that governed the orbits of leadership, the great centrifugal power controlling earthly leaders.

What would have been startling, yet logical, was the reasoning that if there were two facts, one was higher than another and there must be yet another higher still (see v. 8). Thus, if Pharaoh was above the king of Kush, it stood to reason that someone was above Pharaoh. Abraham's assertion would have been that this series of successions continued, not merely until Pharaoh was reached but until God was reached. The paradigm presented to Pharaoh was that he was not the most high ruler after all.

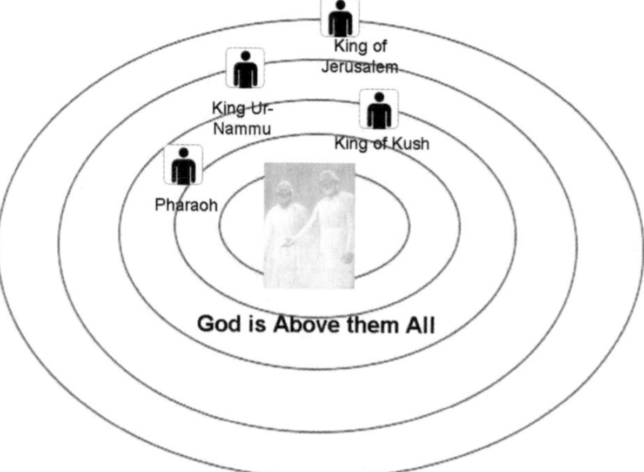

Fig. 4. Universe governed by higher powers

The teaching of astronomy would have gotten the king's attention. The principles of government apperceptively taught would have made sense. This allowed Abraham to teach that mankind must fear God, not man (even a man considered semidivine). But the lesson did not necessarily stop there. These concentric circles of governance and order could also be used to teach of the organization of the kingdom of God on earth, which in Abraham's day operated under the patriarchal order. Thus we, Abraham, and Pharaoh understand that we follow the orbits of governance from ourselves to our parents, grandparents, and so forth, until the person who reports to God is reached, and thus we again find God as the focal, governing point.

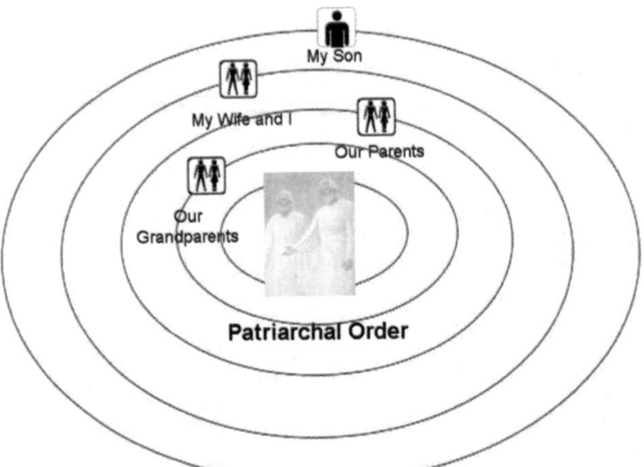

Fig. 5. Patriarchal order

Incidentally, this can be used to understand current Church government as well, demonstrating that the symbolism in Abraham 3 speaks not only to Abraham's generation but to ours as well.

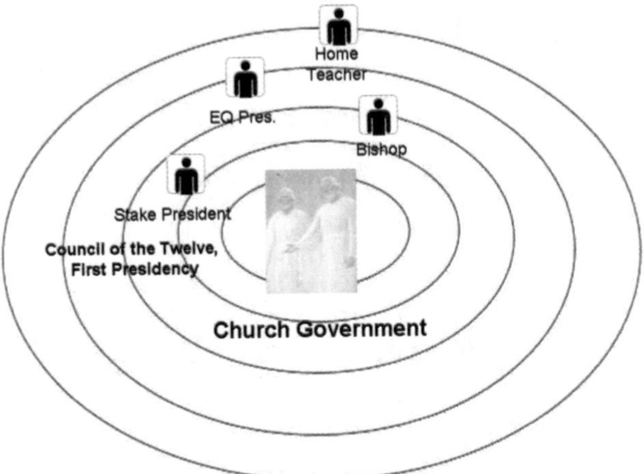

Fig. 6. Church government

This God-centered view of the universe teaches Abraham, the Egyptians, and us another powerful message. Even within a gospel context it is easy to focus on various principles without tying them in to the great center, God. For example, it is easy to discuss modesty, honesty, the Word of Wisdom, or the law of tithing without connecting them to the center of the gospel: God, His Son, and the Atonement. Even such edifying principles as these can be distracting if they are disassociated from that central focus. President Boyd K. Packer described the Atonement as being "the very root of Christian doctrine. You may know much about the gospel as it branches out from there, but if you only know the branches and those branches do not touch that root, if they have been cut free from that truth, there will be no life nor substance nor redemption in them."[29] As Thomas B. Griffith said in a BYU devotional, "If you cannot figure out the link between the topic you are to teach and the Atonement of Christ, you have either not thought about it enough or you shouldn't be talking about it at church."[30] When properly understood, the God-centered vision that Abraham 3 presents us should help us to remember that every aspect of the gospel is governed by its great center: God, His Son, and the Atonement.

The analogies Abraham is able to draw from the heavens increase because God seems to immediately show him an expanded vision of His creations: "And he said unto me: My son, my son (and his hand was stretched out), behold I will show you all these. And he put his hand upon mine eyes, and I saw those things which his hands had made, which were many; and they multiplied before mine eyes, and I could not see the end thereof" (Abraham 3:12). Not only did Abraham see more in the vision, but God also taught him more.

God's Relationship with Abraham and with Us

For example, God expounded on the blessings of the Abrahamic covenant. It is difficult to know how much of the covenant had been established with Abraham at this point. In Genesis 12, just before going to Egypt, Abraham is told that the Lord will make of him a great nation and that the Lord will bless those that bless Abraham and curse those that curse Abraham (see Genesis 12:2–3). These are two of the most important aspects of the Abrahamic covenant.[31] It is tempting to consider the vision that is recorded as Abraham 3 as an extended record of when the Lord brought Abraham "forth abroad, and said, Look now toward heaven, and tell the stars, if thou be able to number them: and he said unto him, So shall thy seed be" (Genesis 15:5), except that in the Genesis account this takes place after the trip to Egypt. Perhaps there is a problem with the chronology of the Genesis account. During this same incident, Abraham makes sacrifices, divides the portions into halves, and walks before them in what is almost certainly symbolic of "cutting a covenant"—a literal translation of the Hebrew phrase—with God. As the sacrifice is accepted, the Lord covenants that Abraham will have a land of promise (see Genesis 15:9–21), another important aspect of the covenant. Yet only later is Abraham told, "I will make my covenant between me and thee," and then has other aspects of the covenant confirmed and his name changed (Genesis 17:2–8).

It is difficult to tell if the covenant was established in stages—as it seems to be with us, who enter the covenant at baptism but more fully partake of it in the marriage covenant—or if it was given wholly at once and then reconfirmed in various ways at various times or if there is a problem with the Genesis text as we have received it.[32] Thus, we cannot be certain at what stage of the covenant Abraham was when he received the vision recorded in Abraham 3, but he at least knew something of it. He also had the covenant's aspect of progeny reconfirmed when, in the midst of supernaturally seeing the stars,[33] God told him, "I will multiply thee, and thy seed after thee, like unto these; and if thou canst count the number of sands, so shall be the number of thy seeds" (Abraham 3:14). It is interesting that in the midst of seeing a vision designed to instruct him as to what he should teach the Egyptians, Abraham is reminded of how the heavens tie into God's covenant with him.

The apperception analogies that God employs in this fuller vision take a step beyond those He had employed in the first. In those explanations God had focused on nondescript entities with God at the center, allowing for organizational and institutional comparisons. In the second vision God applies the same principles to the individual. After showing Abraham the vastness of His creations, He again speaks of the orbiting bodies, that Kolob is the greatest of the stars—significantly, again because it is nearest to Him—and that the moon, the earth, and all the stars coexist with celestial bodies both above and below them in the order of orbits (see Abraham 3:16–17). Yet immediately this is followed by a comparison to spirits, or intelligences, which God makes clear have always existed and always will exist (see Abraham 3:18). All individual beings, like the stars, will find that there is a being less intelligent than they and a being more intelligent than they. The exception is God: "There are two spirits, one being more intelligent than the other; there shall be another more intelligent than they; I am the Lord thy God, I am more intelligent than they all" (Abraham 3:19). This point is similar to that made after Abraham's first vision, except that it focuses more on the universality and simultaneous individuality of the application.

Almost as if to demonstrate this clearly, after this declaration the Lord makes an immediate transition. The very next thing He says is, "The Lord thy

God sent his angel to deliver thee from the hands of the priest of Elkenah" (Abraham 3:20). How curious this insertion is! On the face of it there is no connection between this statement and the grand principles God had just been elaborating. Yet it proves exactly the point of the individuality God is emphasizing. God has just made His greatness clear. Not only is He the Creator of the vast expanse and numberless bodies Abraham has just seen—and not seen, for he "could not see the end thereof" (Abraham 3:12)—but He is all-powerful, for "there is nothing that the Lord thy God shall take in his heart to do but what he will do it" (Abraham 3:17). Finally He emphasized that He is greater than everything else.

I would imagine that seeing the Lord face to face and beholding these vast creations (seemingly more than Moses initially saw in Moses 1) must have been overwhelming and humbling, and I suppose God intended that effect to some degree. Yet God did not leave Abraham at that point. Immediately after helping Abraham realize how small he is, and how immense God is, God also reminds Abraham of their relationship with each other; after all, it was this glorious God who had cared so much about Abraham that He had reached out and saved him. The reminder of the covenant in verse 14 must have done something similar. Abraham is in the midst of seeing the greatness of God's creations, and God reminds him that He intends to make Abraham just as great a creator in the realm of progeny. Abraham here encounters a God that overwhelms him with His magnitude and then reminds him how personal their relationship is and how much God cares for Abraham, demonstrated both in what He has done and what He will do. We must understand that as it was with Abraham, so it is with us. We are dealing with a magnificent yet magnanimous and personal God who will help deliver us from our own difficulties.

Abraham has learned much about God and his relationship with God, but he has also learned about the relationship of every individual with God.

However, there is more. In the model of orbiting spheres, each being is affected by those above it, and in turn affects those below it. While we are ultimately dependent upon God, we are also indubitably intertwined with each other in our approach to God. We cannot come unto God irrespective of our relationships with others. As the Lord said, "Therefore if thou bring thy gift to the altar, and there rememberest that thy brother hath ought against thee; leave there thy gift before the altar, and go thy way; first be reconciled to thy brother, and then come and offer thy gift" (Matthew 5:23–24).

Intelligence in God's Eyes

As we look at God's description of our interrelationships and the clear declaration that some beings are more intelligent than others, students often feel some discomfort. The wording and apperceptive comparison establishes something akin to the Great Chain of Being.[34] Clearly a hierarchy is a part of this description of the universe. The natural question that arises from our egalitarian-oriented societies is, why are some beings more intelligent than others? This question lends itself to a discussion of what seems to be God's next topic in His revelation to Abraham. As we entertain this concept, we must be cognizant of two scriptural definitions of *intelligence*: (1) the uncreated identity of each individual and (2) "light and truth." I am not convinced that the two definitions are completely separate and unrelated. We must also keep in mind that the principles we are about to discuss concerning intelligences are connected to the astronomical principles we have just reviewed. Both are designed to help us understand our nature and our position in relation to God. It is God who makes the transition within the revelation, and as we follow His reasoning, we will come to further understand what he is trying to teach Abraham and *us*—Abraham's posterity—about our intelligences and our standing with God.

Section 93 of the Doctrine and Covenants is most illustrative in our attempts to answer the question of why some beings are more intelligent than others. It first helps us define intelligence. We are told, "Intelligence, or the light of truth, was not created or made, neither indeed can be" (D&C 93:29), and, "The glory of God is intelligence, or, in other words, light and truth" (D&C 93:36). This indicates that the degree of intelligence depends upon the amount of light and truth we have received.

The section also illustrates how to receive light and truth. It describes this process for the Savior, saying, "He received not of the fulness at the first, but received grace for grace; and he received not of the fulness at first, but continued from grace to grace, until he received a fulness" (D&C 93:12–13). The example set by Christ is then applied to us: "And no man receiveth a fulness unless he keepeth his commandments. He that keepeth his commandments receiveth truth and light, until he is glorified in truth and knoweth all things. . . . All truth is independent in that sphere in which God has placed it, to act for itself, as all intelligence also" (D&C 93:27–28, 30). Knowing all things, or obtaining knowledge, is important. As the Prophet Joseph Smith taught, "A man is saved no faster than he gets knowledge for if he does not get knowledge he will be brought into Captivity by some evil power in the other world as evil spirits will have more knowledge & Consequently more power than many men who are on the earth. Hence it needs Revelation to assist us & give us knowledge of the things of God."[35]

The passages in section 93 suggest that the amount of intelligence we receive depends directly on what we do with the light and truth already received. When we obey the light and truth we have, we receive more. When we disobey or ignore it, we lose that which we have (see 2 Nephi 28:30). It has been my experience that as we contemplate this principle, if we take a moment to quietly ask the Lord which principles of light and truth we currently possess but are not obeying, the Spirit will answer the question.

All this information about the need to obey light and truth as it is given to us is echoed in Abraham's visions: "We will prove them herewith, to see if they will do all things whatsoever the Lord their God shall command them" (Abraham 3:25). His visions also teach the principles that if we obey the truth we have been given, we will be given more until we are full of light and truth, and if we don't obey what we have, we will lose what light and truth we have thus far been given: "They who keep their first estate shall be added upon; and they who keep not their first estate shall not have glory in the same kingdom with those who keep their first estate; and they who keep their second estate shall have glory added upon their heads for ever and ever" (Abraham 3:26).

We may ask, Why would God want to prove us herewith? And why would He give to those who receive and take away from those who do not? The principle that answers these questions is lucidly illustrated by Elder Dallin H. Oaks:

> In contrast to the institutions of the world, which teach us to *know* something, the gospel of Jesus Christ challenges us to *become* something.
>
> Many Bible and modern scriptures speak of a final judgment at which all persons will be rewarded according to their deeds or works or the desires of their hearts. But other scriptures enlarge upon this by referring to our being judged by the *condition* we have achieved. . . .
>
> From such teachings we conclude that the Final Judgment is not just an evaluation of a sum total of good and evil

> acts—what we have *done.* It is an acknowledgment of the final effect of our acts and thoughts—what we have *become.* It is not enough for anyone just to go through the motions. The commandments, ordinances, and covenants of the gospel are not a list of deposits required to be made in some heavenly account. The gospel of Jesus Christ is a plan that shows us how to become what our Heavenly Father desires us to become.[36]

Coupling Elder Oaks's teachings with those found in section 93, we are led to conclude that the amount of light and truth we obey determines the amount of light and truth with which we will be filled. Our prospects at the judgment bar will largely be determined by the type of being we have become and whether we have become a being of light—full of light and truth. Of course, the amount of light and truth we receive is affected both by our obedience and by our reception of grace in these efforts (see D&C 93:12–13, 20). In many ways, the reception of grace is akin to God rescuing Abraham while he is on the altar. In the midst of our gaining light and truth and our efforts for progress, we must never forget what God wants to do for us, nor His ability to enact His desires.[37] After all "there is nothing that the Lord thy God shall take in his heart to do but what he will do it" (Abraham 3:17).

These principles seem to be the culminating doctrines of Abraham's vision. The Abrahamic analogy of astronomic principles ably illustrates that there is an order to things and that there are levels of progress to be made within that order. The central principle it teaches is that the goal of that progress converges on one point, God. We may ask, What did God want Abraham to learn when He showed him this vision? What did He want Abraham to teach the Egyptians? And what did He want Abraham to teach us by making record of this vision? Among many things, the most salient principles include that God wanted to teach Abraham, the Egyptians, and us about our relationship with Him, on a variety of levels. God is the focal point of everything; He is the Creator of and driving force behind all things in the universe. Finally, the culminating point appears to be that even though God is above us, our progression is toward Him. Simply put, Abraham chapter 3 masterfully teaches us about our relationship with God.

Notes

1. Orson F. Whitney, "Latter-day Saint Ideals and Institutions," *Improvement Era*, August 1927, 851, 861.

2. For a succinct summary of this, see Richard D. Draper, S. Kent Brown, and Michael D. Rhodes, *The Pearl of Great Price: A Verse-by-Verse Commentary* (Salt Lake City: Deseret Book, 2005), 273.
3. Sinuhe B 212–13, as in Friedrich Vogelsang and Alan H. Gardiner, *Literarische Texte des Mittleren Reiches* (Leipzig, Germany: H.C. Hinrichs'sche Buchhandlung, 1908), table 7a. This text originates in the Abrahamic era.
4. For an excellent discussion on this point of view, see John Gee, William J. Hamblin, and Daniel C. Peterson, "'And I Saw the Stars,' The Book of Abraham and Ancient Geocentric Astonomy," in *Astronomy, Papyrus, and Covenant*, ed. John Gee and Brian M. Hauglid (Provo, UT: FARMS, 2005), 1–16.
5. Michael D. Rhodes and J. Ward Moody, "Astronomy and the Creation in the Book of Abraham," in *Astronomy, Papyrus, and Covenant*, ed. John Gee and Brian M. Hauglid (Provo, UT: FARMS, 2005), 17–35. For an excellent discussion on how the two systems work together, see Richard Lyman Bushman, *Joseph Smith: Rough Stone Rolling* (New York: Alfred A. Knopf, 2005), 454–55.
6. Kerry Muhlestein, "Approaching Understandings in the Book of Abraham," in *The FARMS Review of Books* 18, no. 2 (2006): 231.
7. Dan Vogel and Brent Lee Metcalfe, "Joseph Smith's Scriptural Cosmology," in *The Word of God*, ed. Dan Vogel (Salt Lake City: Signature Books, 1990), 218n78.
8. Gee, Hamblin, and Peterson, "I Saw the Stars," 4.
9. On the effectiveness of teaching via apperception, see Boyd K. Packer, *Teach Ye Diligently* (Salt Lake City: Deseret Book, 1975), 20–27.
10. Pyramid Text, 442.
11. Otto Neugebauer and Richard A. Parker, *Egyptian Astronomical Texts,* vol. 1: *The Early Decans* (Providence, RI: Brown University Press, 1960); Otto Neugebauer and Richard A. Parker, *Egyptian Astronomical Texts,* vol. 2: *The Ramesside Star Clocks* (Providence, RI: Brown University Press, 1964), 3–7.
12. Pyramid Text, 519.
13. Pyramid Text, 214, 570.
14. Pyramid Text, 503, 509, 570.
15. Pyramid Text, 412, 504.
16. Pyramid Text, 263, 265, 266, 473, 609.
17. Pyramid Text, 366, 609.
18. Pyramid Text, 477.
19. Pyramid Text, 302.
20. Pyramid Text, 412, 442.

21. Pyramid Text, 691.
22. Pyramid Text, 473, 609.
23. Pyramid Text, 509.
24. Stephen Quirke, *The Cult of Ra: Sun-Worship in Ancient Egypt* (New York: Thames & Hudson, 2001), 116.
25. Michael Zeilik, Stephen A. Gregory, and Elske V. P. Smith, *Introductory Astronomy and Astrophysics*, 3rd ed. (New York: Saunders College Publishing, 1992), 446–47, 451.
26. Pyramid Text, 274; see also Robert K. Ritner, "The Mechanics of Ancient Egyptian Magical Practice," *Studies in Ancient Oriental Civilizations*, no. 54 (Chicago: University of Chicago, 1993), 61–62. I am grateful to Dr. John Gee for reminding me of this reference. See also Coffin Text, 16.
27. Pyramid Text, 454.
28. Michael D. Rhodes, "The Joseph Smith Hypocephalus . . . Seventeen Years Later," (Provo, UT: FARMS, 1994), 8.
29. Boyd K. Packer, in Conference Report, May 1977, 80.
30. Thomas B. Griffith, "The Root of Christian Doctrine," *BYU Magazine*, Fall 2006, 46.
31. John Van Seters, *Abraham in History and Tradition* (New Haven, CT: Yale University Press, 1975), 288.
32. The eighth article of faith (as well as the very existence of the Joseph Smith Translation) makes it clear that there are some problems with the Bible as we have received it. This is why Joseph Smith said, "I believe the Bible as it read when it came from the pen of the original writers" (*Discourses of Joseph Smith*, comp. Alma P. Burton [Salt Lake City: Deseret Book, 1977], 245). Of course, many of those who collected and redacted the sacred texts had good intentions (see 2 Nephi 29:4–5).
33. While the imagery of verse 12, wherein the Lord "put his hand upon mine eyes, and I saw those things which his hands had made, which were many; and they multiplied before mine eyes," indicates this is above and beyond that which mankind can see on his own, in verse 14 Abraham makes the point that it was nighttime when he saw these things, almost as if they could be seen because he was out looking around at night. Still, the nature of the vision combined with the language of verse 12 seems to indicate a seerlike vision.
34. Bushman, *Rough Stone Rolling*, 537.
35. Joseph Smith, as quoted in Bushman, *Rough Stone Rolling*, 436.
36. Dallin H. Oaks, in Conference Report, October 2000, 40–41.

37. Joseph Smith, comp., *Lectures on Faith* (Salt Lake City: Deseret Book, 1985), 38–44.

Latter-day Saints value the inspired changes in the Joseph Smith Translation of the Bible.

Photo by Bruce R. Nordgren

New Discoveries in the Joseph Smith Translation of the Bible

Kent P. Jackson

Kent P. Jackson *is a professor of ancient scripture at BYU.*

In November 2004 the Religious Studies Center at Brigham Young University published a facsimile transcription of all the original manuscripts of the Joseph Smith Translation of the Bible.[1] I was privileged to be one of the editors of the project and worked with those manuscripts in preparing the publication. A facsimile transcription seeks to reproduce in print—as much as is humanly and typographically possible—the writing found on a handwritten document. Thus the transcription includes the writers' original spelling, grammar, punctuation, line endings, omissions, errors, insertions, and deletions. The purpose of the publication is to provide scholars and lay readers with an accurate reproduction of the text as found on Joseph Smith's original manuscripts. Its importance is in the fact that those documents had never been made public before but were stored in archives that were only available for study to a limited number of researchers.

The last Latter-day Saint leader with any hands-on involvement in the JST was Joseph Smith himself. After his death, the manuscripts were in the possession of his family and then the Reorganized Church of Jesus Christ of Latter Day Saints (RLDS, now Community of Christ). Today they are carefully preserved in the Library-Archives of the Community of Christ in Independence, Missouri. None of those who assisted the Prophet as scribes came west with the Saints, and so from the time of his death, contact between The Church of Jesus Christ of Latter-day Saints and the Bible translation was for the most part severed. It was not until the 1960s that the contact was reestablished, when Brigham Young University professor Robert J. Matthews undertook the first serious and systematic study of the original manuscripts.[2] More recent efforts by others, including recent scholarly publications on the JST, build on the foundation established by Professor Matthews. Now, thanks to the cooperation of the Community of Christ in making possible the publication of the manuscripts, the texts are available for continued research and exploration.

During the course of our work with the New Translation (the term used by Joseph Smith and his contemporaries),[3] we learned many things. Some confirmed what was already known, but there were also some surprises. This article will touch briefly on a few of the things we discovered.

How the Translation Was Done

Although the Prophet left no written account of the process by which the translation was accomplished, there are important clues in the manuscripts, and thus we understand the work better now than ever before.

Like many other important people of his generation, Joseph Smith did almost all of his writing with the help of scribes. In the 446 pages of the New Translation manuscripts, his handwriting is found on only four pages where he served as his own scribe[4] and on seven other pages where he wrote small, isolated corrections.[5] Otherwise, he dictated the text, and his scribes wrote down what they heard from him.

The translation was done sequentially—not by topic, as some have supposed. And it was done from one end of the Bible to the other, but not exactly in that order. Joseph Smith translated Genesis 1–24 between June 1830 and March 1831. Then he was instructed in a revelation to leave the Old Testament and translate the New Testament (see D&C 45:60–61), which he did from March 1831 to July 1832. He then returned to Genesis 24, and he translated from there to the end of the Old Testament, finishing in July 1833. But the translation was not complete with the original dictation. There is much evidence on the manuscripts that Joseph Smith went over sections already translated and made additional refinements and corrections—until he felt that the translation was as the Lord wanted it to be.

Before the translation began, Oliver Cowdery had purchased a Bible for Joseph Smith and himself.[6] The Prophet used that Bible for the New Translation, apparently from the very beginning. Much of the work was done with

Joseph Smith dictating the text in full. The evidence tells us that he had the Bible in front of him, likely in his lap or on a table, and that he read from it while his scribes wrote. When he came to a passage needing revision, he would dictate words not found in the King James text until he came back to that text and continued with it. The writing on the manuscripts shows no indication of when the text was coming out of the printed Bible and when it was coming through revelation. The scribes may not have known when he was simply reading and when he was uttering words not found on the printed page. The translations of Genesis 1–24 and Matthew 1–John 5 were recorded that way.

But many Bible chapters required no changes at all, and thus midway through the translation, Joseph Smith (perhaps with some pleading by his scribe) developed a system in which only the corrections and additions would be recorded, rather than the entire text including passages with no changes. On the pages where the short-notation system was used, we see the following system at work: Joseph Smith dictated to his scribes the chapter and verse references and then only the new words or sentences. In his Bible, he marked the words to be replaced and the locations for insertions and changes. Thus the Prophet's Bible contains the deletion and insertion points, and the manuscripts contain only the new words to be inserted. So in order to understand fully what Joseph Smith had in mind with the changes in Genesis 24–Malachi and John 6–Revelation, readers and researchers need to study both the marked Bible and the original manuscripts. In our publication of the documents, we made that possible by printing photographs of almost fourteen hundred marked verses from Joseph Smith's printed Bible on pages directly facing the corresponding manuscript transcriptions.

Scribes and Dates

Modern technology has allowed us to confirm and clarify some important points regarding the scribes and the dates they worked. In the 1970s Robert Matthews developed the general chronological outline of the translation, based on evidence on the manuscripts. Our work in recent years made use of high-definition scanned images that allowed magnification and computer enhancement. As a result, we were able to see things in the electronic images that are not visible on the original manuscripts, even with a magnifying glass. But much of our progress in recent years was the result not of high technology but of good detective work. In the summer of 1995, my coeditors, Robert Matthews and Scott Faulring, were examining the pages of the first Old Testament manuscript at the RLDS archives in Independence, Missouri. Faulring was a research historian with the Joseph Fielding Smith Institute for Church History. Professor Matthews had a hunch years ago that Emma Smith may have served as one of the Prophet's scribes.[7] When looking at some handwriting attributed to John Whitmer that did not look quite as expected, they decided to act on his hunch and check the writing against some Emma Smith letters in the archives. A positive match was established that was later confirmed when Faulring did an extensive examination with other examples.[8]

Thanks to the handwriting expertise of Faulring and my student assistant Brenda Johnson, we now are quite certain of the exact locations where one scribal hand ends and another begins, and we have been able to correlate some of that information with known events and dates in Church history. Oliver Cowdery, John Whitmer, Emma Smith, Sidney Rigdon, Jesse Gause, and Frederick G. Williams were the scribes. Gause's handwriting was not identified until after the book came out.[9] There is one unidentified scribe who copied just a few lines from one manuscript to another. Others, probably assistants working with Joseph Smith, added verse breaks and corrections to the capitalization and punctuation. RLDS archivists later added a few small notations for organizational purposes, like page numbers. A very few small corrections, written lightly in pencil, appear to be in the handwriting of Joseph Smith III, the Prophet's son and president of the RLDS Church (1860–1914). Almost all of them repair copying errors made by scribes. One small insertion he made to an awkward but correct King James phrase (perhaps thinking it was an error by a scribe) was mistakenly made into a footnote in the LDS edition of the Bible: ". . . *and worthy* of death" at Matthew 26:66.[10]

Scott Faulring found some important historical sources that allowed us to make significant improvements in the internal dating. Two documents relating to the scribal work of Frederick G. Williams now let us know when the New Testament translation was finished (July 1832) and help us understand the timing of the corrections the Prophet made after the initial dictation.[11] This revised dating is significant because it helps us correlate revelations in the Doctrine and Covenants with the progress of the JST, and it helps us deal with the question, When was the JST finished?

Types of Changes in the JST

I believe that parts of the Joseph Smith Translation restore original biblical text that had become lost since the time of the Bible's authors.[12] There are some things in the translation that, in my opinion, cannot be explained in any other way. For example, I have found wording on the first Old Testament manuscript that I believe can only be explained as a very literal translation from a Hebrew original. The wording is so odd in English that editors after Joseph Smith's time took it out, so it is not in the book of Moses today.[13] Even though I believe that the JST restores original text, it is likely that most changes have other explanations. Joseph Smith taught that some truths pertaining to our salvation were lost even before the Bible was compiled, and thus some JST corrections may reveal teachings or events that never were recorded in the Bible in the first place.[14] Some JST changes probably edit the text to bring it into harmony with truth found in other revelations or elsewhere in the Bible. The Prophet taught: "[There are] many things in the Bible which do not, as they now stand, accord with the revelation of the Holy Ghost to me,"[15] necessitating latter-day correction.

Many changes edit the wording of the Bible to make it more clear and understandable for modern readers. As I examined the changes the Prophet made, I was surprised to see that more individual corrections appear to fall into this last category than into any other. Few are aware of that (nor was I), because the JST footnotes in our LDS Bible rightly focus on the more important matters of doctrine and history. There are many instances in which the Prophet rearranged word order or added words to make the text easier to read and modernized the language to replace archaic King James features with current grammar and vocabulary. There are numerous changes from *saith* to *said*, from *that* and *which* to *who*, and from *thee* and *ye* to *you*. He even modernized the language of his original dictations in some instances. When refining one passage, he changed "this earth upon which *thou standest*, and *thou shalt* write" to "this earth upon which *you stand*, and *you shall* write."[16] But by no means were the modernizations done consistently through the manuscripts, and alternative forms like "*mine* hands" and "*my* hands" and *hath* and *has* are very frequent.

Translation and Revelation

From observing the writing on the manuscripts, it seems to me that Joseph Smith's process for translating the Bible was different from that used for the Book of Mormon. On the original Book of Mormon manuscript, there is very little evidence that he struggled with wording, changed his mind, or made later revisions to his translation. His calling was to render the text of the gold plates into the English language, and it appears that he was to do so without modifying, enlarging, or embellishing what Mormon and the other authors had written. When he prepared the second printing of the Book of Mormon, he made spelling and grammatical revisions. He also made some word changes for clarification, but considering the size of the book, those were relatively few.

On the JST manuscripts, we frequently see remarkable writing that suggests that the words flowed spontaneously from the Prophet's lips without the slightest contemplation, hesitation, or uncertainty. The first page of the translation, which begins Moses 1, gives that impression. But other passages show evidence of exertion as the Prophet sought to obtain the right words to convey the intended meanings. There are instances in which he changed his mind, tried different words until he felt he had them right, or dictated words with which he later was dissatisfied. And even on pages in which the text seemed to flow easily, the Prophet sometimes returned later to make additional refinements. All of that evidence shows that Joseph Smith was very concerned to have the translation be consistent with the Lord's will and never content until it was. It seems that in the New Translation, more so than in the Book of Mormon, the Lord's instructions for translators were applicable: "You must study it out in your mind; then you must ask me if it be right, and if it is right I will cause that your bosom shall burn within you; therefore, you shall feel that it is right" (D&C 9:8).

As we researched the JST manuscripts, my student assistant Peter Jasinski discovered that Joseph Smith translated Matthew 26 twice, each with the help of a different scribe. The translations were done several months apart, and it appears that the Prophet simply forgot that he had translated the chapter already. We studied the duplicate translations carefully, believing that they would help us understand the nature of the JST better.[17] The two new translations are not identical; in fact, there are considerable differences. The rewordings for clarity and modernizations of archaic language were done without great consistency, with both of the translations contributing in unique ways. For example, in one of the translations, Joseph Smith modernized most of the King James pronouns, but he changed few in the other.

The most important changes were those that introduced new content or changed a verse's meaning. What we found when we examined those changes amazed us and added to our appreciation of Joseph Smith and his inspired work. Although some content changes were unique to one new translation or the other, the majority were found in *both*. Yet the new thoughts the Prophet added to the two translations were rarely expressed in the same words, and often they were not even inserted at the same locations in the text. In other words, he made the same corrections but not in the same words or the same places.

Why were the two inspired translations of the same chapter not identical? Joseph Smith taught that when the Holy Ghost gives us "pure intelligence," it serves in "expanding the mind [and] enlightening the understanding" with "sudden strokes of ideas."[18] Our conclusion was as follows: "Perhaps it would be reasonable to propose that as Joseph Smith worked his way through Matthew 26, dictating the text to his scribe Sidney Rigdon in spring 1831 and again to his scribe John Whitmer the next fall, impressions came to his mind in the form of pure intelligence, enlightened understanding, and sudden strokes of ideas—but not necessarily in exact words. Responding to those impressions, the Prophet himself supplied the words that corrected the problem or emphasized the point or otherwise caused the verse to express the ideas that the Lord wanted it to communicate."[19] This suggestion may explain why the duplicate translations are verbally different.

The Text of the Book of Moses

In an earlier article, I gave a general review of how the JST and the book of Moses came to be.[20] Many Latter-day Saints still do not know that the book of Moses in the Pearl of Great Price is an excerpt from the JST. It includes the vision Moses experienced before God revealed to him the creation account (now Moses 1), and it includes the JST of Genesis 1:1–6:13 (now Moses 2–8). Our book of Moses text did not come from Joseph Smith's original manuscripts, however, because those were not available to Latter-day Saints when the Pearl of Great Price was created and when subsequent editions were prepared.

Joseph Smith made his initial translation of the early Genesis chapters between June 1830 and February 1831. Sometime during the next two years, he made additional corrections and refinements to the translation. Years later, Joseph Smith III headed a committee to prepare the publication of the *Inspired*

Version, which is a printed version of the Joseph Smith Translation, edited, prepared in Bible format, and published by the RLDS Church beginning in 1867. Unfortunately, the committee did not fully understand the intent of the original manuscripts, and as a result, many of the Prophet's corrections were not included in the *Inspired Version* text. Because Latter-day Saints in Utah had no access to the original manuscripts, the *Inspired Version* was the best text available to them, and thus in the 1878 Latter-day Saint Pearl of Great Price, the RLDS *Inspired Version* text through Genesis 6:13 was copied and included verbatim, creating what we now call the book of Moses.[21] With modifications in editions of 1902, 1921, and 1981, it has remained our text ever since. The 1902 edition made many changes in the text of the book of Moses, but changes in the later editions were minor.[22]

When Was the JST Finished?

It is sometimes heard that Joseph Smith's Bible translation was never finished, an assumption that stems from later in the nineteenth century when Latter-day Saints had no access to the manuscripts and virtually no institutional memory about the translation. But careful study of the manuscripts and early historical sources teach us that Joseph Smith considered the translation finished. At the conclusion of the Old Testament, where the translation ends, the following words are written: "Finished on the 2d day of July 1833."[23] That same day, the Prophet and his counselors, JST scribes Sidney Rigdon and Frederick G. Williams, wrote to Church members in Missouri and told them, "We this day finished the translating of the Scriptures for which we returned gratitude to our heavenly father."[24] Could more have been done with the translation? Yes, but it was not designed to be. The Lord could have revealed other things in the New Translation, but He did not. Instead, beginning in July 1833, Joseph Smith no longer spoke of translating the Bible but of printing it, which he wanted and intended to do "as soon as possible."[25] As Robert Matthews pointed out years ago, the Prophet's own words show that from then on, his efforts were to have it printed as a book, and he repeatedly encouraged Church members to donate money for its publication. But other priorities and a lack of funds caused that it was not printed in his lifetime, which was a matter of considerable disappointment to him.[26]

The Bible Dictionary in the English LDS Bible states that Joseph Smith "continued to make modifications" in the translation "until his death in 1844."[27] Based on information available in the past, that was a reasonable assumption, and I taught it for many years. But we now know that it is not accurate. The best evidence points to the conclusion that when the Prophet called the translation "finished," he really meant it, and no changes were made in it after the summer (or possibly the fall) of 1833.

The primary evidence is in the handwriting on the manuscripts. In the process of translating the Bible, Joseph Smith made an initial dictation of the text and then later went back over parts of it to make further refinements and corrections. He called that second stage of the process the "reviewing." The historical sources tell us that the review of previously translated material was going on while the initial translation of other parts of the Bible was still under way. In July 1832 Joseph Smith announced the completion of the New Testament translation and the shift back to the Old Testament, which had been set aside some time earlier.[28] Then in February 1833, during the time he was engaged in the Old Testament translation with Frederick G. Williams as scribe, he announced that the "reviewing" of the New Testament had just been completed, for which Sidney Rigdon was the primary scribe.[29] The manuscripts show a frequent pattern of translating with one scribe and making additional corrections with another.

What does the handwriting tell us about when the final corrections were completed? Richard P. Howard, an RLDS historian who did early research on the JST manuscripts, wrote that the later corrections were "most likely in the handwriting of Joseph Smith, Jr."[30] Based on that assessment, he and others concluded that the Prophet continued to refine the translation, even until his death in 1844. But, in fact, extremely few of the later corrections are in Joseph Smith's handwriting. Of the hundreds of corrections made after the original dictation, only fifteen small revisions are in Joseph Smith's hand. Of the rest, roughly 10 percent are in the hand of Frederick G. Williams, and most of those are in the New Testament and thus were made by February 1833. The remaining 90 percent are in the hand of Sidney Rigdon, and the vast majority of those are early in the New Testament (made by February 1833) and in Old Testament sections that had been translated in 1830 and early 1831. Elder Rigdon served as the Prophet's scribe only until the fall of 1833, which is therefore probably the last possible date for any translation changes. Both men were out of Joseph Smith's favor by 1839.

The manuscripts show that after Joseph Smith finished the translation, much work was done to get the text ready for printing. The Prophet, or assistants working under his direction, went through the text systematically to provide capitalization, punctuation, and verse divisions. The original scribes were inconsistent in the use of punctuation and capitalization as they took dictation from Joseph Smith, so an edit to standardize punctuation and capitalization was required before the JST could be printed. That edit was done, though perhaps not to modern standards of consistency. In the same process, ampersands (&) were spelled out to *and*. More than one handwriting is found on the manuscripts engaged in this editing work.

Except in a very few places, the chapter breaks of traditional Bibles were retained on the JST manuscripts. But the verses on the manuscripts are very different from those in traditional Bibles, which were invented by a French printer in the sixteenth century. Most of the JST verses are large, paragraph-size verses, dividing complete thoughts instead of sentences. When the RLDS publication committee prepared for the printing of the *Inspired Version* in 1866–67, they discarded those verse divisions and created short verses similar to those found in other Bibles. When verses were added to the book of Moses and Joseph Smith–Matthew in preparation for the 1902 Pearl of Great Price, Latter-day Saints did not have the original manuscripts and thus were not aware of the JST verse divisions.[31]

The spelling on the manuscripts reflects the idiosyncrasies of the individual scribes, but no effort was made to edit spelling for consistency. Perhaps the Prophet decided to leave that refinement to be taken care of during the typesetting and proofing process.

The Miracle of the New Translation

The Joseph Smith Translation is a miracle—a divine act of God. Its origin is expressed on the manuscripts in words like these: "A Revelation given to Joseph the Revelator,"[32] "A Revelation given to the Elders of the Church of Christ,"[33] and "A Translation of the New Testament translated by the power of God."[34] To these can be added the Lord's words about it in the Doctrine and Covenants: "And the scriptures shall be given, even as they are in mine own bosom, to the salvation of mine own elect" (D&C 35:20). Given these statements, it is hard to imagine that any Latter-day Saint would not take the New Translation seriously and earnestly seek to learn from it.

My work with the manuscripts increased my appreciation for what this collection of revelation adds to our religion. Consider the following list of doctrines for which the JST makes unique contributions or is our only or best source:[35] the nature of God, the scope of the Father's work, the mission of

Jesus Christ, the plan of salvation, the character and motives of Satan, the Fall of Adam, the antiquity of the gospel, Enoch and the establishment of Zion, the doctrine of translation, Melchizedek and his priesthood, the destiny of the house of Israel, the purpose of animal sacrifice, the age of accountability, the origin of the law of Moses, the Second Coming of Jesus Christ, and the degrees of glory.

As one of the editors of Joseph Smith's New Translation texts, I labored over the Prophet's manuscripts most working days and many Saturdays for over six years, a privilege that I will always consider to be among the high points of my life. On numerous occasions I felt to say, as Oliver Cowdery did regarding his service as scribe for the Book of Mormon: "These were days never to be forgotten."[36] On the wall of the office where we worked, my student assistants placed pictures of each of Joseph Smith's scribes for his Bible revision. We felt honored to be in their company as we worked to make more fully available to the Latter-day Saints this great work of revelation—Joseph Smith's New Translation of the Bible.

Notes

1. See Scott H. Faulring, Kent P. Jackson, and Robert J. Matthews, eds., *Joseph Smith's New Translation of the Bible: Original Manuscripts* (Provo, UT: Religious Studies Center, Brigham Young University, 2004).
2. See Robert J. Matthews, *"A Plainer Translation": Joseph Smith's Translation of the Bible—A History and Commentary* (Provo, UT: Brigham Young University Press, 1975).
3. For example, see Doctrine and Covenants 124:89.
4. Old Testament Manuscript 2, pages 81, 82, 83, and 86.
5. Old Testament Manuscript 1, page 7; New Testament Manuscript 2, folio 2, page 9; New Testament Manuscript 2, folio 4, pages 109, 110, 114, 146, and 147.
6. See Kent P. Jackson, "Joseph Smith's Cooperstown Bible: The Bible Used in the Joseph Smith Translation in Its Historical Context," *BYU Studies* 40, no. 1 (2001): 41–70.
7. Matthews, *"A Plainer Translation,"* 95.
8. See "Emma and the Joseph Smith Translation," *Insights: An Ancient Window: The Newsletter of the Foundation for Ancient Research and Mormon Studies*, August 1996.

9. Jesse Gause was a member of the First Presidency for a few months in 1832, after which he left the Church (see Erin B. Jennings, "The Consequential Counselor: Restoring the Root(s) of Jesse Gause," *Journal of Mormon History* 34, no. 2 [Spring 2008]: 182–86).
10. The JST footnotes came from the printed RLDS *Inspired Version* (1944 edition), not from the manuscripts. See New Testament Manuscript 2, folio 2, page 4, line 9; and RLDS Committee Manuscript, Matthew, page 73, line 6, Library-Archives, Community of Christ, Independence, Missouri. The words "and worthy" are inserted on both manuscripts in Joseph Smith III's handwriting.
11. Frederick G. Williams, undated statement concerning his employment as scribe, Frederick G. Williams Papers, Church History Library, The Church of Jesus Christ of Latter-day Saints, Salt Lake City, Utah; and Joseph Smith to W. W. Phelps, July 31, 1832, Joseph Smith Collection, Church History Library; published in Dean C. Jessee, ed., *The Personal Writings of Joseph Smith*, rev. ed. (Salt Lake City: Deseret Book, 2002), 274.
12. For an extended discussion of the possible types of changes in the JST, see Faulring, Jackson, and Matthews, *Joseph Smith's New Translation of the Bible*, 8–11.
13. See Kent P. Jackson, "Behold I," *BYU Studies* 44, no. 2 (2005): 169–75.
14. See Joseph Smith, *History of the Church of Jesus Christ of Latter-day Saints*, ed. B. H. Roberts, 2nd ed. rev. (Salt Lake City: Deseret Book, 1957), 1:245.
15. Andrew F. Ehat and Lyndon W. Cook, eds., *The Words of Joseph Smith: The Contemporary Accounts of the Nauvoo Discourses of the Prophet Joseph* (Provo, UT: Religious Studies Center, Brigham Young University, 1980), 211, spelling and capitalization standardized.
16. Old Testament Manuscript 2, page 3, lines 30–31, spelling standardized.
17. See Kent P. Jackson and Peter M. Jasinski, "The Process of Inspired Translation: Two Passages Translated Twice in the Joseph Smith Translation of the Bible," *BYU Studies* 42, no. 2 (2003): 35–64.
18. Ehat and Cook, *Words of Joseph Smith*, 4–5, spelling standardized. I thank my friend Richard D. Draper for bringing this quotation to my attention in this context.
19. Jackson and Jasinski, "The Process of Inspired Translation," 61–62.
20. See Kent P. Jackson, "How We Got the Book of Moses," page 137 in this book.
21. The book of Moses material in the 1851 Liverpool *Pearl of Great Price* was fragmentary, out of order, and came from preliminary manuscripts. The 1878 edition contained a much more accurate and complete text.

22. For a detailed history of the Book of Moses text, see Kent P. Jackson, *The Book of Moses and the Joseph Smith Translation Manuscripts* (Provo, UT: Religious Studies Center, Brigham Young University, 2005).
23. Old Testament Manuscript 2, page 119, line 5.
24. Joseph Smith, Sidney Rigdon, and Frederick G. Williams to the Brethren in Zion, July 2, 1833, Joseph Smith Collection, Church History Library, published in Smith, *History of the Church*, 1:368.
25. "You will see by these revelations that we have to print the new translation here at kirtland for which we will prepare as soon as possible" (Joseph Smith, Sidney Rigdon, and Frederick G. Williams to Edward Partridge, August 6, 1833, Joseph Smith Collection, Church History Library).
26. See Robert J. Matthews, "Joseph Smith's Efforts to Publish His Bible Translation," *Ensign*, January 1983, 57–64.
27. Bible Dictionary, "Joseph Smith Translation," 717. The Guide to the Scriptures says the same thing. For example, see the Spanish "Guía para el estudio de las escrituras," 112.
28. "We have finished the translation of the New testament . . . , we are making rapid strides in the old book [Old Testament] and in the strength of God we can do all things according to his will" (Joseph Smith to W. W. Phelps, July 31, 1832, Joseph Smith Collection, Church History Library; published in Jessee, *Personal Writings of Joseph Smith*, 274).
29. "This day completed the translation and the reviewing of the New Testament" (Kirtland High Council Minute Book, February 2, 1833, 8, Church History Library; published in Joseph Smith, *History of the Church*, 1:342).
30. Richard P. Howard, *Restoration Scriptures: A Study of Their Textual Development* (Independence, MO: Herald, 1969), 122. In the revised and enlarged edition (Herald, 1995), Howard identifies the insertions as "mostly in the handwriting of Joseph Smith, Jr." (107).
31. It is interesting to note that in the first printing of the book of Abraham, the Prophet provided similar large verses (see *Times and Seasons* 3, no. 9 [March 1, 1842]: 703–6; 3, no. 10 [March 15, 1842]: 719–22).
32. Old Testament Manuscript 1, page 1, line 1.
33. Old Testament Manuscript 1, page 3, line 15.
34. New Testament Manuscript 1, page 1, line 2.
35. The following list summarizes Faulring, Jackson, and Matthews, *Joseph Smith's New Translation*, 20–25. References can be found there.
36. *Latter Day Saints' Messenger and Advocate* 1, no. 1 (October 1834): 14.

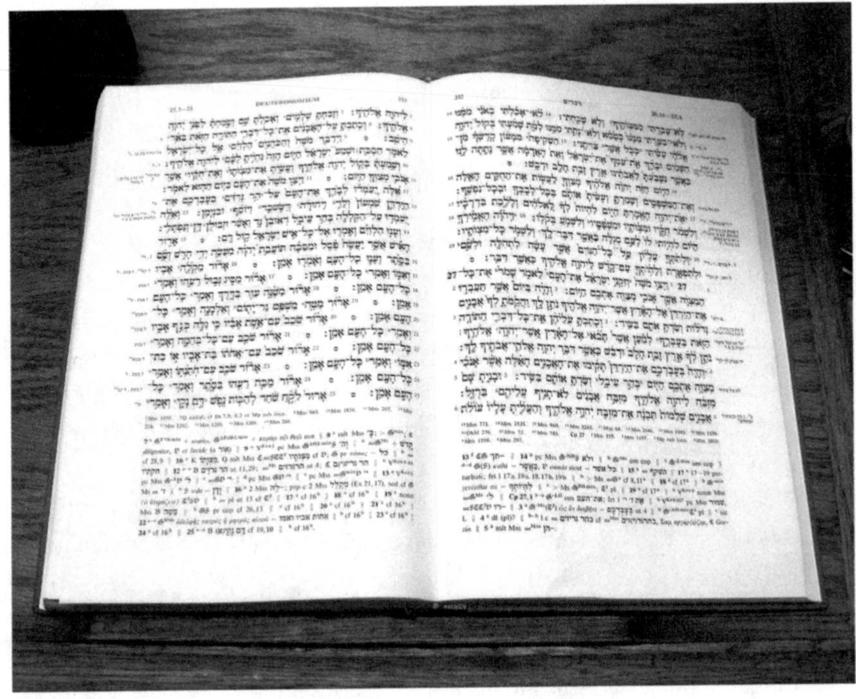

Whether we realize it or not, when we read scriptures and sing hymns we often say Hebrew words.

Photo by Brent R. Nordgren

Biblical Hebrew Words You Already Know and Why They Are Important

Dana M. Pike

Dana M. Pike *is a professor of ancient scripture at BYU.*

Whether we realize it or not, when we read scriptures and sing hymns we often say Hebrew words. Our pronunciation may not be quite right, but this observation is true nonetheless. Why don't some of us realize this? Because Hebrew words have successfully made their way into our modern religious terminology without our knowledge of the origin of these words or the process of their transmission. What difference does it make whether we know their origin? Since many of these words are religious terms and titles, knowing their meaning in their original language can instruct and remind us of important concepts every time we use them. But this can only happen if we know what they mean and how they were employed in the Hebrew Bible. We miss a complete dimension of understanding and spiritual reinforcement if we do not know the meaning of these terms. The Prophet Joseph Smith certainly shared this perspective when he commented on the value of studying the scriptures in their original language: "Our latitude and longitude can be determined in the original Hebrew with far greater accuracy than in the English version."[1]

Certain Hebrew words made their way into English through a process called transliteration. A transliterated word is one in which the general sound of the letters (*-literate*) of a word in one language cross (*trans-*) into another language, creating a new word, so to speak, in the second language. This process contrasts with "translation," through which a word in one language is replaced by a word with the same meaning in another language but rarely sounds anything like the word in the original language. Biblical names are good examples of words that are routinely transliterated, not translated. For example, 1 Samuel 13:16 begins, "And Saul, and Jonathan his son, and the people that were present with them. . . ." *Saul* is the transliterated form of the Hebrew name *šāʾūl* (pronounced *shah-OOL*), which means "asked," while *Jonathan* comes into English from *yônātān*, "Jehovah has given." If these names had been *translated*, the verse would read, "And *Asked*, and *Jehovah-has-given*, his son, and the people that were present with them. . . ." This example sufficiently illustrates the occurrence of transliterated words (in this case names) in the Old Testament. It also shows that some Hebrew letters are not available in English (such as *ʾaleph*, the letter in the middle of *šāʾūl/Saul*), so there is not always an exact match between the original form and its transliterated counterpart.[2] Furthermore, there are no capital letters in Hebrew, and there is no "j" sound. The Hebrew "y" (*yod*) ended up being pronounced like a "j" in English due to the linguistic influence of French on Middle English (AD 1100–1500) in the centuries following the Norman invasion of Britain.[3]

The following discussion of six biblical Hebrew words, including the name *Jehovah*, indicates what these words originally meant and demonstrates how they were employed by biblical authors. It also suggests how knowing the meaning and usage of these words can make our experience more meaningful when reading or speaking them, whatever their context.

Amen

The English word *Amen* (commonly pronounced *ay-MEN*) is transliterated from the Hebrew אָמֵן/ *ʾāmēn*, pronounced *ah-MEN* (or *ah-MAIN*). It means "surely" or "may it be so" and has the sense of confirming what has just been spoken or done. The Hebrew word *ʾāmēn* derives from the lexical root *ʾMN*, which conveys the sense "to be faithful, to be established, to believe, to be confirmed." This explains why *Amen* is even used as a title for Jesus in Revelation 3:14: "the Amen, the faithful and true witness."

The confirming nature of *ʾāmēn/Amen* is very evident when David, shortly before his death, gave orders to "cause Solomon my son to ride upon mine own mule. . . . And let Zadok the priest and Nathan the prophet anoint him there king over Israel. . . . For he shall be king in my stead. . . . And Benaiah the son of Jehoiada answered the king, and said, Amen: [may] the Lord God of my lord the king say so too. As the Lord hath been with my lord the king, even so be he with Solomon" (1 Kings 1:33–37). Not only did Benaiah verbalize his consent to David's orders with his "Amen," he also expressed his desire that the Lord ratify Solomon's kingship. About three and a half centuries later, when the Lord instructed Jeremiah to remind his contemporaries about the Lord's covenant promise to their ancestors, Jeremiah responded, "So be it [*'āmēn*], O Lord" (Jeremiah 11:5). In both of these passages, *'āmēn* was spoken to show affirmation of and commitment to what had just been said.

Latter-day Saints regularly conclude their prayers, teachings, and testimonies with the word *Amen*. When this occurs in a public context, the class or congregation responds, "Amen," in unison. This practice has its antecedent as early as Mosaic times, as illustrated in several passages in the Old Testament. For example, Moses instructed the Israelites that they should have a covenant-renewal ceremony in Shechem after entering the land of Canaan. As part of that occasion, the Levites would "say unto all the men of Israel with a loud voice. . . . Cursed be he that maketh the blind to wander out of the way. And all the people shall say, Amen. Cursed be he that perverteth the judgment of the stranger, fatherless, and widow. And all the people shall say, Amen. . . . Cursed be he that confirmeth not all the words of this law to do them. And all the people shall say, Amen" (Deuteronomy 27:14, 18–19, 26).

Similarly, when David brought the ark of the covenant to Jerusalem, he delivered a psalm of praise and thanksgiving as part of the public festivities (see 1 Chronicles 16:7–36). When he concluded, "all the people said, Amen, and praised the Lord" (v. 36; see also Nehemiah 5:13; 8:6; Jeremiah 28:6). Several psalms also preserve the liturgical use of this word. Psalm 106 concludes with the line, "Blessed be the Lord God of Israel from everlasting to everlasting: and let all the people say, Amen. Praise ye the Lord" (v. 48; see also Psalms 41:13; 72:19; 89:52). These passages illustrate how the public pronouncement of *'āmēn/Amen* was an important part of Israelite worship involving all who were present as they witnessed their acceptance of what was said or done.

Thus, when a Latter-day Saint utters the word *Amen* after an ordinance, or at the conclusion of their own prayer or testimony, the person declares to the Lord and to others (when uttered in a public setting) his or her approval and acceptance of the preceding action, teaching, or prayed request: "May it be so—or, I am convinced that it is so—just as I have said (or done)." The individual thereby declares personal responsibility for what has been requested, taught, or done in the sacred name of the Lord Jesus. And when other Latter-day Saints respond to a public testimony or prayer by collectively declaring "Amen"—just as ancient Israelites did—they indicate that they are witnesses to and accepting of what has been said: "So be it" or "Let it be so." As such, they become participants in the proceedings, praying the same prayer, testifying of the same truths, renewing the same covenant. Obviously, *Amen* should not be uttered thoughtlessly.

Hallelujah

The expression *Hallelujah* is always translated, not transliterated, in the KJV Old Testament, so it does not appear therein. But the Hebrew from which it derives, הַלְלוּ־יָהּ/(*halĕlû-yāh*) occurs two dozen times in the Bible, always in the book of Psalms.

Hallelujah (*halĕlû-yāh*) consists of the plural imperative form (*halĕlû*) of the verb *HLL*, "to praise," plus an abbreviated form of the divine name *Jehovah* (*yāh*). As noted above, the "j" sound in English is not present in Hebrew. Furthermore, ancient Israelites pronounced the name of their God more like "Yahweh" than "Jehovah" (see discussion below). Thus, *yāh* at the end of *halĕlû-yāh* represents Yah, a short form of the name of the God of Israel. This form of the divine name occurs independently about twenty times in the Hebrew Bible, but only once in the KJV, in Psalm 68:4, where it is spelled with a "j" and rendered in all capitals: "Sing unto God, sing praises to his name: extol him . . . by his name JAH, and rejoice before him." Elsewhere, it is rendered "the Lord."[4]

Hallelujah thus means "praise Yah/Jehovah." It is translated in the KJV as "praise (ye) the Lord" because English Bibles substitute "the Lord" for the name *Jehovah/Yahweh*. For example, Psalm 106:48 (quoted above) reads: "And let all the people say, Amen. Praise ye the Lord [*halĕlû-yāh*]." The Hebrew title of the book of Psalms, *sefer tĕhillîm*, also derives from the lexical root *HLL*, "to praise," and literally means "book of praises."[5] Psalm 150:6, the last verse of the last psalm in the book of Psalms, reads, "Let every thing that hath breath praise the Lord [*tĕhallēl yāh*]. Praise ye the Lord [*halĕlû-yāh*]." This phrase, *halĕlû-yāh*, is therefore an ancient and well-attested expression of worship, communicating praise to and for the Lord.

Throughout history, various psalms have been referred to as "Hallel psalms" because they are particularly expressive of praise (*HLL*) to Jehovah for His saving acts and for His continued blessings (see Psalms 111–18; 146–50).

Psalm 136 is often called the "Great Hallel." This psalm proclaims thanks and praise to Jehovah, "for his mercy endureth for ever," the phrase with which all twenty-six verses conclude. By Jesus's day the singing of Hallel psalms was a standard part of the celebration of several Jewish holidays, including Passover. For this reason, it is often assumed that the hymn Jesus and His eleven Apostles sang together at the end of their Passover meal was a Hallel psalm (see Matthew 26:30).[6]

The Hebrew phrase *halělû-yāh* was transliterated into Greek as *hallēlouia*, the form in which it occurs four times in the Greek New Testament (see Revelation 19:1–6). However, in the Greek alphabet there is no letter equivalent to *h*; rather, the "h" sound is indicated by a "rough breathing" mark that is not represented in the Roman alphabet. Therefore the Greek-to-English form of the Hebrew *halělû-yāh* is *Alleluia*. So Revelation 19:4 reads: "And the four and twenty elders and the four beasts fell down and worshipped God that sat on the throne, saying, Amen; Alleluia." Just as in the Hebrew Bible, *Alleluia* occurs here in the context of worship.

The expression *Halělû-yāh/Hallelujah/Alleluia* contains the name of the Lord Jehovah and has functioned as a joyful yet reverent expression of praise for His goodness and mercy for thousands of years. When modern disciples of Christ encounter either form of this phrase—"Hallelujah" or "Alleluia"—in scripture or in hymns,[7] or employ it in some other form of worship, it can only be hoped that they will appreciate the full extent of its meaning, thereby giving heartfelt expression to their gratitude and joy by saying, "Praise the Lord."

Sabbath

The English word *Sabbath* is transliterated from the Hebrew noun שַׁבָּת/*šabbāt* (*shabbat* or *shabbath*), which occurs over one hundred times in the Hebrew Bible. It is related to a verb from the lexical root *ŠBT*, which means "to cease labor, rest." The concept of resting from one's weekday labors on the seventh day of the week is first introduced in scripture when the Lord rested after six periods of creative activity: "And on the seventh day God ended his work which he had made; and he rested [*wayyišbōt*] on the seventh day from all his work which he had made. And God blessed the seventh day, and sanctified it: because that in it he had rested [*šābat*] from all his work which God created and made" (Genesis 2:2–3). The seventh day is not specifically called the Sabbath in this passage, but the verb indicating the cessation of God's labor (*šābat*) is the basis for the day's name, which provides an apt description of one purpose of the day—resting from regular productivity. Genesis 2:2–3 therefore provides a practical model for humans (resting after six days of work), based on divine example (God's resting), and teaches the nature of the day—it was "sanctified," making it literally a holy day.

These features are reiterated in the fourth of the Ten Commandments: "Remember the sabbath day, to keep it holy. . . . The seventh day is the sabbath of the Lord thy God: in it thou shalt not do any work. . . . For in six days the Lord made heaven and earth . . . and rested [*wayyānaḥ*] the seventh day: wherefore the Lord blessed the sabbath day, and hallowed it" (Exodus 20:8–11). Interestingly, the Israelites were practicing this pattern even before the revelation at Mount Sinai (see Exodus 20), since the manna the Lord provided for them was not given on the seventh day of the week (see Exodus 16:22–30). When Moses recounted the Ten Commandments in Deuteronomy 5, he provided an additional reason for the Israelites' Sabbath observance: their families, slaves, and livestock were to rest in remembrance of God giving them rest by delivering them from their servitude in Egypt (see vv. 12–15). Sabbath observance is thus connected in these two renditions of the Ten Commandments with the significant acts of creation and redemption by Jehovah, who is Jesus Christ.[8]

By virtue of being "sanctified," or "hallowed," by the Lord, the Sabbath takes on greater significance than just a day of rest. Exodus 31 is an important indicator of the Lord's view of the Sabbath:

> And the Lord spake unto Moses, saying,
>
> Speak thou also unto the children of Israel, saying, Verily my sabbaths [*šabtōtay*] ye shall keep: for it is a sign between me and you . . . that ye may know that I am the Lord that doth sanctify you.
>
> Ye shall keep the sabbath [*šabbāt*] therefore; for it is holy unto you. . . . Six days may work be done; but in the seventh is the sabbath of rest [*šabbāt šabbātôn*], holy to the Lord. . . .
>
> Wherefore the children of Israel shall keep the sabbath [*šabbāt*] . . . for a perpetual covenant.
>
> It is a sign between me and [them] . . . for in six days the Lord made heaven and earth, and on the seventh day he rested [*šābat*], and was refreshed. (Exodus 31:12–17)

The Lord indicates in this instructive passage that Sabbath observance is a sign of His covenant relationship with His people, and that Sabbath observance demonstrates recognition that it is He, Jehovah, who sanctifies His people.

These scriptures outline the following sequence: (1) Jehovah rested on and sanctified, or *made* holy, the seventh day (see Genesis 2:3); (2) He has commanded His disciples to *keep* the Sabbath holy (see Exodus 20:14)—it comes to us already holy, we are charged to maintain its holy status; and (3) our Sabbath observance—maintaining the sanctity of the day—is both a sign of our commitment to the Lord and a reminder to us that it is He, and only He, who has the power to sanctify us (see Exodus 31:13). This means true Sabbath observance is not just resting from labor, but is a major means through which we enter into the "rest of the Lord," which is a "state of peace . . . [and] spiritual enjoyment resulting from the power or presence of the Lord. Ultimately, it is the fulness of God's glory (D&C 84:24)."[9] Moving beyond worldly rest to divine rest on and through *yôm haššabbāt*, "the day of Sabbath," brings the blessings of heaven in various and powerful ways, as promised by the Lord in Isaiah 58:13–14 and elsewhere.

After Jesus's Resurrection and Ascension to heaven, members of Christ's Church transitioned to observing the first day of the week, the Lord's day, as holy.[10] Our weekly observance of the Sabbath is thus a combination of celebration and worship. As we call the Sabbath "a delight" (Isaiah 58:13), we rest from our weekday labors, we gather to worship and renew covenants, we commemorate the mighty acts of God (in the lives of our ancestors as well as our own, and especially Jesus's atoning sacrifice and Resurrection), and we participate with the Lord in the rest and sanctification of our souls (see D&C 59:8–13).[11]

Sabaoth

Not to be confused with the word *Sabbath*, which looks somewhat similar in English, צְבָאוֹת/ *ṣĕbā'ôt*/*Sabaoth*[12] is a plural Hebrew noun meaning "hosts, armies." It occurs only twice in the KJV in its transliterated form, both in the New Testament: Romans 9:29 ("the Lord of Sabaoth") and James 5:4 ("the Lord of sabaoth").[13] But *ṣĕbā'ôt*/*Sabaoth* and the collective singular form *ṣābā'* occur about five hundred times in the Hebrew Bible.

Sometimes "host(s)" refers collectively to the inanimate creations of the Lord, such as the stars and planets, as in Moses's warning to the Israelites about false worship: "Take ye therefore good heed unto yourselves; . . . lest thou lift up thine eyes unto heaven, and when thou seest the sun, and the moon, and the stars, even all the host of heaven [*ṣĕbāʾ haššāmayim*], shouldest be driven to worship them, and serve them" (Deuteronomy 4:15, 19).

More often, "host(s)" refers to large numbers of people (see Exodus 12:41), particularly an army, as in David's statement to Solomon: "Moreover thou knowest also what Joab the son of Zeruiah did to me, and what he did to the two captains of the hosts [*ṣibʾôt*] of Israel . . . whom he slew" (1 Kings 2:5).[14] The concept of a nonmortal, heavenly host fighting for and with Israel is also attested in the Old Testament. For example, the being who appeared to Joshua shortly before the Israelite attack on Jericho said, "As captain of the host [*ṣĕbā*] of the Lord am I now come. And Joshua fell on his face to the earth, and did worship. . . . And the captain of the Lord's host [*ṣĕbā*] said unto Joshua, Loose thy shoe from off thy foot; for the place whereon thou standest is holy" (Joshua 5:13–15).[15] Such passages clearly demonstrate the use of the singular *ṣĕbāʾ* and the plural *ṣĕbāʾôt/Sabaoth* to designate human and heavenly armies. Such usage is not surprising, since the Lord, Jehovah, is depicted as a warrior several times in the Bible, such as in Exodus 15:3–4: "The Lord is a man of war: the Lord is his name. Pharaoh's chariots and his host [ḥêl, "army, strength"] hath he cast into the sea."[16]

The Lord's heavenly host is not just composed of fighters, but all the holy beings who surround Him and do His will: "The Lord hath prepared his throne in the heavens. . . . Bless the Lord, ye his angels, that excel in strength, that do his commandments. . . . Bless ye the Lord, all ye his hosts [*sĕbāʾāyw*]; ye ministers of his, that do his pleasure" (Psalm 103:19–21). Likewise: "Praise ye him, all his angels: praise ye him, all his hosts [*sĕbāʾô*]" (Psalm 148:2). This is perhaps the main connotation of *yhwh ṣĕbāʾôt*, "the Lord of Sabaoth," a phrase that occurs almost 250 times in the Hebrew Bible, most commonly in prophetic texts. Jehovah as King of heaven is Lord of all the many heavenly beings and spirits, as well as of people on earth.

Although the specific sense of "hosts" in the designation *yhwh sĕbāʾôt* is not certain in every biblical passage (divine beings in general, heavenly fighters, stars, some combination of these), it is evident that the expression "the Lord of hosts"—"Lord of Sabaoth"—is meant to encapsulate and convey Jehovah's exalted status in the midst of other heavenly beings and His power to accomplish all His purposes in heaven and on earth. It is therefore not surprising that this phrase occurs a few times in uniquely Latter-day Saint scripture.

The transliterated word *Sabaoth* is attested four times in the Doctrine and Covenants (see 87:7; 88:2; 95:7; 98:2), always in relation to a prayer that has or will "come up into the ears of the Lord of Sabaoth." For example, Doctrine and Covenants 95:7 emphasizes the Lord's creative power: "Call your solemn assembly, that your fastings and your mourning might come up into the ears of the Lord of Sabaoth, which is by interpretation, the creator of the first day, the beginning and the end." The phrase "by interpretation" here does not indicate that the word *Sabaoth* literally translates to "creator of the first day," but rather it correlates the concepts of creation and hosts. This, of course, makes good scriptural sense, based on Genesis 2:1 ("Thus the heavens and the earth were finished, and all the host of them [*ṣĕbāʾām*]") and Doctrine and Covenants 45:1 ("give ear to him who laid the foundation of the earth, who made the heavens and all the hosts thereof").[17] Doctrine and Covenants 87:7 correlates with the military sense of many of the occurrences of *yhwh ṣĕbāʾôt* in the Hebrew Bible: "That the cry of the saints, and of the blood of the saints, shall cease to come up into the ears of the Lord of Sabaoth, from the earth, to be avenged of their enemies." These attestations of "Lord of Sabaoth" (from *yhwh ṣĕbāʾôt*) in the Doctrine and Covenants provide a demonstrable link between modern revelation and an age-old concept and tradition of scripture language, although in this case represented in the KJV Old Testament only in translation—"the Lord of hosts"—not transliteration.

The phrase "Lord of Sabaoth" expresses the majesty and dominion of the Lord, who reigns over all. Our use of this phrase expresses our conviction of the Lord's supremacy and conveys worship and confidence. The Lord and His righteous host, both in heaven and on earth, will not be defeated.

Satan

The name-title *Satan* is the transliterated form of the Hebrew common noun שָׂטָן/*śāṭān* (pronounced *sah-TAHN*), which means "adversary, slanderer." [18] The related Hebrew verb from the lexical root *ŚṬN* means "to accuse, slander, be an adversary."[19]

Perhaps surprisingly, the Hebrew noun *śāṭān* occurs in the following passages to designate humans who were adversaries to someone else: David (see 1 Samuel 29:4); Abishai and his brothers (see 2 Samuel 19:22); and the collective enemies of Solomon, from whom the Lord had given him rest (see

1 Kings 5:4; v. 18 in the Hebrew Bible). Specific enemies of Solomon who harassed him later in his reign are also labeled *śāṭān*/"adversary": "Then the Lord raised up an adversary [*śāṭān*] against Solomon, Hadad the Edomite. . . . God raised up another adversary [*śāṭān*] against Solomon, Rezon son of Eliadah. . . . He was an adversary [*śāṭān*] of Israel all the days of Solomon, making trouble as Hadad did" (1 Kings 11:14, 23, 25; New Revised Standard Version; hereafter cited as NRSV). Thus, in the Hebrew Bible, *śāṭān* is sometimes used in reference to human "satans," enemies who posed a political or military threat to the well-being of a person or nation.

The Hebrew noun *śāṭān* also refers to nonhuman adversaries in the Bible. In such cases, it occurs three times without the definite article (see Numbers 22:22, 32; 1 Chronicles 21:1) and twenty-three times with the definite article (*ha-*): *haśśāṭān*, literally, "the satan" (see Job 1–2; Zechariah 3:1–2). Demonstrating the wide-ranging use of this common noun, even an "angel of the Lord" acted as a *śāṭān*: "And God's anger was kindled [against Balaam] because he went [with Balak's messengers]: and the angel of the Lord stood in the way for an adversary [*lĕśāṭān*] against him. . . . And the angel of the Lord said unto him, Wherefore hast thou smitten thine ass these three times? behold, I went out to withstand thee [*lĕśāṭān*], because thy way is perverse before me" (Numbers 22:22, 32; the NRSV reads, "I have come out as an adversary," in v. 32).

Only 1 Chronicles 21:1 contains the noun *śāṭān* without the definite article in what can be considered a proper name-title for the demonic Satan, the adversary of God and His people: "Satan stood up against Israel, and incited David to count the people of Israel" (NRSV). This of course is the way the term *śāṭān* is usually used in post–Old Testament Jewish and Christian literature. Latter-day Saints generally understand *haśśāṭān* ("the adversary") in Job 1 and 2 and Zechariah 3 to also be "the adversary," Satan, the one who slandered Job's integrity and acted as an adversary to that righteous man. The KJV and most other modern translations render *haśśāṭān* as "Satan" in these passages, ignoring the definite article.[20]

The name-title *Satan* occurs numerous times in the New Testament and in Restoration scripture as a designation for the adversary of the Lord.[21] When Latter-day Saints use the term *Satan* to refer to the devil, they will hopefully recall that, even more than human adversaries, this being is an eternal enemy. He rebelled against God, is "the father of all lies," and seeks "to deceive and to blind" people "to lead them captive at his will" if they choose not to follow the Lord (see Moses 4:4). No wonder he is labeled "adversary."

Jehovah

Surprisingly, the name *Jehovah* occurs only four times in the King James translation of the Old Testament. It is printed in capital letters, as in Psalm 83:18: "That men may know that thou, whose name alone is JEHOVAH, art the most high over all the earth" (see also Exodus 6:3; Isaiah 12:2; 26:4).[22] It also occurs three times as a component of altar or place names: "And Moses built an altar, and called the name of it Jehovah-nissi" (Exodus 17:15; see also Genesis 22:14; Judges 6:24). The name *Jehovah* does not appear in the KJV New Testament at all. Despite this minimal indication, the Hebrew form of this name, יהוה/*yhwh*, occurs about 6,500 times in the Hebrew Bible! It is important for students of scripture to understand the cause of this great disparity.

Jehovah does not appear more often in the King James Version and other translations of the Bible because the translators were influenced by a Jewish custom, developed sometime after 500 BC, of not pronouncing the divine name *yhwh* out of respect for its sacred nature. This necessitated substituting a title in its place when reading the biblical text (the consonants *yhwh* were still written when biblical texts were copied). This development contributed to the eventual loss of the pronunciation of *yhwh*.[23] The substitute title most often used was, and still is, *'ădōnāy*, "lord" (literally, "my lords," but conventionally translated "Lord" or "my Lord"; the independent form is *'ădōn*, "lord"; *'ădōnî* is "my lord").[24] Copies of the Hebrew Bible print the letters of the divine name, *yhwh*, but usually place the vocalization "points," or vowel indicators, for the word *'ădōnāy* around these four letters to remind readers to substitute the title *Lord* for the divine name *yhwh*.[25] This substitution is exhibited in English translations every time the divine name *yhwh* is printed as "the Lord." [26] Printing "Lord" in all capitals allows readers of the English translation to distinguish between the occurrences of *yhwh* in the Hebrew text, which would be read *'ădōnāy*, and actual occurrences of the noun *'ădōn*, "lord." The latter term sometimes refers to God and is printed "Lord" in translation and sometimes refers to human rulers and is printed "lord" (except at the beginning of sentences, when the "l" is always capitalized and context must indicate who the Lord is). This practice is evident in many passages, such as 1 Kings 1:36 ("And Benaiah . . . answered the king, and said, Amen: the Lord [*yhwh*] God of my lord [*'ădōnî*] the king say so too") and Exodus 4:13–14 ("And [Moses said to God], O my Lord [*'ădōnāy*], . . . and the anger of the Lord [*yhwh*] was kindled against Moses").

The consonants in the name "**J**e**h**o**v**a**h**" are transliterated from the four Hebrew letters of the divine name *yhwh* (again, the Hebrew "y" is represented in English as "j").[27] And the vowels in "J**e**h**o**v**a**h" are derived from the vowels in the substitute title *'ădōnāy*, with a slight variation in the first vowel.[28] Thus, the name *Jehovah*, which is very familiar to us, is a hybrid form that was written as early as the twelfth or thirteenth century, but is not well attested in English until the early sixteenth century.[29] It was never actually pronounced "Jehovah" in antiquity. Based on evidence such as the shortened forms of *yhwh* that appear in Israelite personal names[30] and in the Hebrew Bible (for example, *Yah/JAH* in Psalm 68:4, and the last portion of the expression *halĕlû-yāh*, discussed above), scholars postulate that the divine name was originally pronounced "Yahweh" or something similar.[31]

The name *Yahweh/Jehovah* seems related to the Hebrew verb "to be," and is usually translated "he is" or "he causes to be." Those who favor the meaning "he is" correlate it with the form of the name *Jehovah* Moses was taught at the burning bush: "I AM" (Exodus 3:14).[32] Understood this way, the name *Yahweh/Jehovah* does not mean "He is . . . (something, like love or mercy)," but rather "He exists," which conveys the duration of the Lord's power, superiority, and eternal dominion—Yahweh/Jehovah just *is*. This is the reason Church-related publications sometimes translate "Jehovah" as "Unchangeable One" or "Self-existent One."[33] But based on the preserved vocalization of short forms of the divine name, many scholars translate "Yahweh" as a causative, "he causes to be/exist."[34] This emphasizes Yahweh/Jehovah's ongoing power to create and uphold all things. The last phrase in Doctrine and Covenants 88:41 nicely captures the sense of the divine name when understood this way: "all things are by him."

The tradition of rendering Hebrew *yhwh* as "the Lord" has produced some unusual combinations, such as "the Lord God," a phrase that occurs about three hundred times in the KJV. One well-known example is "Surely the Lord God will do nothing, but he revealeth his secret unto his servants the prophets" (Amos 3:7). In such cases, the Hebrew reads *'ădōnāy yhwh*, literally "(my) Lord, Yahweh/Jehovah." But since the translators were rendering *yhwh* as "the Lord" and not as *Yahweh/Jehovah* and because they wanted to avoid the odd-looking "Lord Lord," the name *yhwh* in these passages was rendered as "God." Printing it in all capitals indicates that the underlying Hebrew word is the divine name *yhwh.* [35] This phrase, "Lord God," should not be confused with the well-attested phrase "the Lord God," which renders the Hebrew words *yhwh 'ĕlōhîm*, as found in Genesis 2:4 ("the Lord God made the earth and the heavens"), Psalms 106:48 ("Blessed be the Lord God of Israel [*yhwh 'ĕlōhê yiśrā'ēl*]"), and hundreds of other passages.

The name *Jehovah* is not limited to the Bible. It occurs twice in the Book of Mormon, six times in the Doctrine and Covenants, and twice in the book of Abraham.[36] It often occurs in Latter-day Saint prophetic statements, hymns, and other Church contexts, including the temple. Even though Jehovah is a nonancient, hybrid version of the name of God the Son, Latter-day Saints and the Lord continue to use it because it represents the form of His name in our Restoration religious heritage. Similarly, English speakers do not use the original pronunciations of *John* (*Yohanan*), or *Jesus* (*Yeshua*/*yēšûa'*), or the names of any other ancient Saints whose names have come to us in transliteration, impacted to a lesser or greater degree by their transition to English.

As Keith H. Meservy has observed, "We can find Jesus Christ in the Old Testament by substituting *Jehovah* for Lord whenever it appears. Then something wonderful happens. Jehovah, who is Jesus Christ, appears from beginning to end of this great book as the God of the Old Testament."[37] Additionally, the meaning of *Jehovah* can remind us of the enduring nature of His love, His plans, and His creative and saving power. When ancient Saints "called on the name of the Lord [*yhwh*]," they employed *yhwh*, Yahweh/Jehovah, the one of whom it is rightly said there is no other name under heaven by which salvation comes (see Acts 4:12; Mosiah 3:17).

Conclusion

Biblical names, terms, and titles that have been transliterated into English all have meaning in their original Hebrew form. Our scripture study is much richer and more productive when we know how these words are used in scripture so we can reflect on their meanings. This discussion of terms that have been transliterated from biblical Hebrew to English has sought to demonstrate this premise. Thoughtful consideration of transliterated terms employed in our worship of Jehovah (*Hallelujah, Sabbath*), that express faithful involvement with and commitment to Him and His teachings (*Amen*), and that convey His power and superiority over all opposition (*Sabaoth*), including the adversary (*Satan*), can be instructive and edifying to Latter-day Saints, whether we encounter these terms in scripture, hymns, or preaching. The importance of understanding the meaning and significance of *Jehovah*, a name of our Redeemer, cannot be overstated. Other Hebrew terms that appear in transliterated form in scripture and in our religious language that could have been discussed here include hosanna (*hộšaʾ-nāʾ*), cherubim (*kĕrubîm*), seraphim (*śĕrāpîm*), Sheol (*šĕʾôl*), and Messiah (*mašîaḥ*). But these must await your own study, a future article, or both.[38]

Notes

I express thanks to my colleagues Gaye Strathearn and Charles Swift, and to my wife, Jane Allis-Pike, for reading and commenting on drafts of this article.

1. Joseph Smith, *Teachings of the Prophet Joseph Smith*, comp. Joseph Fielding Smith (Salt Lake City: Deseret Book, 1976), 290–91 (commenting on the "images of beasts" in Daniel 7 versus actual beasts mentioned in the book of Revelation). Consider also this comment from Joseph Smith in *History of the Church of Jesus Christ of Latter-day Saints*, ed. B. H. Roberts, 2nd ed. rev. (Salt Lake City: Deseret Book, 1957), 2:396: "Attended the school and read and translated with my class as usual. My soul delights in reading the word of the Lord in the original [Hebrew], and I am determined to pursue the study of the languages, until I shall become master of them, if I am permitted to live long enough."
2. Note, for example, that the Hebrew letter שׁ (*shin*) is represented by *š* in transliteration and has the sound "sh." Occasionally, this "sh" sound is carried through the transliteration process into English, as in the name *Shelemiah/šelemyāh*, but oftentimes (for various reasons) it becomes "s" as in *Sabbath* (from *šabbāt*) and *Saul* (from *šāʾūl*). Transliteration schemes, including the one used in this article, often require extra symbols to indicate sounds not natively available in the alphabet into which the original word is transliterated.
3. The *Oxford English Dictionary*, s.v. "J," http://www.dictionary.oed.com/ (accessed April 19, 2006) provides an informative overview of the history of the pronunciation and shape of the letter *J*. Originally, *j* was an *i* with a tail on it. This can be see in a number of English publications, including the 1611 edition of the KJV in which, for example, the number eight is printed in lowercase Roman type as *viij* rather than *viii*. I thank Royal Skousen and Don Chapman, both in BYU's Department of Linguistics and English Language, for sharing their insights on this matter. See further discussion of this issue below in connection with the name *Jehovah*.

4. See, for example, Exodus 15:2; 17:16; Isaiah 38:11.
5. The Hebrew title *tĕhillîm* was translated into Greek as *psalmoi*, "songs of praise." This was transliterated into Latin as *Psalmorum*, which was eventually transliterated into English as *Psalms*.
6. See Steven R. Swanson, "Hallel," in *Anchor Bible Dictionary*, ed. David Noel Freedman, 3:30, for a convenient overview and discussion.
7. A number of hymns in the Latter-day Saint hymnal contain one or more forms of *Hallelujah/Alleluia/* "Praise the Lord." Classic examples include Hymns 72 and 200.
8. That Latter-day Saints believe Jehovah is Jesus is well attested in both canonical scripture and latter-day prophetic statements. For example: "The God of Abraham, and of Isaac, and the God of Jacob, yieldeth himself . . . to be lifted up . . . to be crucified. . . . The God of nature suffers; . . . they crucify the God of Israel" (1 Nephi 19:10, 12–13); "the Lord, . . . even the voice of Jehovah, saying: I am the first and the last; I am he who liveth, I am he who was slain; I am your advocate with the Father" (D&C 110:2–4); "we commemorate the birth of Jesus Christ two millennia ago. . . . He was the Great Jehovah of the Old Testament, the Messiah of the New" ("The Living Christ: The Testimony of the Apostles," *Ensign*, April 2000, 2). See also LDS Guide to the Scriptures, s.v. "Jehovah" and "Jehovah is Christ," http://scriptures.lds.org/en/gs/contents.
9. M. Catherine Thomas, "Rest of the Lord," in *Book of Mormon Reference Companion*, ed. Dennis L. Largey and others (Salt Lake City: Deseret Book, 2003), 679. See also Robert L. Millet, "The Holy Order of God," in *The Book of Mormon: Alma, the Testimony of the Word*, ed. Monte S. Nyman and Charles D. Tate Jr. (Provo, UT: Religious Studies Center, Brigham Young University, 1992), 61–88, especially 71–75.
10. Bible Dictionary, "Sabbath," 765.
11. Latter-day prophets have repeatedly emphasized the importance of appropriate Sabbath observance and worship. See, for example, the First Presidency letter on "Sabbath Day Observance," dated September 28, 1992, which was to be read in Church sacrament meetings.
12. The *s* with a dot under it, *ṣ*, represents the Hebrew letter *ṣade*, an emphatic *s*. It is sometimes transliterated as "ts," and has a sound similar to the two *z*'s in *pizza*.
13. Most modern translations, such as the NRSV, render "Sabaoth" in these verses as "hosts."
14. Readers will notice that in this example the spelling is a little different. This is due to the particular grammatical construction of the word in relation to other

words in the sentence. Other passages in which "host(s)" refers to a human army include Judges 4:2, 7; 8:6; 2 Kings 5:1; and Psalm 60:10.

15. 2 Kings 6:16–17 recounts the appearance of the heavenly host/army, but this passage does not contain the word *host.*
16. Some other examples of this concept include Exodus 14:14; Judges 5:4; 2 Samuel 5:23–24; Psalm 68:7; Habakkuk 3:9–12.
17. See also Nehemiah 9:6; D&C 38:1. For comments on D&C 95:7 see Joseph Fielding McConkie and Craig J. Ostler, *Revelations of the Restoration* (Salt Lake City: Deseret Book, 2000), 691; and Stephen E. Robinson and H. Dean Garrett, *A Commentary on the Doctrine and Covenants* (Salt Lake City: Deseret Book, 2004), 3:209. I strongly disagree with the suggestion of Robinson and Garrett that "Sabaoth" in D&C 95:7 is not a transliteration of *ṣĕbāʾôt,* but of *šabbāt,* Sabbath, and with their conclusion that "creator of the first day" indicates that Jehovah is Lord of the Jewish Sabbath on Saturday and the Christian Sabbath on the first day of the week.
18. The other two common name-titles for Satan—*devil* and *Lucifer*—have their own interesting etymological histories. In brief, the word *devil* is an anglicized, transliterated form of the Greek term *diabolos*, which means "accuser, slanderer," thus having a similar range of meaning as "satan," and can be seen as a translation of *śāṭān. Lucifer* was transliterated into English from Latin (*lux* + *ferre*, "light-bringer"). It is a translation of the Hebrew in Isaiah 14:12: "How art thou fallen from heaven, O Lucifer [*hêlēl* ("bright/shiny one")], son of the morning [*ben-šāḥar*]!"
19. The verb occurs only six times in the Hebrew Bible: Psalms 38:21 (38:20 in English versions); 71:13; 109:4, 20, 29; and Zechariah 3:1.
20. Textually, this is a complicated situation because other nouns, such as *ʾĕlōhîm* (Elohim; God), sometimes occur with the definite article *hāʾĕlōhîm* as in Job 1:6, similar to *haśśāṭān*. The definite article is not translated in these cases when it is understood that *ʾĕlōhîm* refers to God, not "the gods," as it sometimes does in the Hebrew Bible (see, for example, Exodus 12:12; Joshua 24:15; Judges 10:6).
21. This raises a tricky issue. Given the paucity and late date of most attestations of the concept of a demonic Satan in the Hebrew Bible, one can more easily understand why some scholars, without the benefit of a Restoration view, accept a developmental or evolutionary approach to the human invention of Satan. Linguistically, it is clear that English *Satan* is a transliteration from Hebrew *śāṭān*. But it may not be clear to everyone what should be made of the fact that the

"fallen one" is called "Satan" in premortal (see Moses 4:3–4) and early mortal (see Moses 5:13, 18) contexts. Presumably, this indicates that *śāṭān* was part of the vocabulary of the Israelites from at least Moses's day onwards. Since it is not certain what the link between the Adamic language and Hebrew is, occurrences of *Satan* in Moses 4 and 5 should not be taken as evidence that Satan was called "Satan" in the language(s) of heaven or Adam.

22. There are no capital (uppercase) letters in Hebrew. The practice of rendering JEHOVAH in all capitals represents a decision on the part of the translators and printers to show respect for the divine name.
23. It seems that the divine name *yhwh* was pronounced until after the Babylonian Exile and building of the Second Temple in Jerusalem 515 BC. According to the traditional explanation, in the following centuries the full form of the name was only pronounced by the Aaronic high priest alone in the Holy of Holies on Yom Kippur (the Day of Atonement), and eventually became lost to all. (As a point of interest, Yom Kippur is transliterated from Hebrew *yôm kippūrîm* and translates as "Day of Atonement.") The divine name *yhwh* is sometimes called the Tetragrammaton, a Greek term that means "four letters."
24. This (*'ădōnāy*) is the most common form of *'ădōn* used in relation to deity in the Hebrew Bible. The grammatical plural ("my lords") is generally thought to convey majesty.
25. Actually, only the first and last of the three vowels are usually indicated in print. The Hebrew alphabet consists only of consonants. Vowel sounds are part of the language but not originally indicated in written texts since there were no vowel letters. Systems were developed in the second half of the first millennium AD to indicate vowel sounds by placing dots and other small marks in relation to the consonantal letters.
26. The word *the* in the phrase "the LORD" is not in the Hebrew text, but is added to make sense in English, since the name is replaced by a title. Technically, the "L" in "LORD" is capitalized and the "ORD" are printed as small capitals: LORD.
27. Because the Hebrew letter *waw* (ו) is pronounced *vav* in modern times (and because the pronunciation of "w" and "v" alternates in other languages as well; for example, "w" in German is pronounced "v"), the four letters of the divine name are variously written as YHWH, YHVH, JHVH, and so on. Whatever the variations in English, the Hebrew letters are always the same: יהוה.
28. The first vowel in English is different because the first vowel in *'ădōnāy* is a shortened sound that would normally be represented by a short "eh." But because

ʾădōnāy begins with the letter *ʾaleph*, what would be a short "eh" is pronounced as a short "ah."

29. The Hebrew *yhwh* went into Latin as IHVH, the form by which it transferred into English and other European languages. The letter *J* "is, in its origin, a comparatively late modification of the letter I. In the ancient Roman alphabet, I, besides its vowel value [in certain words] had the kindred consonantal value of modern English Y" (*Oxford English Dictionary*, s.v. "J" (accessed April 19, 2006). On the historical relationship between the letters *u* and *v*, see the discussion in *Oxford English Dictionary*, s.v. "U" and "V."

    The *Oxford English Dictionary* indicates that "Jehovah," spelled "Iehouah," appeared in William Tyndale's translation of the five books of Moses, the Pentateuch, in 1530. This form, sometimes with minor variations, is how it was commonly spelled in other attestations at that time. In the first edition of the KJV (1611) the block Roman print of the divine name in Exodus 6:3 is "IEHOVAH," while the blackletter script of the rest of the biblical text utilizes a capital *J*, (an *I* with a tail), illustrating the ongoing process that eventually culminated in the distinction between these two letters.

    It is often claimed that the English word *Iehouah/Jehovah* was first used in the early 1500s; however, it has been observed that "the writers of the sixteenth century, Catholic and Protestant (e.g. Cajetan and Théodore de Bèze), are perfectly familiar with the word [*Iehouah*]. Galatinus himself (Areana cathol. veritatis, I, Bari, 1516, a, p. 77) represents the form as known and received in his time [early 1500s]. Besides, Drusius (loc. cit., 351) discovered it in Porchetus, a theologian of the fourteenth century. Finally, the word is found even in the Pugio fidei of Raymund Martin, a work written about 1270 (ed. Paris, 1651, pt. III, dist. ii, cap. iii, p. 448, and Note, p. 745). Probably the introduction of the name Jehovah antedates even R. Martin" (*Catholic Encyclopedia*, s.v. "Jehovah (Yahweh)," www.newadvent.org/cathen/08329a.htm; I thank Stan Thayne for this reference). Similarly, *Anchor Bible Dictionary*, s.v. "Yahweh," claims, without providing support, that "this confused usage [the hybrid *Iehouah/Jehovah*] may, however, have begun as early as 1100 a.d." For other remarks on this issue, see Kent P. Jackson, *The Restored Gospel and the Book of Genesis* (Salt Lake City: Deseret Book, 2001), 6, 15–16.

30. A very brief description of this is contained in the Bible Dictionary, "Names of persons," 737. See also Dana M. Pike, "Names, Theophoric," *Anchor Bible Dictionary*, 4:1018–19.

31. This is briefly mentioned in the Bible Dictionary, "Jehovah," 710–11. See also Henry O. Thompson, "Yahweh," in *Anchor Bible Dictionary*, 6:1011–12.
32. Hebrew *yhwh* is related to *yihyeh*, the *Qal* third masculine singular imperfect form of the verb "to be." Exodus 3:14 contains the *Qal* first singular imperfect form of this verb, *'ehyeh*. The imperfect aspect, or tense, in Hebrew conveys present, ongoing, and future action. So "I AM" is a translation, not a transliteration of the Hebrew.
33. See, respectively, Bible Dictionary, "Jehovah," 710, and James E. Talmage, *Jesus the Christ* (Salt Lake City: Deseret Book, 1981), 36. Talmage's rendition "*Self-existent One*" is probably the basis for all later uses of this in other Church-related publications.
34. See for example, Jackson, *Restored Gospel and the Book of Genesis*, 7; and Thompson, "Yahweh," in *Anchor Bible Dictionary*.
35. Rendering *'ădōnāy yhwh* as "the Lord God" is based on the practice of the Hebrew Bible, which in these cases places the vocalization of the word *'ĕlōhîm*, "God," in conjunction with *yhwh*, rather than the vowels of *'ădōnāy*, to remind readers to say this substitute for the divine name. Combinations that are more rare than "Lord God" in the KJV include: "Lord God" (in Isaiah 3:15 and Zechariah 9:14; the rendering of Hebrew *'ădōnāy yhwh*, which is "Lord God" elsewhere in the KJV); "Lord JEHOVAH" (the KJV rendition of Hebrew *yh yhwh*, the short and full form of the divine name, in Isaiah 2:12; 26:4); and "O God the Lord" (Psalms 109:21; 141:8; the Hebrew here is *yhwh 'ădōnāy*, literally "Yahweh, Lord," or "Lord, Lord").
36. See 2 Nephi 22:2 (where it is rendered in all capitals as in the KJV of Isaiah 12:2); Moroni 10:34; D&C 109:34, 42, 56, 68; 110:3; 128:9; Abraham 1:16; 2:8. It is presently impossible to know how many times *yhwh/Yahweh* may have been written in Nephite scripture prior to its translation into English.
37. Keith H. Meservy, "Lord = Jehovah," *Ensign*, June 2002, 29.
38. These terms can be further researched by consulting the LDS Bible Dictionary and other more in-depth resources such as *The HarperCollins Bible Dictionary* (1996), *Eerdmans Dictionary of the Bible* (2000), and *Anchor Bible Dictionary* (1992), as well as a good concordance. Some are also discussed in *Book of Mormon Reference Companion*.

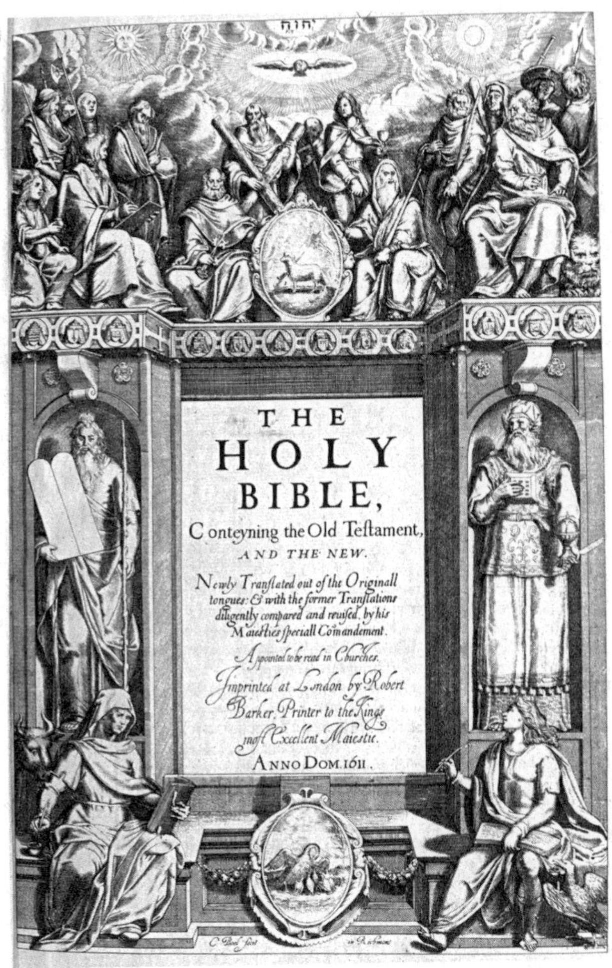

Title Page of the 1611 King James Version

All 1611 images courtesy of L. Tom Perry Special Collections, Harold B. Lee Library, Brigham Young University

Chapters, Verses, Punctuation, Spelling, and Italics in the King James Version

Kent P. Jackson, Frank F. Judd Jr., and David R. Seely

***Kent P. Jackson** is a professor of ancient scripture at BYU. **Frank F. Judd Jr.** is an assistant professor of ancient scripture at BYU. **David R. Seely** is a professor of ancient scripture at BYU.*

The Bible was written in Hebrew, Aramaic, and Greek, the everyday spoken languages of the ancient Israelites and the early Christians.[1] But because few readers today know those languages, we must rely on translations and hope the translators accurately conveyed the words, thoughts, and intents of the original writers as recorded on the original manuscripts.

The English Bible

William Tyndale (1494–1536) is the father of the English Bible; unfortunately, however, few Latter-day Saints know of him and of his profound contributions to the scriptures.[2] In violation of the law and in constant danger of imprisonment and death, Tyndale translated and published parts of the Bible into English and created the translation from which much of the King James Version ultimately descended.[3] Tyndale, like Martin Luther and other Reformers of their time, believed that the Bible should be in the language of the people and available to believers individually. The medieval Christian church, in contrast, taught that access to the Bible should be controlled by the church through the priests and that the only legitimate Bible was the Latin Vulgate translation that had been in use in the church for a thousand years—though very few Christians could read it.[4] Tyndale knew that the original Hebrew and Greek texts, in the words of the ancient prophets and apostles themselves, were more authoritative than any man-made translation could be. And he knew that the manuscripts in those languages that were closest to the writers' originals should be the sources from which translations should come. Using editions of the Hebrew Old Testament and the Greek New Testament that only recently had appeared in print, he undertook the first English translation of the Bible from the original languages.

He succeeded wonderfully. In addition to being a courageous Reformer and advocate of religious freedom, Tyndale was also a master linguist and wordsmith.[5] His goal was to make the Bible so accessible that every plowboy in England could own and read a copy. To that end, the New Testament and the Old Testament sections he translated and published were small, portable, and relatively inexpensive. Tyndale's translation is characterized by what Nephi called "plainness" (2 Nephi 25:4). It is in clear and simple English, the language of middle-class people of Tyndale's own time, and it is deliberately free of the elegant and affected literary trappings of the monarchy and the church. His choice of words has endured. Computer-based research has shown that over 75 percent of the King James Old Testament (of the sections on which Tyndale worked) comes from Tyndale as well as over 80 percent of the King James New Testament.[6]

Tyndale translated and published the New Testament (editions of 1526, 1534, 1535), Genesis to Deuteronomy (1530, 1534), and Jonah (1531). He probably also translated Joshua to 2 Chronicles (published after his death).[7] Before he could translate more, however, he was captured, imprisoned, strangled to death, and burned at the stake for his heresy. Other Protestant translations followed in succession, and all were built on Tyndale's foundation, including the Coverdale Bible, Matthew's Bible, and the Great Bible. The most important successors to Tyndale's Bible came next—the Geneva Bible, the Bishops' Bible, and the King James Bible.

The Geneva Bible (1560) was translated and published by exiled Reformers who had fled to Protestant Switzerland to avoid persecution in Britain when it was under a Catholic monarch. It was an excellent translation that, for the most part, was a revision of Tyndale. Its translators shared Tyndale's vision of making the Bible accessible to ordinary people in their own tongue. To assist readers, they added explanatory marginal notes, maps, illustrations, cross-references, and numerous study helps. It was what we now call a "study Bible," and it enabled readers to drink deeply from the words of the prophets and apostles without the mediation of priests or the church. More than any other Bible in English, the popular Geneva Bible liberated the word of God from its medieval past and placed it in the hands of hundreds of thousands of readers. It was also the Bible of Shakespeare and his contemporaries and was an important foundation of modern English.

In contrast, the Bishops' Bible (1568) was created with a different intent, and it produced a different outcome. It was prepared by conservative Anglican bishops who were not altogether comfortable with the idea of giving ordinary people free access to the word of God. Thus, they produced a translation further removed from the common language of the people than the Geneva Bible was. The vocabulary and sentence structure were throwbacks to earlier times, with an increase of less-familiar Latinate words and Latinate word order. It was intended primarily to be used in churches; and, to that end, its large, heavy, volumes were chained to pulpits all over England. It also lacked many of the study helps and all of the marginal notes that the bishops found offensive in the Geneva Bible. Predictably, people found the Bishops' Bible unappealing, bought few copies of it, and continued to purchase the Geneva Bible instead.[8] It soon became apparent to authorities of the Church of England that the Bishops' Bible would not do, so they decided to undertake another revision, the one that is known to us as the Authorized Version or King James Version (KJV).

The King James translation was motivated as much as anything else by the politics of the day, including the continuing popularity of the Geneva Bible. Geneva was popular with the nonconformist Puritans, whose loyalty to the monarchy and the Church of England was under suspicion. Its abundant marginal notes, written to assist readers to study the Bible on their own, reflected independence from both the church and the crown and, in some places, reflected Calvinist ideas that the king and his advisors found bothersome. The decision was made to undertake a new translation free of undesirable influences and under the careful watch of authorities. All but one of the committee of approximately fifty translators appointed under King James's direction were bishops or priests of the Church of England, and among them were the best Hebrew and Greek scholars in Britain. Their instructions were to make a revision of the Bishops' Bible, and thus each member of the committee was given a fresh unbound copy (or part of a copy) to work from.[9] They also had before them the Hebrew Old Testament and the Greek New Testament, as well as earlier English translations, including Geneva and Tyndale.

The translators worked patiently through all parts of the Bible, scrutinizing every passage. The outcome was the most consistent and carefully produced of all the English Bibles to that date. In general, their work succeeded best when they followed the original languages and Geneva (and hence Tyndale); it succeeded least when they remained true to their instructions to follow the Bishops' Bible. Awkward passages from the Bishops' Bible survived in many instances, as in Matthew 6:34: "Sufficient unto the day is the evil thereof" (compare with "The day hath enough with his own grief" [Geneva], and "The day present hath ever enough of his own trouble" [Tyndale]).[10] But in other instances, the translators wisely abandoned the Bishops' Bible and followed Geneva instead, often improving upon Geneva's wording. On the whole, the language of the King James translation is strongest in the Gospels, where it is most firmly based on the genius of William Tyndale. It is least strong in the Old Testament prophetic books, which Tyndale never translated.

When the King James Bible was published in 1611, it included an eleven-page, small-print introduction titled "The Translators to the Reader." That work, rarely included in Bibles now, makes the translators' strong case for the necessity of publishing the Bible in the contemporary language of its readers. Interestingly, the introduction's frequent quotations from scripture come not from its own translation but from the Geneva Bible instead. And sadly, it never mentions the King James translation's debt to William Tyndale, who was still viewed with suspicion by some. The bishops who produced the King James Version were themselves less enthusiastic than Tyndale and the Geneva translators about turning the Bible over to lay readers. This attitude is reflected in interesting ways. Whereas the first Geneva title page had an illustration of Moses parting the Red Sea, inviting readers into the promised land of reading the Bible in their own language, the King James title page depicted a massive stone wall, guarded on all sides by statues of prophets and evangelists. The King James Version's title contained the words "Appointed to be read in Churches" (after "by his Maiesties Speciall Commandment"). Thankfully, that phrase was not included in the title in the Latter-day Saint edition, first published in 1979. Although most Geneva editions were small and portable and were printed in roman type—by then the type familiar in most books and the same type in which this article is printed—the 1611 King James Bible was huge (11 by 16 inches), very expensive, and printed in archaic black-letter type. Fortunately, the people's desire for the word of God prevailed, and the King James Version was soon printed in much more economical and reader-friendly formats.

Many of the Puritans left England to escape persecution from King James and the very bishops who had produced the new translation. Included among them were the Pilgrims who colonized New England. They brought with them the Geneva Bible, and thus it became the Bible of most of America's earliest English-speaking settlers. The king soon outlawed the printing of the Geneva translation in England, but it was printed elsewhere in Europe for three more decades, and English readers continued to use it.[11] Over the following decades, the King James Bible became more appreciated, both by scholars and by lay readers, and political, commercial, and cultural factors combined to bring about its eventual success.[12] In the meantime, it underwent numerous changes, evolving in practically each new edition until it arrived at its present state in 1769.

By the time of Joseph Smith's birth in 1805, the King James translation had become the Bible of the English-speaking world, and most people were not even aware of other translations. When English speakers said "the Bible," they meant the King James Version. For the most part, it remained that way until midway through the twentieth century.

Whereas the Bible in modern languages is the word of God "as far as it is translated correctly" (Articles of Faith 1:8), much of what we see in our Bibles is the work of men. The King James translators and their predecessors, like all Bible translators from ancient times to the present, had to make hundreds of thousands of decisions while choosing words and phrases to convey as best they could the intent of the ancient writers. Our interest in this article, however, is not with the word choices in the Bible but with the other things that scholars, translators, editors, and printers invented to organize and present those words on the page—the chapters, verses, punctuation, spelling, and italics.

Books of the Bible

The Bible is a huge book—containing 766,137 words in English (KJV). And yet the modern reader can instantly turn to any particular passage in this massive book by following the data given in a simple formulaic reference such as Matthew 7:7. From this reference, a reader knows to turn to the book of Matthew, chapter 7, verse 7, where the reader finds the passage, "Seek, and ye shall find." But this system was not part of the original texts of the Bible. The book divisions occur because the Bible is a collection of many different books; the divisions into paragraphs, chapters, and verses are all artificial and were done centuries after the texts were written.

The English word *Bible* is derived from a Greek word *biblia*, meaning "books," reflecting the fact that the Bible is a collection. Many books were written in antiquity that were considered sacred by various groups in various places and at different times. Whereas there is much scholarship that deals with the canonization of the books of the Bible, there is little if any explicit information from the earliest historical circumstances of why and how certain ancient books were preserved and considered as canonical or standard works.[13] At some point in ancient times, a collection of those books was made that eventually became what we call the Old Testament. One of the earliest examples we have of such a collection is the plates of brass from 600 BC, which contained the books of Moses, a history of Israel, a collection of prophetic books, and genealogy (see 1 Nephi 5:10–14). Early Jews thought of the Bible as a collection of three different kinds of material, as reflected by the fact that Jesus spoke of "the law of Moses, and the prophets and the psalms" (Luke 24:44).

The earliest list of the thirty-nine specific books of the Old Testament is from the end of the first century AD and records that those books were originally found on twenty-four scrolls—because several of the smaller books could fit onto a single scroll (see 4 Esdras 14:44–46). Because the texts were written on separate scrolls, there was little need to organize them in any particular order. But there was a sense that the Bible contained three types of books and that, just as on the plates of brass, the Law or Torah (the five books of Moses) had preeminence. The rabbis and Jesus often referred to the Old Testament collection of books as "the Law and the Prophets." The Jewish canon established a tradition that organized the books according to the three categories: Torah, Prophets, and Writings. The Christian canon, preserved in all Christian Bibles to the present, followed a slightly different order, with historical books (Genesis through Esther), poetic books (Job to Song of Solomon), and prophetic books divided between the Major Prophets (longer books: Isaiah, Jeremiah, Ezekiel, and Daniel), and the twelve Minor Prophets from Hosea through Malachi.[14]

Just as in the case of the Old Testament, we know very little about the process by which twenty-seven of the many ancient Christian books came to be considered as scripture. The earliest canonical list is the Muratorian Canon, perhaps from the third century AD, which lists most of the books that make up the New Testament today—and in a similar order. It appears that the New Testament came about as a compilation of three different collections: a collection of four Gospels, a collection of fourteen epistles of Paul, and a collection of seven epistles from other church leaders, completed with the addition of two texts: the Acts and Revelation.

From the various Gospels that circulated anciently, the church by the middle of the second century had accepted four: Matthew, Mark, Luke, and John. The book of Acts was inserted between the Gospels and the letters to provide a link between the life of Jesus and the ministries of the Apostles in the early Church. The fourteen Pauline epistles were eventually organized more or less by length from the longest to the shortest—from Romans to Philemon—followed by Hebrews because early Christians were uncertain about its authorship. The seven surviving epistles from other Church leaders were added, followed by the book of Revelation.

Divisions of the Biblical Text

Divisions of the texts in the Hebrew Old Testament and the Greek New Testament have their own history and can be treated separately.[15] It was only when the Christian Bible combined the two Testaments, and especially as the Bible was translated into various languages, that the texts were treated similarly, and a uniform system of numbered chapters and verses was superimposed upon the text that presently survives. Because the earliest surviving texts of the Bible date from centuries after the original authors, no one knows the nature of the original divisions. From what is known about the history of the divisions of the texts in the various manuscript traditions, three simple necessities can be identified that motivated the gradual creation of various units and later the systems of numbering those units. First, there was a need to identify and isolate specific units that could be read in worship services in the synagogue or the church. Second, the need occurred to provide a simple way of referring to a specific passage in the Bible to facilitate preaching, teaching, study, discussion, and debate. Finally, both Jewish and Christian scholars created concordances of the language of the Bible—and small numbered divisions of the text were almost a necessity for such concordances.

Old Testament Paragraphs and Verses

The oldest surviving Hebrew Old Testament texts are among the Dead Sea Scrolls, found beginning in 1947 in the caves at Qumran—the earliest dating to about 250 BC. These scrolls were written with pen and ink on pieces of leather that were sewn together to form scrolls. The Hebrew text was written in horizontal lines reading from right to left, in columns that were also read from right to left, and the scribes usually left slight spaces between the words. Interestingly enough, the system of division attested in these earliest biblical texts is neither chapters nor verses but paragraphs according to thematic or sense units.

The system of division into paragraphs was preserved in the Jewish tradition and eventually became part of the Masoretic Text of the Hebrew Bible (see below). The logic of paragraph divisions can be illustrated by several examples. In the Hebrew text of the Creation story in Genesis 1:1–2:3, the text is divided into seven paragraphs coinciding with the seven days of creation. Within historical narrative, the paragraphs divide a story into episodes. Thus, 1 Samuel 1 is divided into five episodes that trace the life of Hannah and the birth of Samuel, and Isaiah 1 is divided into six paragraphs of varying lengths that indicate different topics. Paragraph divisions dramatically illustrate the episodic nature of biblical narrative and help the reader see the basic sense units of the text.

In addition to the division of the text into small paragraph units, the Jewish tradition also developed a system of dividing the Torah into fifty-four larger units, each consisting of many paragraphs called *parashoth*. Those divisions provided suitable units to be read in the synagogue each Sabbath with the intent that the whole of the Torah could be read in a calendar year. Each of those sections received a title based on the first word or words of the passage, but they were never numbered. The titles provided a label as a point of reference for teachers and students in the discussion of a text. The whole of the Hebrew Bible, except for the Psalms, is divided into paragraphs, but only the Torah is divided into *parashoth*.

The division into verses preceded the division into chapters. Within the paragraph divisions, Jewish scribes in the Mishnaic period (AD 70–200) developed a system of dividing the biblical text into verse units that roughly coincided with sentences. In addition to ordering the text for easier study, the verse divisions had a function in the reading of the Torah in the synagogue. Because it was customary to read a section of the Bible in the original Hebrew and then stop and translate the passage into Aramaic, verses provided convenient places for the reader to stop and allow the interpreter to speak.[16] Just as with the paragraphs and *parashoth*, the scribes never numbered those verses.

About AD 500, a group of rabbinic Jewish scribes and scholars, called the Masoretes, saw that the text of the Bible as it was being transmitted began to show signs of changing through the years. The Masoretes standardized the Hebrew text by developing a system to write vowels. They also formalized word divisions; developed a set of accents to indicate ancient traditions of reciting the text; created concordances; counted all of the paragraphs, words, and letters; and inserted notes of explanations, references, and statistics in the margins and at the end of the texts to help future scribes. Their work is called the Masoretic Text. It became the model for all future scribal copying and the standard Bible for most Jews in the world to the present day.

Elements of the paragraph and verse divisions that were preserved in the Masoretic Text were later superimposed in various ways on the texts of the Greek and Latin translations of the Bible that were used by Christians. The King James translators had access to the Masoretic Text and implemented in their translation the original Jewish system of verse divisions together with the system of numbering that they had inherited from other Christian Bible editions and translations. Following the model of the Hebrew paragraph divisions, the KJV translators or editors also created a system of paragraph markers throughout the Old Testament (¶) that most often parallels the divisions found in the Hebrew Bible.

New Testament Paragraphs

As with the Old Testament, we do not have any original New Testament texts. But we do have very early textual evidence of the New Testament from the beginning of the second century, and those earliest manuscripts were written in the tradition of Greek texts of their day, in all capital letters, with no division between the words or sections. Although the modern reader may be bewildered by a text that has no apparent breaks, the ancient Greek has a set of rhetorical particles that indicate natural pauses and breaks in the text. Most New Testament texts were written on parchment or papyrus, and by the second century, they began to be written in codices (books with leaves bound together—singular, *codex*) rather than on scrolls.[17]

Just as in the Hebrew tradition, the first system of division in the New Testament text was the paragraph, which naturally followed the rhetorical and grammatical particles in the text. One of the earliest systems of division in the New Testament is attested in the Greek Bible manuscript Vaticanus, dating from the fifth century AD. In Vaticanus, the scribes used a system of unknown origin in which the text was divided into sections corresponding to the break in sense. Those divisions were called in Greek *kephalaia*, which means "heads" or "principals." They were named and numbered in the margins and are the first attested form of a sort of chapter division in the New Testament. In Vaticanus, for example, the Gospel of Matthew was divided into 170 such units—62 in Mark, 152 in Luke, and 50 in John. The *kephalaia* were much smaller in length than the present-day chapters and are much closer to the paragraphs. In other Greek manuscripts, Acts, the epistles, and Revelation were similarly divided into chapters and smaller sections.[18]

As they did with the Old Testament, the King James translators indicated paragraph divisions in the New Testament with paragraph markers (¶). Often, but not always, their paragraph divisions coincide with ancient chapter divisions known from early manuscripts, but for some reason that mystifies scholars to the present day, they end at Acts 20:36.[19]

At the same time the *kephalaia* divisions in the New Testament were being made, rudimentary smaller divisions, indicated by simple forms of punctuation (sixth–eighth centuries), were beginning to be marked in the Greek texts; these divisions would eventually be reflected in the chapter and verse divisions after the thirteenth century.

Today's Chapters and Verses

Eventually, the Christians developed a need for a more precise way of citing scriptural passages for the Old and New Testaments, especially in the creation of concordances. The Christians incorporated in their biblical texts the Jewish paragraph and verse divisions of the Old Testament and the medieval chapter system of the New Testament.

The creator of the system of chapters that is used to the present time is Stephen Langton (1150–1228), a professor of theology in Paris and later the archbishop of Canterbury.[20] Langton introduced his chapter numbers into the Latin Bible—the Vulgate—in 1205, from which they were transferred in the ensuing centuries to Hebrew manuscripts and printed editions of the Old Testament as well as to Greek manuscripts and printed editions of the New Testament.

The system of verse divisions that has prevailed to the present was the work of a Parisian book printer, Robert Estienne (Latinized as *Stephanus*; 1503–59). In the printing of his fourth edition of the Greek New Testament in 1551, he added his complete system of numbered verses for the first time.

For the Old Testament, Stephanus adopted the verse divisions already present in the Masoretic Text of the Hebrew Bible, and within Langton's chapters, he assigned numbers to the verses. Following his own sense of logic as to the sense of the text, Stephanus took it upon himself, also within the framework of Langton's chapters, to divide and number the verses in the New Testament. His son reported that he did this work as he regularly traveled between Paris and Lyon. Whereas he probably did much of the work in his overnight stays at inns, his detractors spread the story that he did it while riding on his horse, and they attributed what they thought to be unfortunate verse divisions to slips of the pen when the horse stumbled. In 1555, Stephanus published the Latin Vulgate—the first whole Bible divided into numbered chapters and verses. Soon, those divisions became standard in the printed editions of the scriptures in Hebrew, Greek, Latin, and eventually in all of the modern languages. The first English Bible to have the numbered chapters and verses of Langton and Stephanus was the Geneva Bible in 1560.

Some scholars have criticized Stephanus's verse divisions as seemingly arbitrary, citing the fact that although they often coincide with a single sentence in English, sometimes they include several sentences, sometimes they divide a single sentence, and sometimes they separate direct quotations from the situation of the speaker. But clearly the advantages of organizing the text for reading and finding passages far outweigh any disadvantages. In the King James Bible, the translators typographically created a new, separate paragraph in each verse by indenting the verse number and first word and captitalizing the first letter of the first word, even if it was in the middle of a sentence.[21] For the casual reader, this procedure can provide a rather serious obstacle, giving the false impression that the Bible is composed of a collection of disconnected sentences and phrases and making it difficult to see and understand any particular verse in its larger context. Consequently, a conscientious reader of the King James Version should always make a concentrated effort to see the bigger context of any particular verse of scripture, being aware that the chapter and verse divisions are artificial and subjective additions to the text that should not constrain us in the interpretation of the Bible.

The preference of Joseph Smith and the early Latter-day Saints seems to have been for longer content-based paragraphs rather than short verses. On the original manuscripts of the Joseph Smith Translation, the Prophet's assistants, presumably working under his direction, created verses that are much larger than those in traditional Bibles, corresponding more with paragraphs.

For example, Genesis 1 contains nine verses in the JST but thirty-one in the King James translation.[22] Similarly, in the first printing of the Book of Abraham, Joseph Smith or his assistants divided the text into nine large paragraph-length verses, as opposed to the thirty-one verses in the same chapter in the Pearl of Great Price today.[23] And the first edition of the Doctrine and Covenants (1835) had numbered verses much longer than those we use now.[24] Most modern Bible translations preserve Stephanus's verses but do not create separate paragraphs for each verse, dividing the chapters instead into paragraphs based on the internal content of the scriptural text.

Punctuation

The 1611 King James Bible was published by the firm of Robert Barker of London. Barker's family had been in the printing business for decades, and he had the distinction of being "Printer to the Kings most Excellent Maiestie," as is noted on the Bible's title page. With that designation, his company held the new Bible's franchise (sometimes with partners) into the 1630s, when the concession went to other printers, most often university presses. The origin of the punctuation in the 1611 KJV is not well understood. In large part, it was determined by the translators, based on the Hebrew and Greek texts, earlier English versions, and the current usage of the time. But it likely also contains influence from editors in Barker's shop. The punctuation in the 1611 edition was not done very consistently. Readers today are often surprised to learn that the punctuation in our current KJV differs in thousands of places from that of the 1611 first edition. Note the following example from Matthew 26:47–48, with the 1611 text (left) compared with the text of the 1979 Latter-day Saint edition (right):

47 ¶ And *while he yet ſpake, loe,
Iudas one of the twelue came, and
with him a great multitude with
ſwords and ſtaues from the chiefe
Prieſts and Elders of the people.
48 Now he that betrayed him gaue
them a ſigne, ſaying, Whomſoeuer I
ſhall kiſſe, that ſame is he, hold him faſt.

47 ¶ And while he yet spake, lo,
Judas, one of the twelve, came, and
with him a great multitude with
swords and staves, from the chief
priests and elders of the people.
48 Now he that betrayed him gave
them a sign, saying, Whomsoever I
shall kiss, that same is he: hold him
fast.

Usually, punctuation differences are inconsequential, but sometimes they affect meaning. Note Acts 27:18, which also has a word difference and an italic difference:

18 And being exceedingly tossed with a tempest the next day, they lightned the ship:	18 And we being exceedingly tossed with a tempest, the next *day* they lightened the ship;

The edition of 1612 made punctuation changes, and every printing thereafter for a century and a half made more. Each printing house that published the Bible modified the punctuation in some way in virtually every edition, and thus of the numerous editions between 1611 and the late eighteenth century, none were identical. Mathew Carey, an American printer of the early 1800s, noted that the punctuation differences between various Bibles were "innumerable." He gave as an example Genesis 26:8, which had "eight commas in the Edinburgh, six in the Oxford, and only three in the Cambridge and London editions."[25]

In 1762, Professor F. S. Parris produced an important revised edition for the Cambridge University Press, continuing the process of revision and modernization that had been underway since 1611—not only in punctuation but in all areas of the text. In 1769, the Oxford University Press, under the direction of Professor Benjamin Blayney, revised the Parris edition further. Blayney made numerous punctuation changes, adding much punctuation to the text.[26] He also made many other changes, such as strictly applying to the text archaic grammatical rules that neither were part of the language in 1611 nor were intended by the translators. (For example, in the current KJV, the pronoun *ye* is always used for the second-person plural when the subject of the sentence, and *you* is used for the second-person plural in all other cases. This is an artificial consistency imposed on the text by Blayney. In the 1611 KJV, the two forms were used more interchangeably; and even long before 1611, both forms were in common usage in the singular as well as in the plural. The fluid use of the pronouns in the Book of Mormon reflects these developments in the language.[27]

Blayney's new edition soon came to be viewed as the standard for British publishing houses and eventually for American publishers as well. It remains so today, and most King James printings now, including the Latter-day Saint edition, are virtually identical to Blayney's Oxford edition of 1769.[28]

But punctuation usage in modern English has continued to evolve since 1769, and thus Bible readers today see commas, colons, and semicolons used in ways that are different from how we use them now.

As we discussed earlier, the verses in the Hebrew Bible are most often self-contained grammatical units, although there are many exceptions. But the earliest manuscripts of the Old Testament contained no punctuation. The Masoretes, working about a millennium after most of the original writers, formalized a system of punctuation that included sentence-ending marks and various marks within sentences to show major and minor breaks. The evidence suggests that in some cases, the Masoretes may have made mistakes in sentence division; but, on the whole, they did an extraordinarily good job, and their work was a profound accomplishment. When the translators and editors of the King James Bible and its predecessors applied European punctuation, in most cases they honored the Masoretic sentence endings because they kept the verse divisions of Stephanus from the previous century. Thus, sentences in the King James Old Testament almost always end where sentences end in the Masoretic Text. But within sentences, the English translators frequently subdivided the text differently.

In New Testament manuscripts, rudimentary punctuation marks began to appear gradually in the sixth and seventh centuries, usually indicating breaks in sentences. It was not until the seventh century that marks for breathing and accents began to appear, and it was not until the ninth century that the continuous writing in the texts began to be broken into individual words.

The texts of the manuscripts Sinaiticus and Vaticanus contain a system of punctuation as indicated by a single point of ink on the level of the tops of the letters, or occasionally by a small break in the continuous letters or by a slightly larger letter, to indicate a pause in the sense of the text—a break that usually corresponds with a sentence. Later New Testament manuscripts from the sixth and seventh centuries developed a more complex system of marks, usually made by dots indicating a pause, a half-stop, and a full stop, and later a mark of interrogation, corresponding to the English usage of a comma, semicolon, period, and question mark. Occasionally, there were slight spaces between words to indicate a break in the sense. Ninth-century manuscripts show that the scribes began to insert breaks between the words in their texts, and punctuation marks were more frequently put at the end of words rather than above the letters as before. It should be noted that any markings or spaces added to the original continuous writing of the earliest New Testament manuscripts involved a subjective act of interpretation by the scribe. There is evidence of ancient scribal disagreement in terms of punctuation and even word divisions. In addition, later scribes often went back and inserted marks of punctuation above the lines of earlier manuscripts (as in the case of Vaticanus) to reflect their own interpretations.

Therefore, the Greek texts used by the translators of the Bible into English, including Tyndale and the King James translators, already contained systems of word division, punctuation, breathings, and accents that certainly influenced the way the texts were interpreted and translated. The translators of each different English version had the ancient markings and divisions before them, but they variously punctuated their translations according to their understanding and interpretation of the text.[29]

Absent in the King James translation are quotation marks, which did not appear commonly until long after 1611. Capital letters are used to show where a quotation begins, but the end of a quotation can be determined only from the context. That is not always easy, as is seen in Genesis 18:13–14: "And the Lord said unto Abraham, Wherefore did Sarah laugh, saying, Shall I of a surety bear a child, which am old? Is anything too hard for the Lord?"[30]

The punctuation in today's KJV, dating to Blayney's edition of 1769, is generally systematic and quite consistently done. It uses periods to end sentences, colons and semicolons for major breaks within sentences, and commas for smaller breaks. On the whole, the colons, semicolons, and commas seem to have been applied according to the objectives of the translators and later editors—not necessarily with the intent of reflecting the punctuation in the Hebrew and Greek texts.

By today's standards—and even by the standards of 1611 and 1769—the King James Version often feels overpunctuated, and readers sometimes find themselves tripping over its many tiny clauses that interrupt the flow of the text and occasionally make the meaning less clear. But this is neither unexpected nor accidental; it was intended to be that way. We should recall that when the translation was originally conceived and published, it was "Appointed to be read in Churches." Its creators filled it with punctuation, believing that the congregational reading for which it was primarily intended would be enhanced by the short clauses, each set apart by a pause. Had they known that the Bible's greatest use would eventually be with families in private homes, perhaps they would have done otherwise.

Spelling

The printing of the Bible in English contributed greatly to the standardization of English spelling. In Tyndale's day, there was much variety in spelling, and indeed Tyndale's own publications showed considerable inconsistency while at the same time contributing to the establishment of spelling norms. Early in the next century, when the King James translation appeared, English spelling was still in flux, and it differed in many instances from the spelling in use today, as can be seen in the comparison of the 1611 KJV of Isaiah 7:13–14 (left) and the current Latter-day Saint edition (right).

Spelling conventions evolved rapidly in the seventeenth century, as is reflected in early printings of the KJV. Barker's 1611 first edition has the spellings "publique" (Matthew 1:19), "musicke" (Luke 15:25), and "heretike" (Titus

13 And hee said; Heare ye now, O house of Dauid; Is it a small thing for you to weary men, but will ye weary my God also?
14 Therefore the Lord himselfe shal giue you a signe: * Beholde, a Virgine shall conceiue and beare a Sonne, and || shall call his name Immanuel.

13 And he said, Hear ye now, O house of David; *Is it* a small thing for you to weary men, but will ye weary my God also?
14 Therefore the Lord himself shall give you a [a]sign; [b]Behold, a [c]virgin shall conceive, and bear a [d]son, and shall call his name [e]Immanuel.

3:10), with three separate spellings for the same grammatical ending. Within a few decades, all of those were standardized to "-ick." At 1 Timothy 4:16, the 1611 edition reads, "Take heed unto thy selfe." Barker's 1630 edition uses "heede," and his edition of only four years later uses "heed" again. His edition of 1639 changes "selfe" to "self," but the spelling "thyself" (one word) was not standardized until the mid-eighteenth century. Spelling in the KJV began changing as early as in the second impression of 1611. It continued to evolve in later printings—but inconsistently in the hands of various publishers, who clearly had the intent to keep its spelling current with the times. It was not until Blayney's edition of 1769 that publishers considered the spelling standard and finalized (although not entirely consistent), when today's King James spelling was set in place.[31] Thus, our current Bible has words and grammar from before 1611 but spelling from 1769.

The English spellings of biblical names evolved over the centuries until the 1611 King James translation, when the spellings of most names were fixed. The 1611 printing had some inconsistencies (including the spelling of *Mary* as *Marie* in several places in Luke 1), but most variants were standardized by the 1629 Cambridge edition.[32] The spelling of names in the KJV is heavily influenced by the Latin Vulgate; and, in many cases, the spellings are far removed from how the ancient people actually pronounced their own names. Some examples include *Isaac*, pronounced anciently "Yitz-haq" (Geneva, *Izhák*; Bishops', *Isahac*); *Isaiah*, "Ye-sha-ya-hu"; *John*, "Yo-ha-nan"; *James*, "Ya-a-qov"; and *Jesus*, "Ye-shu-a."[33]

The spelling of the Lord's name in the KJV Old Testament is a special case. The divine name that is written "the LORD" in the King James translation is spelled with four letters in Hebrew—*y h w h*. It probably was pronounced *Yahweh* in ancient times.[34] The form of the name that is familiar to us is *Jehovah*, with spelling and pronunciation brought into English by Tyndale in the early 1500s.[35] After the end of the Old Testament period, the Jews adopted a custom, based perhaps on an exaggerated reading of Exodus 20:7, that it was blasphemous to pronounce God's name, so in the place of *Yahweh*, they used substitute words. As they read their Hebrew texts, when they came upon God's name, they would not pronounce it but substituted in its place the word *'ădōnāy*, which means "my Lord(s)." Greek-speaking Jewish translators in the third century BC replaced the divine name with the common Greek noun *kyrios*, "lord." Most modern translations have continued the custom. In the King James translation, whenever God's name *Yahweh* appears in the Hebrew text, the translators have rendered it as "the LORD."[36] Capital and small capital letters are used to set the divine name apart from the common English noun *lord*.

Italics

The use of italics in today's King James Bible has an interesting but complex history.[37] The practice of using different type within a text for various reasons seems to have begun in the early part of the sixteenth century. During the years 1534–35, Sebastian Münster and Pierre Robert Olivetan—who printed Latin and French translations of the Bible, respectively—were two of the earliest individuals to indicate, by means of a different type, words in the translation not represented precisely in the exemplar. The first English Bible to follow this practice was the Great Bible, which was printed in 1539 under the editorship of Miles Coverdale, who made use of both Münster's Latin and Olivetan's French translations. In this English translation, which was printed in black-letter type, Coverdale employed both brackets and a smaller font to indicate variant readings from the Latin Vulgate that were not in the Hebrew or Greek manuscripts.

William Whittingham's 1557 edition of the New Testament was printed in roman type and was the first English translation to use italic type for words not in the manuscripts. In his preface, he noted that he inserted those words "in such letters as may easily be discerned from the common text."[38] Three years later, Whittingham and other Protestant scholars at Geneva published the entire Bible in English—the Geneva Bible. Geneva's preface stated the following: "[When] the necessity of the sentence required anything to be added (for such is the grace and propriety of the Hebrew and Greek tongues, that it cannot but either by circumlocution, or by adding the verb or some word be understand of them that are not well practiced therein) we have put it in the text with another kind of letter, that it may easily be discerned from the common letter."[39] The 1560 Geneva Bible, printed in roman type, was the first edition of the entire Bible in English that used italics. In 1568, the Bishops' Bible followed the Geneva Bible in this practice, but because it was printed in a black-letter type, the added words were printed in roman type.[40]

Like the Bishops' Bible, the 1611 King James Bible was printed in black-letter type and used a smaller roman font for words not represented in the original languages, as in this example from Genesis 1:12 in the 1611 KJV (left) and the current text (right).

In 1618, the Synod of Dort explained some of the rules used for translating the KJV: "That words which it was anywhere necessary to insert into the text to complete the meaning were to be distinguished by another type, small roman."[41] Later editions of the KJV printed in roman type, including

12 And the earth brought foorth grasse, and herbe yeelding seed after his kinde, and the tree yeelding fruit, whose seed was in it selfe, after his kinde: and God saw that it was good.	12 And the earth [a]brought forth grass, *and* herb yielding seed after his kind, and the tree yielding fruit, whose seed *was* in itself, after his [b]kind: and God saw that *it was* good.

the LDS edition, have followed the lead of the Geneva Bible in using italics for those words not represented in the Hebrew or Greek manuscripts.

Some important observations should be made concerning italics in the King James translation. First, the primary use of italics is to identify words not explicitly found in the Hebrew or Greek manuscripts that are necessary in English to make the translation understandable. There are a number of examples of these elliptical constructions. Most instances of italics in the Bible are for the verb "to be" (for example, "I *am* the Lord thy God," Isaiah 51:15). Italics were often used to supply unexpressed but implied nouns (for example, "the dry *land*," Genesis 1:9, 10), possessive adjectives (for example, "*his* hand," Matthew 8:3), and other verbs (for example, "his tongue *loosed*," Luke 1:64). Sometimes in Greek conditional sentences, the subordinate clause (or protasis) is expressed, whereas the main clause (or apodosis) is implied. A noteworthy example is found in 2 Thessalonians 2:3: "Let no man deceive you by any means: *for that day shall not come*, except there come a falling away first." In this case, the subordinate clause of the condition is "except there come a falling away first," and the implied main clause, added in italics, is "for that day shall not come."[42]

Second, a closer look at italics in the KJV reveals other uses, besides supplying unexpressed but implied words.[43] Some italics indicate that the words are poorly attested among the ancient manuscripts. An example of this is at John 8:7: "Jesus stooped down, and with his finger wrote on the ground, *as though he heard them not*." The phrase "as though he heard them not" was not in a different type in the 1611 edition, but it was placed in italics in later editions, including the LDS edition. In this case, the Greek phrase is not in the earliest manuscripts of the New Testament, and subsequent editors of the KJV indicated their uncertainty about its authenticity by placing the words in italics.[44]

Another interesting example of this usage is at 1 John 2:23: "Whosoever denieth the Son, the same hath not the Father: [*but*] *he that acknowledgeth the Son hath the Father also*." Since the 1611 edition, the KJV has set apart the clause "but he that acknowledgeth the Son hath the Father also" in special type. The Greek clause is in the earliest manuscripts but is absent from many important later manuscripts. Because the words "hath the Father" precede and end the clause, it seems that a scribe's eye inadvertently skipped from one instance of "hath the Father" to the other and accidentally omitted the clause.[45] Thus, even though the clause is not in many later manuscripts, it does seem to be original.[46] Because the KJV translators did not have access to the early manuscripts that have this reading, the italics in 1 John 2:23 may be indicating that the clause comes from the Latin Vulgate, similar to the practice of the Great Bible.[47]

Third, there are many inconsistencies in the use of italics in the King James translation. The original KJV translators seem to have been fairly conservative in their use of italics, but their 1611 edition contained numerous inconsistencies, many of which continue today. For example, Hebrews 3:3 states "this *man*," whereas the same construction in Hebrews 8:3 is rendered "this man."[48] Over the years, editors greatly expanded the practice of using italics, a process that continued until Blayney in 1769, who added many to the text. For instance, John 11 in the 1611 edition contains no italicized words, but in a 1638 edition, it has fifteen italicized words, and in a 1756 edition, it has sixteen.[49] The same chapter in the 1979 LDS edition has nineteen italicized words.[50] Note the example from John 11:41, in 1611 (left) and the current text (right):

Concerning this increased use of italics in later editions, F. H. A. Scrivener concluded, "The effect was rather to add to than to diminish the manifest inconsistencies."[51] In today's edition, types of words that are italicized in one location are not necessarily italicized in another. For example, Acts

41 Then they tooke away the ſtone from the place where the dead was layd. And Ieſus lift vp his eyes, and ſaid, Father, I thanke thee, that thou haſt heard me.	41 Then they took away the stone *from the place* where the dead was laid. And Jesus lifted up *his* eyes, and said, Father, I [a]thank thee that thou hast heard me.

13:6 has "whose name *was* Bar-jesus," whereas the same construction in Luke 24:18 is rendered "whose name was Cleopas." There is sometimes inconsistency within the same verse. Luke 1:27 contains both "a man whose name was Joseph" and "the virgin's name *was* Mary."[52]

Although the translators and editors were not consistent in their use of italics, "it appears that generally, though not always, their judgment was justified in their choice of italicized words."[53] The question remains, however, whether italicized words in the Bible are really necessary at all.[54] One scholar has proposed that "it is impossible to make any message in one language say exactly what a corresponding message says in any other," and because the words rendered in italics are necessary to make the English understandable, "they are not extraneous additions but are a legitimate part of the translation and need not be singled out for special notice." That is the case because the primary goal of any translator is "to transmit the meaning of the message, not to reproduce the form of the words."[55] With that in mind, publishers of the Bible in modern languages have abandoned the custom of using italics, and the King James Version is now unique in employing them. For the same reason, when the Book of Mormon, the Doctrine and Covenants, and the Pearl of Great Price are translated from English into other languages, no attempt is made to identify in italics the words in the translations that do not come from the original English.

Conclusion

In recent years, despite a general decrease in Bible reading in the Western world, there has been an increased interest in the fascinating history of the English Bible and the King James Version.[56] Although it is no longer the most widely used or the most influential Bible translation in English, the KJV is still in print and still sells well.

In 2005, the venerable Cambridge University Press published a new edition of the KJV that may eventually become the most important edition since Benjamin Blayney's of 1769. Cambridge University Press, the oldest printing establishment in the world, has been publishing the English Bible since 1591 and the King James Version since 1629. It is the press that prepared the text and set the type for the English Latter-day Saint edition that is still in use today. In the same spirit that led to the recent restorations of Michelangelo's paintings in the Sistine Chapel and Leonardo da Vinci's *Last Supper*, Cambridge's editor cautiously removed most of the well-meaning but often misguided "repairs" of earlier editors (including Parris and Blayney) to restore the KJV more fully to the text and intent of its 1611 creators. Where justifiable, the grammatical changes and word choices of the post-1611 editors were peeled back to reveal the grammar and words of the original. The original intent of keeping the KJV's spelling contemporary was applied, so the new edition is now standardized to modern spelling. The punctuation was taken back to the system of 1611 but simplified and made consistent, and quotation marks were added. All the italics were removed. Poetic sections were reformatted to reflect the poetic intent of the ancient prophets and psalmists, instead of prose, and the separate paragraphs for each verse were replaced with paragraphs based on the Bible's content.[57] Thus, despite the fact that the King James Bible is now four hundred years old, it is still very much alive.

Like the Prophet Joseph Smith, we Latter-day Saints "believe the Bible as it read when it came from the pen of the original writers."[58] Modern languages, like English, were not part of the Bible "as it read when it came from the pen of the original writers," nor were the chapters, verses, punctuation, spelling, and italics that we see in printings of the Bible today. But because very few Latter-day Saints can read the languages in which the Bible was first written or have access to the earliest manuscripts, we need those medieval and modern tools that translators, scholars, editors, and printers have provided over the centuries that deliver the word of God to us on the printed page. Together, they were all designed to help us better read and understand the scriptures—to help us seek, that we may find (see Matthew 7:7).

Notes

1. The Old Testament was written in Hebrew, with a few chapters in the related language Aramaic. The New Testament was written in what is called *koine* Greek, the common Greek used throughout the biblical world in the days of Jesus and the Apostles.
2. See Robert D. Hales, "Preparations for the Restoration and the Second Coming: 'My Hand Shall Be over Thee,'" *Ensign*, November 2005, 88–92. Calling Tyndale the "father of the English Bible" does not overlook the importance of the work of John Wycliffe and his collaborators, who produced an English Bible in the late fourteenth century, translated from the Latin Vulgate. Later English Bibles, however, did not descend from Wycliffe's translation but from Tyndale's.
3. Recent histories of the English Bible include Benson Bobrick, *Wide as the Waters: The Story of the English Bible and the Revolution It Inspired* (New York: Simon and Schuster, 2001); Alister E. McGrath, *In the Beginning: The Story of the King James Bible and How It Changed a Nation, a Language, and a Culture* (New York: Doubleday, 2001); Adam Nicolson, *God's Secretaries: The Making of the King James Bible* (New York: HarperCollins, 2003); and David Daniell, *The Bible in English* (New Haven and London: Yale University Press, 2003). The best biography of William Tyndale is David Daniell, *William Tyndale, A Biography* (New Haven and London: Yale University Press, 1994).
4. The Latin Vulgate was, in large part, the work of Jerome (ca. 342–420). The word *vulgate* in the title means that it was translated into the common tongue of Western Christians in Jerome's time. But by the fifteenth century, Latin had ceased to be a spoken language of the common people, and few could read it. Even many priests could not read it adequately.
5. See David R. Seely, "Words 'Fitly Spoken': Tyndale's English Translation of the Bible," in *Prelude to the Restoration: From Apostasy to the Restored Church* (Provo, UT: Religious Studies Center, Brigham Young University; Salt Lake City: Deseret Book, 2004), 212–27.
6. See John Nielson, "Authorship of the King James Version of the Bible," unpublished MA thesis, Brigham Young University, 1994, especially 93; and John

Nielson and Royal Skousen, "How Much of the King James Bible is William Tyndale's?" *Reformation* 3 (1998): 49–74.

7. See David Daniell, ed., *Tyndale's New Testament: Translated from the Greek by William Tyndale in 1534* (New Haven and London: Yale University Press, 1989), vii–xxxii; and Daniell, ed., *Tyndale's Old Testament: Being the Pentateuch of 1530, Joshua to 2 Chronicles of 1537, and Jonah* (New Haven and London: Yale University Press, 1992), ix–xxxix.
8. Altogether, despite the official recognition of the Bishops' Bible and the official disdain of the Geneva Bible, there were forty-nine printings of the Bishops' Bible and 153 printings of the Geneva Bible, not including at least seven editions of the KJV that included the Geneva Bible's notes (see A. S. Herbert, ed., *Historical Catalogue of Printed Editions of the English Bible, 1525–1961* [London: British and Foreign Bible Society; New York: American Bible Society, 1968], 60–291).
9. They were given a copy of the 1602 edition of the Bishops' Bible; see David Norton, *A Textual History of the King James Bible* (Cambridge: Cambridge University Press, 2005), 35–36.
10. Spelling modernized in both examples. The Tyndale text is from his 1536 edition.
11. See Herbert, *Historical Catalogue*, 192.
12. See the discussion in Daniell, *Bible in English*, 451–60.
13. For information about the process of canonization, see Bible Dictionary, 630–31. "Canon," For a broad overview, see F. F. Bruce, *The Canon of Scripture* (Downer's Grove, IL: Intervarsity Press, 1988).
14. For the sake of brevity, we will not deal here with the Apocrypha. See Bible Dictionary, "Apocrypha," 610–11; also C. Wilfred Griggs, "Apocrypha and Pseudepigrapha," in Daniel H. Ludlow, ed., *Encyclopedia of Mormonism* (New York: Macmillan, 1992), 1:55–56.
15. Basic information on the writing and divisions of the Old Testament text can be found in Ernst Würthwein, *The Text of the Old Testament*, 2nd ed. (Grand Rapids, MI: Eerdmans, 1995), 1–44. For the New Testament, see Bruce M. Metzger and Bart Ehrman, *The Text of the New Testament*, 4th ed. (New York and Oxford: Oxford University Press, 2005), 1–51. For illustrations of biblical texts, see also Bruce M. Metzger, *Manuscripts of the Greek Bible* (New York and Oxford: Oxford University Press, 1981).

16. The Mishnah (ca. AD 200), in *Megillah* 4.4, already speaks of verses and specifies how many verses the reader may read in Hebrew before the interpreter translates into Aramaic.
17. See Metzger and Ehrman, *Text of the New Testament*, 12–13.
18. See Metzger and Ehrman, *Text of the New Testament*, 34–36.
19. Metzger and Ehrman note that the paragraph divisions end in Sinaiticus in Acts 15 (*Text of the New Testament*, 34).
20. Langton was famous in English history for his role in encouraging King John to agree to the terms of the Magna Carta in 1215.
21. In this they followed the precedent of the Geneva and Bishops' Bibles.
22. See Scott H. Faulring, Kent P. Jackson, and Robert J. Matthews, eds., *Joseph Smith's New Translation of the Bible: Original Manuscripts* (Provo, UT: Religious Studies Center, Brigham Young University, 2004), 595–97.
23. See *Times and Seasons* 3, no. 9 (March 1, 1842): 703–6; 3, no. 10 (March 15, 1842): 719–22.
24. The 1830 Book of Mormon had very large paragraphs, presumably created by compositor John H. Gilbert.
25. Mathew Carey, "Autobiography of Mathew Carey," *New England Magazine* 6 (January–May 1834): 232; Carey, "Preface" in his 1801 quarto Bible. The 1611 edition had only four commas in Genesis 26:8, and the Latter-day Saint edition has six.
26. See Norton, *Textual History*, 153–55.
27. See *The Oxford English Dictionary*, 2nd ed., 20 vols. (Oxford and New York: Oxford University Press, 1989), s.vv. "ye," "you"; Norton, *Textual History*, 111–13.
28. Blayney was a professor of Hebrew at Oxford University. See Herbert, *Historical Catalogue*, 282–83; Norton, *Textual History*, 103–14, 195–97; F. H. A. Scrivener, *The Authorized Edition of the English Bible (1611), Its Subsequent Reprints and Modern Representatives* (Cambridge: Cambridge University Press, 1884), 28–36, 101–5, 238–42.
29. See Scrivener, *A Plain Introduction to the Criticism of the New Testament*, ed. Edward Miller, 4th ed. (London, 1894), repr. (Eugene, OR: Wipf and Stock, 1997), 1:48–49.
30. Modern quotation marks would render the passage as follows:
    And the Lord said unto Abraham, "Wherefore did Sarah laugh, saying, 'Shall I of a surety bear a child, which am old?' Is anything too hard for the Lord?"
31. See Norton, *Textual History*, 62–114.

32. See Norton, *Textual History*, 84–85.
33. Neither Hebrew nor Greek has a "J" sound.
34. See David Noel Freedman and M. P. O'Connor, "*YHWH*," in *Theological Dictionary of the Old Testament*, ed. G. Johannes Botterweck and Helmer Ringgren, trans. David E. Green (Grand Rapids, MI: Eerdmans, 1986), 5: 500–21. Variations in the name include *Yah*, *Yaw*, and *Yahu*.
35. Tyndale's 1530 Pentateuch is the earliest attestation of *Jehovah* in print in English (see Daniell, *William Tyndale: A Biography*, 284–85. See also "Jehovah" in Tyndale's "A Table Expounding Certain Words," following Genesis in his 1530 Pentateuch, in Daniell, ed., *Tyndale's Old Testament*, 82).
36. In four exceptions, it is rendered "JEHOVAH" because of special emphasis given to the name in the text (see Exodus 6:3; Psalm 83:18; Isaiah 12:2; 26:4).
37. For more on the history of italics, see Dewey M. Beegle, *God's Word into English* (Grand Rapids, MI: Eerdmans, 1960), 112–19; Jack Lewis, "Italics in English Bible Translation," in *The Living and Active Word of God: Studies in Honor of Samuel J. Schultz*, ed. Morris Inch and Ronald Youngblood (Winona Lake, IN: Eisenbrauns, 1983), 255–66; and Walter F. Specht, "The Use of Italics in English Versions of the New Testament," *Andrews University Seminary Studies* 6 (1968): 88–93.
38. Alfred W. Pollard, ed., *Records of the English Bible* (London: Oxford University Press, 1911), 276–77, spelling modernized.
39. Pollard, *Records of the English Bible*, 281–82, spelling modernized.
40. Some editions followed the Great Bible in printing added words in small black-letter type and with brackets.
41. Pollard, *Records of the English Bible*, 339.
42. See F. F. Bruce, *1 & 2 Thessalonians* (Waco, TX: Word, 1982), 166; and Abraham J. Malherbe, *The Letters to the Thessalonians* (New York: Doubleday, 2000), 418.
43. For more examples of different types of italicized words in the KJV, see John Eadie, *The English Bible* (London: MacMillan, 1876), 2: 280–87; Scrivener, *Authorized Edition*, 64–71; and Specht, "Use of Italics," 93–96.
44. See Bruce, *The Gospel of John* (Grand Rapids, MI: Eerdmans, 1983), 415; Alfred Plummer, *The Gospel According to John* (Cambridge: Cambridge University Press, 1893), 184–85; and Specht, "Use of Italics," 94.
45. See Metzger, *A Textual Commentary on the Greek New Testament*, 2nd ed. (Stuttgart: Deutsche Bibelgesellschaft, 1994), 641; and Raymond E. Brown, *The Epistles of John* (New York: Doubleday, 1982), 354.

46. The famous Johannine Comma of 1 John 5:7–8 ("in heaven, the Father, the Word, and the Holy Ghost: and these three are one. And there are three that bear witness in earth") is not in any Greek manuscript before the sixteenth century nor in any Latin manuscript before the fourth century (see Metzger, *Textual Commentary*, 647–49). Yet this phrase appears neither in special type in the 1611 edition nor in italics in the 1979 LDS edition. The phrase was placed in italics in the Cambridge 1873 edition edited by F. H. A. Scrivener and subsequent editions based upon it (see Scrivener, *Authorized Edition*, 69).
47. The 1611 edition rendered the phrase in small roman type but did not place the word "but" in brackets. The brackets in the 1979 LDS edition seem to be a way that later editions of the KJV drew attention to the fact that among those manuscripts that have the phrase, the word *but* is absent in the Latin and the Greek but is supplied in the English to connect the phrase to the first clause in John 2:23.
48. For more examples from the 1611 edition, see Scrivener, *Authorized Edition*, 69–71.
49. See also Eadie, *English Bible*, 280.
50. Specht concluded: "In 1769, the Oxford edition by Benjamin Blayney made more corrections and further extended the use of italics, probably beyond the limits that the original famous 47 revisers would have approved" (Specht, "Use of Italics," 92).
51. Scrivener, *Authorized Edition*, 71.
52. For more on inconsistencies, see Eadie, *English Bible*, 280–87; Lewis, "Italics in English Bible Translations," 267–69; and Specht, "Use of Italics," 96–102.
53. Bible Dictionary, 708.
54. Early Latter-day Saint Church leaders, including Joseph Smith, seem to have viewed the use of italics in the Bible with suspicion. See Thomas A. Wayment and Tyson J. Yost, "The Joseph Smith Translation and Italicized Words in the King James Version," *Religious Educator* 6, no. 1 (2005): 51–64.
55. William L. Wonderly, "What About Italics?" *Bible Translator* 6 (1956): 114, 116.
56. See the references in note 3. From time to time, modern facsimiles of the 1611 edition have been made available, including *The Holy Bible 1611* (Columbus, OH: Vintage Archives, 2000), and *The Holy Bible 1611 Edition King James Version* (Nashville: Nelson, [1982]). Unfortunately this latter edition replaces the black letter type with roman type.

57. The New Cambridge Paragraph Bible (Cambridge: Cambridge University Press, 2005). See Norton, *Textual History*, 131–64, 198–361. Norton was the editor of this new edition.
58. Joseph Smith, *Teachings of the Prophet Joseph Smith*, comp. Joseph Fielding Smith (Salt Lake City: Deseret Book, 1938), 327; see also Joseph Smith, *The Words of Joseph Smith: The Contemporary Accounts of the Nauvoo Discourses of the Prophet Joseph*, comp. Andrew F. Ehat and Lyndon W. Cook (Provo, UT: Religious Studies Center, Brigham Young University, 1980), 256.

Papyrus Manuscript p[4]
(recto; Luke 6:4–16), A.D. 150–75.
This is the earliest surviving manuscript of the Gospel of Luke.

A Viewpoint on the Supposedly Lost Gospel Q

Thomas A. Wayment

Thomas A. Wayment *is an associate professor of ancient scripture at BYU.*

Over the past few years, it has become increasingly obvious that apathy toward the issues raised by biblical scholars is costing believing Christians a great deal more than we may have anticipated. Of major concern for scholars the past two centuries is the issue of the compositional order of the New Testament and the literary relationship among Matthew, Mark, and Luke—commonly referred to as the synoptic Gospels. The theories presented by scholars are, in some fields of New Testament studies, becoming more controversial, more hostile to faith, and more reform oriented. One such field of study considers the issue now known as the "synoptic problem." The "synoptic problem" refers to the discussion surrounding how the authors of the synoptic Gospels—Matthew, Mark, and Luke—used and referred to one another in the process of writing their own accounts.

Scholarship is quite polarized over how to resolve this issue. Those who advocate a "two-document hypothesis" have heavily influenced the debate among scholars concerning how the Gospels were written and what sources were used in their composition.[1] Their theory is that the Gospel of Mark was the earliest to be written and that it was subsequently used and borrowed from during the composition of the Gospels of Matthew and Luke. This theory can adequately explain how the synoptic Gospels contain much of the same material, but there are also significant portions of the Gospels of Matthew and Luke that are not found in Mark. After looking at those passages where Matthew and Luke contain the same account or saying, for which there is no corresponding account in Mark, scholars concluded that Matthew and Luke borrowed from a second earlier source that has been dubbed "Q," from the German *Quelle* or "source," and hence the idea of two source documents, Mark and Q, from which the "two-document hypothesis" derives its name. The following visual depicts the "borrowing" as reflected in the two-document hypothesis:

The Two-Document Hypothesis

Mark → Luke, Mark → Matthew
Q → Matthew, Q → Luke

(arrows show direction of borrowing)

The compositional theory proposed by many scholars of the New Testament is that Matthew and Luke each independently borrowed a significant amount of their text and order from Mark and that, interspersed between their borrowings from Mark, each evangelist added passages from the theoretical document Q. Scholars determine Q passages by comparing those instances where Matthew and Luke have a verbatim or nearly verbatim parallel between them that is not recorded in Mark. According to the theory, Q can be determined only when Matthew and Luke have copied from it directly and have not altered the saying substantially.

A discussion of Q may appear to many to be merely an academic enterprise, the work of scholars, and to go beyond the realm of faithful scripture searching. In its initial stages, Q was nearly a purely academic enterprise. Today, however, conclusions drawn from it are influencing the faith of thousands and altering the way the New Testament is taught and preached throughout the world. As Latter-day Saints, we have been relatively unaware of this heated discussion among scholars and have often viewed their proceedings as suspicious or beyond the realm of interest.[2] We are rapidly losing ground in this discussion, and, without some opposing influence, scholars may soon declare the two-document hypothesis a proven fact.[3] The issues that this article seeks to address are whether the two-document hypothesis conflicts with Latter-day Saint viewpoints of the New Testament and what ramifications the study of Q could have, if accepted, on our understanding of Jesus of Nazareth.

A Defense of Q?

The idea that the Bible may be incomplete can immediately be defended on the grounds of the eighth Article of Faith, which states, "We believe the Bible to be the word of God as far as it is translated correctly; we also believe the Book of Mormon to be the word of God." The Latter-day Saint belief that the Bible is not infallible and that errors have crept in because of misinformed or intentionally erroneous translations would facilitate our agreement with biblical scholars who likewise argue that the Bible has been corrupted during the process of transmission.[4]

The Q theory, however, is much more than the simple corruption of scripture and mistranslation of texts. Q theorists suggest that the authors of the Gospels of Matthew and Luke knowingly altered and enhanced the teachings they received from Q and Mark. The work of the Evangelists, they propose, as well as their various focal points, can be determined by how the Evangelists changed the materials they received and what materials they added to Mark and Q.

In its most basic form, Q studies have nothing to do with mistranslation but instead lead into a discussion of the tendencies of each author and their different treatments of received traditions. Such a use of biblical traditions could be justified using the model of the Book of Mormon and the way in which Mormon and later Moroni edited the traditions from the large plates of Nephi and the book of Ether. We cannot entirely object to what Q scholars are saying about the way in which Matthew and Luke have handled the traditions that were passed on to them; in fact, we would have to learn to accept the idea that the authors of Matthew and Luke were second-generation Christians who edited the texts of the previous generation and were not eyewitnesses themselves.[5]

Q may also be defended on the grounds that it contains the words of Jesus in their earliest form, and its composition therefore reveals an interest by the earliest disciples of Jesus to record accurately His sayings. One would expect, from a logical standpoint, that the disciples of any great religious leader would collect and gather the sayings of their master immediately upon his death or even during his lifetime. It could be argued that Q represents just such a document. The difficulty with this thesis, however, is that the inner logic of the theoretical Q document would suggest otherwise. Using only those passages contained in Q, scholars have proposed that the Jesus of

Q was a wandering teacher of wisdom who did little to cultivate the master-disciple relationship. The proposed Jesus of Q also had no expectations of a future church or kingdom on the earth and did little if anything to train His disciples for His impending death. Therefore, by the logic of Q, could we really suggest that Jesus had a devout group of followers who worshipped Him and who would have been careful to preserve His teachings? The contents of Q suggest that Jesus had very few personal disciples, and therefore it would be difficult using Q alone to suggest that anyone would be greatly interested in collecting the sayings of Jesus and preserving His name and authority within that collection.

Challenges to Q—The Sermon to the Nephites

One of the founding principles in determining Q and which author of the New Testament most accurately preserved its contents is the belief that the Sermon on the Mount was a composition by the author of the Gospel of Matthew. As is well known among readers of the New Testament, Matthew and Luke contain two very similar sermons: the Sermon on the Mount (see Matthew 5–7) and the Sermon on the Plain (see Luke 6:20–49). The large overlap in wording and order of passages has led to the conclusion that many of the passages of the Sermon on the Mount or Plain were originally contained in Q. By Q's definition, this would be a logical conclusion. The author of the Gospel of Matthew, in this way of thinking, is, in reality, the author of the Sermon on the Mount and qualifies for the honor of having compiled one of the most memorable discourses in history.

This view, however, faces a considerable challenge in the Book of Mormon through Jesus's Sermon to the Nephites (see 3 Nephi 12–14). Scholars argue that the Sermon on the Mount is a composition from the late 70s AD by a second-generation Christian believer. They maintain that Q contained no distinctly organized sermon and that perhaps the Gospel of Luke has given us the most accurate depiction of what Q contained relating to this sermon. The parallel Sermon to the Nephites, however, was given shortly after the death of Jesus. The similarity of wording suggests that the Sermon on the Mount was composed no later than a few years after Christ's death, not forty years later as Q scholars maintain.[6] Latter-day Saints also believe that the composition of the Sermon on the Mount was made during Jesus's own lifetime and that the sermon was actually delivered to an audience of His disciples, although this thinking cannot be absolutely "proven" in a scientific sense.

Evangelists as Editors and Authors

Q in its simplest form raises serious doubts concerning our traditional understanding of who the Evangelists were and what their work consisted of. We would not be surprised to learn their views that the disciple Matthew did not personally pen the Gospel of Matthew or that the Gospel of Luke was penned by another one of Paul's traveling companions whose name has now been lost, but we would be surprised to read that the authors of the New Testament had complete freedom in composing their books and in altering the words of Jesus. Those who advocate Q claim that the earliest historical collection of Jesus's life was devoid of narrative, told no miracles, and contained only short random sayings from Jesus Himself.[7]

Q scholars propose that the Evangelists used this collection of sayings, or *logia*, liberally and that neither Luke nor Matthew showed any great respect for its order, or wording, or tried to transmit it in its entirety. Theoretically, Matthew and Luke used this source freely in their composition and created narrative settings of their own accord, independently inserting passages from Q into their framework, which they had adapted from Mark. What type of record was this that contained the words of Jesus but for which a second-generation Christian author had little, if any, respect for as a valid representation of the life of Jesus? Scholars are arguing with more vigor that the Jesus of Q is the Jesus of history and that the Jesus of the Gospels is the Jesus created by the Church. If the Q theory were indeed valid, then this viewpoint would need to be seriously considered.

An Evolutionary Model

The theory of Q works on an evolutionary model of history, in which the most primitive and concise records were the earliest, and then later authors and editors expanded the history to adapt it for their own circumstances. Q and Mark, the most "primitive" of the Gospels, were the first to be written in this sequence, and the longer Gospels of Matthew and Luke are seen as the final product in the evolution of the Gospel genre. Scholars have argued that Matthew and Luke went through various stages or recensions and that the version we now have is the one that was finally accepted by the church. Such an understanding of textual history may be acceptable to some scholars, but there is an entire stratum of textual critics who defend the position that scribes, especially in the earliest period of textual transmission, tended to delete portions of text rather than expand and enhance.[8]

The normal work of the scribe in correcting the text and harmonizing it to the other New Testament texts is easily identifiable through a study of the textual variants of the New Testament. The opposite, namely the removal of large portions of text, is also easily identifiable in the study of the New Testament. A few examples may suffice:

1. In John 5:2, Jesus performs a miracle at the pool of Bethesda in the city of Jerusalem, but John 6:1 states that "after these things Jesus went over the sea of Galilee," a distance of nearly two hundred miles. The temporal connective "after" suggests that after Jesus did X he did Y, but the two scenes are very different from one another, and it appears that the intervening explanatory text or travel narrative has been removed.

2. In Acts 20:35, we have the statement, "Remember the words of the Lord Jesus, how he said, It is more blessed to give than to receive," yet this saying does not appear in any of the canonical Gospels.

3. From an even earlier period, Paul taught the Thessalonian Saints "by the word of the Lord, that we which are alive and remain unto the coming of the Lord shall not prevent them which are asleep. For the Lord himself shall descend from heaven with a shout, with the voice of the archangel, and with the trump of God: and the dead in Christ shall rise first: then we which are alive and remain shall be caught up together with them in the clouds, to meet the Lord in the air: and so shall we ever be with the Lord" (1 Thessalonians 4:15–17). The Apostle Paul stated in the preceding text that these words originated with the Lord Jesus Christ, yet they are nowhere to be found in the Gospels of the New Testament.

The evidence of the Book of Mormon teaches us that scripture also undergoes corruption through the process of deletions. In Nephi's inspired account, he stated that "the book proceeded forth from the mouth of a Jew; and when it proceeded forth from the mouth of a Jew it contained the fulness of the gospel of the Lord. . . . Wherefore, these things go forth from the Jews in purity unto the Gentiles" (1 Nephi 13:24–25). Although not by any means an absolute statement on all textual variation in the New Testament, the Book of Mormon testifies that the text of the Bible would suffer from deletions but does not mention the proposed expansion of the text as proposed by Q scholars. The transmission process of the Book of Mormon also suggests that inspired records are created through inspired editorial condensation and that the longer text of the Book of Mormon was the earliest. Luke may have had just such a situation in mind when he states, "Forasmuch as many have taken in hand to set forth in order a declaration of those things which are most surely believed among us" (Luke 1:1). Like Mormon, Luke may be giving us an inspired and edited condensation of the traditions that he has received.[9] The evolutionary model should not confine us into thinking that all texts start out primitive and develop over time through the process of uninspired additions.

Ipsissima Vox Iesou—The Very Words of Jesus

An issue that needs to be raised is what relationship the proposed Q document has to the life and teachings of the historical Jesus. Scholars fall into several camps on this issue, with essentially every nuance in between being advocated. The most immediate reaction to the evidence presented by those expounding the two-document hypothesis is that the words of Q most accurately reflect the words of Jesus. This is a logical corollary—if Q is proven to be correct—as Q bears greater chronological proximity to the life of Jesus. We should expect that the earliest accounts would have had access to eyewitness accounts and to those who had been in direct contact with Jesus Himself. If Q represents the most correct collection of the words of Jesus, then we should likely view the later Gospel compilations as confusions of the truth. The editors of Q, namely Matthew and Luke, would, therefore, be the generation of Christians who modified and altered the teachings of Jesus. Almost all additions to Q, unless a historically valid claim can be made for independent reliability, could be understood as alterations of the truth.

This way of thinking leads us to ask ourselves whether our reliance upon the New Testament Gospels is a matter of tradition or whether our reliance upon them as accurate accounts of the life of Jesus is based upon their truthful representation of the facts. Nearly everywhere, Christians today are bristling at the suggestion of such a question, and Q scholars are forcing a decision on the issue. Unfortunately, as believing Christians we are losing the battle in this area, and our silence on this issue is permitting those who would construe things otherwise to gain precedence. For example, a recently aired special on the life of Jesus by Peter Jennings entitled *The Search for Jesus* retold the life of Jesus based on the work of Q scholars. Jennings presented for the first time on national television a documentary on Jesus's life using Q as though it were in many instances a proven fact.[10]

We will never be able to "prove" the historical accuracy of the New Testament, but, as a corollary, it will never be disproved either unless substantial firsthand, eyewitness accounts are discovered. We might rely on the eighth article of faith to affirm our belief in the Bible or the testimonies given in the Book of Mormon, but these witnesses as well as those of the living prophets will never suffice to yield scientific proof. We need to be reminded that the New Testament is not without errors, and those who propose the two-document hypothesis need to be reminded that their proposal is at this stage a theory and that while Q scholars are attempting to reconstruct Christianity upon that new theory, it will always remain simply that, a theory with significant detractors.[11] Faith is not a science, and theory is not an absolute.

Separate and Competing Christianities

The "discovery" of Q has led to a belief that the Gospels represent types or communities of Christian believers and that those communities were in conversation and discourse with one another—for example, in the secondary literature anyone can read about Matthean, Markan, Lukan, and especially Johannine Christianity. Q scholars have proposed that the Gospels represent the work of these communities, and their various alterations to received traditions, namely Q and Mark, help manifest their doctrinal leanings and tendencies. Matthean Christianity is more oriented, for example, to issues of ritual purity, whereas the Gospel of Luke has an overt concern for poverty and the economic poor. This view obliterates the standpoint that all the authors of the New Testament were working within and toward the establishment of the Church left behind in the wake of Jesus's death. The Church, many believe, developed over time and was the product of a dominant group that marginalized its opponents. Scholars have pointed to the conclusion that various early Christian heretical groups could be viewed as more "orthodox" or more historically correct in their understanding of Jesus than those who ultimately triumphed and wrote the New Testament.

There are some points that we should consider before joining these people on the bandwagon. New Testament authors and modern prophets have taught concerning the Apostasy that enveloped the early church. Although we cannot fix the moment of the beginning of the Apostasy, we have traditionally ascribed it to the postapostolic era after the death of the first Quorum of Twelve Apostles. We believe that the Church was organized in the days of the Apostles and that Peter and the other eleven Apostles administered to the needs of the growing Church. Q would radically alter our portrait of the early Church and undermine our belief that Jesus left behind an organized religious community.

Those who advocate that Christian origins should be thus reconstructed often fail to notice that their proposed reconstruction is based on circular reasoning. All passages wherein Jesus overtly teaches, trains, and prepares the Apostles for His upcoming death either derive from Mark or do not originate in Q. Therefore, scholars dismiss those passages that have Church organization or teachings concerning the future Church as late and secondary, but the criteria established by those scholars is the very reason that such evidence has been removed. Their judgment is circular at best because we cannot establish a theoretical document, one in which we have determined its contents, and then make negative statements regarding other traditions based on what was supposedly not in that document. There is no scientific way to verify what was not in Q, and, in fact, if only one author quoted from Q, our methods of detecting Q passages would prove useless because Q passages are determined by verbal similarity between Matthew and Luke. If Luke or Matthew quoted independently from Q, we would never know it. Therefore, many of those passages that speak of Church organization, the training of the Twelve, and what the disciples should do after Jesus's death could derive from Q if they could be shown to not derive from Mark. In reality, only sixty-eight passages are ascribed to Q, but the number could be much greater since Q can be detected only when Matthew and Luke both quote the same passage nearly verbatim.[12]

Paul

Although Paul might first appear to be beyond a discussion of Q, he is not. Paul is our earliest author in the New Testament, and he wrote contemporaneously with the theoretical Q. Therefore, these two sources for the study of the New Testament should be viewed on equal footing. In the era after the "discovery" of Q, scholars began to take a second look at Paul and his familiarity with the traditions of Jesus's life. As is well known, Paul tells us almost nothing of Jesus's ministry or of what Jesus taught.[13]

Two views of this phenomenon have emerged; either Paul did not tell of the traditions of Jesus's life because they were so familiar to his audience, or he was unfamiliar with them because they had not been established by his day. Although not unanimously, Q scholars tend to favor the latter possibility because it lends tacit support to their theory that Christianity was being invented and shaped by the events of the 50s, 60s, and 70s. Paul, in this way of thinking, was a Christian maverick who saw things quite differently from the authors of the synoptic traditions and who was largely responsible for imposing on the early Christian communities a sense of church and central organization.

Conclusion

Q has become many things in our day, probably most of them unanticipated by its original proponents. In reading the early literature on Q, scholars can sense of open debate and concern to establish whether the authors of Matthew and Luke had access to earlier written or oral traditions. The first generation of Q scholars debated whether Q was even a written tradition. Unfortunately, Q has become something unwieldy—a beast with a spirit of its own. Q scholars want to alter our understanding of who Jesus was and present to us a Jesus who did no miracles, did not anticipate His death, did not understand He was the Messiah, and did not leave behind an organized church. The Jesus of Q is essentially a scholar's Jesus who wandered the countryside and taught using conventional wisdom. He had no power to save Himself, and He had no power to save others. Scholars call this the Jesus of history, whereas we worship the Jesus of faith. The following chart shows the directions of borrowing from Q and Mark by Matthew and Luke as proposed by Q scholars.

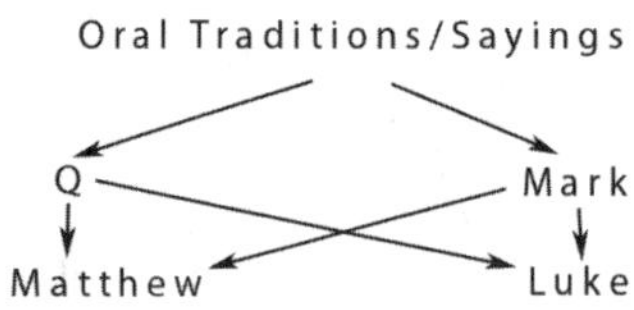

Q studies face serious challenges both from within the ranks and from without. Significant work is being done that reconstructs the textual history of the New Testament using Mark as the first Gospel but without postulating a source such as Q. Others have gone back to the Augustinian hypothesis—that the Gospels were composed in their canonical order. While these arguments may appear too nuanced to be meaningful, the stakes are great. Silence on issues such as Q has permitted those who see things otherwise to have an almost unimpeded voice, which has led many to believe that a consensus is emerging. We as Latter-day Saints have a great interest in Christian origins, probably more so than most.

We do not object to the possible use of sources by the Evangelists, and we expect that if such sources were available to them in the earliest years of the Church, they would make good use of them. We object, however, to what is being said concerning the items that those early sources did not contain, and we openly question whether such a document actually existed. The problem lies not necessarily in Q but in what Q has become.

Notes

1. The "two-document hypothesis" affirms that Matthew and Luke each used the Gospel of Mark as a source in composing their own Gospels as well as an earlier unknown source called Q from the German word for "source," *Quelle.*
2. A great deal of suspicion has surrounded the work of the *Jesus Seminar*, founded in 1985 by Robert Funk and currently located in Santa Rosa, California. The work of the seminar focuses on ascertaining the origins and validity of all traditions about Jesus of Nazareth from His birth until AD 200. The participants of the seminar have garnered a great deal of criticism and suspicion because of their often countercultural theories and dismissal of many of Jesus's sayings as inauthentic and secondary.
3. This trend is hinted at by John S. Kloppenborg in *Excavating Q* (Minneapolis: Fortress, 2000), 11–54.
4. This sentiment was recently expressed by John H. Vandenberg, "What Is Truth?" *Ensign*, May 1978, 54. He states, "We know that the Bible is a compilation of the available messages received by the prophets."
5. I see almost no way of maintaining the tradition that the author of the Gospel of Matthew was an eyewitness if the two-document hypothesis is correct. The only way that he could still be claimed to have any access to eyewitness traditions is through Q and the detection of the method in which he rearranges the material from Mark and Q.
6. John W. Welch, *The Sermon at the Temple and the Sermon on the Mount* (Salt Lake City: Deseret Book, 1990), 164–77.
7. The one instance of a healing in Q is the healing of the centurion's son (see Matthew 8:5–13; Luke 7:1–10). The account of the miracle itself, however, cannot be ascribed to Q because there is little, if any, verbal similarity in the account of the miracle. Q, by definition, contained only the request of the centurion and not the subsequent miracle (see John S. Kloppenborg, *Q Parallels* [Sonoma, CA: Polebridge, 1988], 48–51).

8. Eldon J. Epp, "Issues in New Testament Textual Criticism: Moving from the Nineteenth Century to the Twenty-First Century," in *Rethinking New Testament Textual Criticism*, ed. David A. Black (Grand Rapids, MI: Baker, 2002), 17–76.
9. This has been consistently pointed out by Q scholars, who note that Luke is referring to Q. It may also contain a broader perspective—that Matthew, Mark, and maybe even John had been written and that now Luke proposes to give his account.
10. For the work of the Jesus Seminar, see note 2 above. Jennings has received substantial criticism for his decision to present the Jesus of Q as the accurate, unadulterated Jesus. The special ran on ABC in June 1999.
11. A growing number of scholars are being won over to the Farrer-Goulder hypothesis, made most recently by Mark Goodacre, in *The Case Against Q* (Harrisburg, PA: Trinity, 2002).
12. Kloppenborg, *Q Parallels*, xxxi–xxxiii.
13. For a balanced discussion of what Paul knew and taught concerning Jesus of Nazareth, see Richard Neitzel Holzapfel, "Early Accounts of the Story," in *From the Last Supper through the Resurrection: The Savior's Final Hours*, ed. Richard Neitzel Holzapfel and Thomas A. Wayment (Salt Lake City: Deseret Book, 2003), 401–21.

Index

Entries for images are indicated by italicized page numbers.